TEACHERS AND TEACHING
IN THE DEVELOPING WORLD

REFERENCE BOOKS IN
INTERNATIONAL EDUCATION
(General Editor: Edward R. Beauchamp)
VOL. 8

GARLAND REFERENCE LIBRARY
OF SOCIAL SCIENCE
VOL. 617

Reference Books in International Education

Edward R. Beauchamp
General Editor

1. *Education in East and West Germany: A Bibliography*
   by Val D. Rust
2. *Education in the People's Republic of China, Past and Present: An Annotated Bibliography*
   by Franklin Parker and Betty June Parker
3. *Education in South Asia: A Select Annotated Bibliography*
   by Philip G. Altbach, Denzil Saldhana, and Jeanne Weiler
4. *Textbooks in the Third World: Policy, Content and Context*
   by Philip G. Atlbach and Gail P. Kelly
5. *Education in Japan: A Source Book*
   by Edward R. Beauchamp and Richard Rubinger
6. *Women's Education in the Third World*
   by David H. Kelly and Gail P. Kelly
7. *Minority Status and Schooling*
   by John V. Ogbu and Margaret A. Gibson
8. *Teachers and Teaching in the Developing World*
   by Val D. Rust and Per Dalin

TEACHERS AND TEACHING IN THE DEVELOPING WORLD

Val D. Rust
Per Dalin

GARLAND PUBLISHING, INC. • NEW YORK & LONDON
1990

Library of Congress Cataloging-in-Publication Data

Teachers and teaching in the developing world / [edited by] Val. D.
Rust, Per Dalin.
    p. cm. — (Reference books in international education; vol.
8) (Garland reference library of social science ; vol. 617)
    Papers previously presented at an international seminar, sponsored
by IMTEC, and held in Bali, in November of 1986.
    Includes bibliographical references.
    ISBN 0–8240–3532–1 (alk. paper)
    1. Teachers—Training of—Developing countries—Congresses.
2. Teachers—Developing countries—Congresses. 3. Teaching—
Developing countries—Congresses. I. Rust, Val Dean. II. Dalin,
Per, 1936– . III. International Movement Towards Educational
Change. IV. Series. V. Series: Garland reference library of social
science; vol. 617.
LB1727.D44T43 1990
371.11'009172'4—dc20   89–27603
                                                          CIP

Printed on acid-free, 250-year-life paper
Manufactured in the United States of America

DEDICATED TO
Two teachers: Diane and Astrid

SERIES EDITOR'S FOREWORD

This series of reference works and monographs in education in selected nations and regions is designed to provide a resource to scholars, students, and a variety of other professionals who need to understand the place of education in a particular society or region. While the format of the volumes is often similar, the authors have had the flexibility to adjust the common outline to reflect the uniqueness of their particular nation or region.

Contributors to this series are scholars who have devoted their professional lives to studying the nation or region about which they write. Without exception they have not only studied the educational system in question, but they have lived and travelled widely in the society in which it is embedded. In short, they are exceptionally knowledgeable about their subject.

In our increasingly interdependent world, it is now widely understood that it is a matter of survival that we understand better what makes other societies tick. As the late George Z.F. Bereday wrote: "First, education is a mirror held against the face of a people. Nations may put on blustering shows of strength to conceal public weakness, erect grand façades to conceal shabby backyards, and profess peace while secretly arming for conquest, but how they take care of their children tells unerringly who they are" (*Comparative Method in Education*, New York: Holt, Rinehart & Winston, 1964, page 5).

Perhaps equally important, however, is the valuable perspective that studying another education system provides us in understanding our own. To step outside of our commonly held assumptions about schools and learning, however briefly, and to look back at our system in contrast to another, places it in a very different light. To learn, for example, how the Soviet Union handles the education of a multilingual society; how the French provide for the funding of public education; or how the Japanese control admissions into their universities enables us to understand that there are alternatives to our familiar way of doing things. Not that we can often "borrow" from other societies; indeed, educational arrangements are inevitably a reflection of deeply rooted political, economic, and cultural factors that are unique to a society. But a conscious recognition that there are other ways of doing things can serve to open our minds and provoke our imaginations in ways that can result in new approaches that we would not have otherwise considered.

Since this series is designed to be a useful research tool, the editors and contributors welcome suggestions for future volumes as well as ways in which this series can be improved.

Edward R. Beauchamp
University of Hawaii

CONTENTS

ACKNOWLEDGMENTS

This book is an outgrowth of an international seminar, sponsored by IMTEC Institute, headquartered in Oslo, Norway, which was held on the island of Bali, in Indonesia, in November, 1986. The theme of that seminar was "Improving the Quality of Teaching in the Developing World: Alternative Models." Representatives of research institutes, ministries, and donor agencies gathered together to compare notes and assess teacher education policies and research findings that might contribute to the improvement of teaching in the developing world. We are indebted especially to the Indonesian government, which acted as the host of the seminar, and we acknowledge especially those participating scholars, many of whom have contributed in some way to this volume. I would also like to acknowledge, Maureen Depolo, Christine Carrillo Miner, and Sarah Kincaid who helped prepare the manuscript for publication.

PREFACE

One of the pressing educational issues of our times is the need improve the quality of teaching in the developing world. A significant portion of the limited funds in the developing world is being channeled into the educational sector, and yet, the governments responsible for allocating these funds and the donor agencies that are providing funds from the developed world have a very unclear grasp of the factors that contribute to the improvement of teaching. The reasons for this lack of clarity include the lack of research on teaching and teachers, the need to synthesize the research that has been conducted, and the simple fact that we are at a relatively primitive state in terms of our ability to sort out critical factors that make a difference in education.

In spite of the relative paucity of information available about teaching, some good work is being done by capable researchers and scholars. As might be expected, most of this work is being done in the developed world, where over 3,000 references on teacher effectiveness alone, have been compiled. We are beginning to see movement in the developing world, and over 600 references connected with teacher effectiveness were recently identified (Avalos and Haddad, 1981). Since that time, a great deal more work has been done, and a major objective of this volume is to introduce the reader to recent research and conceptual work on teachers and teaching in the developing world. In conceptualizing a framework for this volume, we relied heavily on a model for research on teaching that has been constructed by Dunkin and Biddle in their book *The Study of Teaching* (1974). This model had been derived from an earlier construct by Mitzel (1960) but tempered by inquiry strategies that had been taking place in the intervening years. Dunkin and Biddle suggested that research on teaching had focused on four classes of variables: Presage Variables (teacher background characteristics, training experiences, and individual properties such as intelligence, motivations, and personality traits); Context Variables (properties of pupils, the school, the community, and classroom contexts); Process Variables (teacher and pupil classroom behaviors); and Product Variables (immediate and long-term learning, attitude changes, and skills). In a simplified model, the variables would follow a linear form, as indicated below:

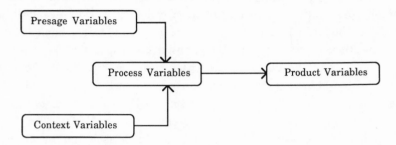

Even though the typical concern of recent research on teachers and teaching in the developing world has been on the relationship between outcome variables, particularly student achievement, and presage, context and process variables (e.g., Avalos and Haddad, 1981; Husen, Saha, and Noonan, 1978; Fuller, 1986), we find this focus too narrow for our purposes. While certain authors in our study pay attention to this research, most are also concerned with clarifying the contextual meaning of variables and identifying alternative ways in which these variables are being operationalized in the developing world. In other words, they and we recognize the need for a much broader knowledge base about teachers and teaching in the developing world, before we focus our attention exclusively on quantitative relationships between variables.

The inquiries of our authors are also tempered by an awareness that the developing world is so multifaceted that it is dangerous to draw too many conclusions of a general nature. A solution to a teaching problem in one geographic area may or may not be appropriate in another. Furthermore, it is clear that teachers and teaching environments within any area are quite varied. Some teachers hold high status and come from the best families, while others are marginal in every sense of the term. Some have extensive training, while others are barely schooled beyond the level of those they are teaching. Consequently, it appears more important at this point in our knowledge level to conceptualize spheres of interest related to teachers and teaching as well as to lay out alternative ways of doing things, of arranging our teaching environments, of training our teachers, of deploying our teachers, appears to us to be a worthy aim.

We have invited leading international experts in the field of teaching research and teacher education to write a chapter of the book or a case study connected with a chapter and include what they feel are the most helpful literature references available. Each chapter is an original piece of writing. In selecting the authors, we attempted to keep two things in balance. First, we wanted to maintain some balance in terms of the geographic distribution of the authors, particularly regarding the developed and developing world but also from various national settings. Second, we attempted to avoid a specific ideological bias and invited authors representing all points of view on the political spectrum.

The book has 20 authors and coauthors, who either come from or live and work in 12 different countries. We are delighted to report that authors from 7 of the countries represented would clearly fall within the sphere of the developing world. It has taken enormous energy to identify such experts to include in the book, and we must confess that we have not been as successful as we had hoped. Such a state of affairs reflects the political economy of educational research in the world today, especially where we are concerned with papers giving an overview of a field. This demands a worldwide network of information, which is simply not available in most countries. Consequently, most of the authors come from the United States, Canada, Great Britain, Norway, Singapore, and Australia.

In terms of ideological orientation, we have also been successful in identifying authors who do represent the full political spectrum. However, we have been impressed that none of the authors has chosen to concentrate on broader political aspects of the problem. Rather, they have treated their topic from a more technical frame of reference. Two conditions may help explain this orientation. First, teaching and teacher education require technical skills and competence. It would be impossible to discuss these issues exclusively from a political vantage point. Second, even those who are politically oriented are beginning to recognize that their struggle is technical as well as political. Scholars in Latin America, for example, recognize that political awareness is no longer enough. Political aims are being confused by technological issues, and they are finding they must come to possess a high level of technical competence if they are to be successful in attaining politically desirable ends.

The book is organized into five major sections, in addition to a Preface. The focus of Section I is on factors surrounding the selection, professional development, and placement of teachers. Cummings summarizes the changes that appear to take place over time in the kinds of people who become teachers and offers a series of provocative hypotheses to account for the typical shift in teacher characteristics. A major portion of this section is devoted to professional development. A chapter and a case study are provided for each of three types of teacher development: pre-service, on-service, and in-service teacher training. While the chapters provide broad overviews of conventional and innovative training policies and practices, the case studies are intended to highlight specific instances of actual training programs. In the concluding chapter of this section, Thompson engages in an elaborate review of issues surrounding the deployment of teachers. He argues that improved deployment patterns and procedures could reduce costs and also contribute to improved schools and learning.

Section II deals with classroom contexts, instruction and outcomes of teaching. Hurst and Rust consider issues such as teachers' pay and their general working conditions. They argue that these are as crucial as any other issue in terms of student learning. Two major chapters in the section focus on instruction but from quite different perspectives. Jones and Bhalwankar draw on research on teaching to derive various teaching models that might be possible to adopt in the developing world, while Avalos provides some overview of what is presently known in the literature about teaching in both the developed and the developing world. She maintains that the crucial thing we must do is accumulate more information about what is actually going on in classrooms of the developing world and draw from this understanding in our recommendations for teacher improvement. Guthrie, who is a member of a development agency in Australia, then makes a case against the wholesale importation of developed world innovations, claiming that traditional teaching has powerful qualities that must not be overlooked.

Section III deals with intervention mechanisms coming mainly from the developed world. In the first chapter, Dalin introduces the topic by reviewing the progress we have made in facilitating professional and institutional renewal. We then turn to actual intervention activities, mainly on the part of bilateral and multilateral agencies that have been undertaken. Nielson asks what level of commitment these agencies have to improve teaching and what directions their support has taken. In the final chapter of the section, Rust and Semali discuss the special case of technological innovations, such as distance learning, radio, computers, etc., and their potential in the teaching equation.

Section IV the editors of this volume draw conclusions and recommendations based largely on the information gathered in the previous sections of the book.

The final section is a comprehensive bibliography of recent work both from the developing and the developed world relevant to teachers, teacher education, and teaching in the developing world.

SECTION I

RECRUITMENT, TRAINING AND
DEPLOYMENT OF TEACHERS

CHAPTER ONE

WHO TEACHES? AN INTERNATIONAL ANALYSIS

William K. Cummings

In most contemporary societies, the profession of teaching employs more adults than any other occupation requiring a similar level of educational preparation. In the United States, there are 4,000,000 teachers compared to 2,000,000 engineers, 500,000 lawyers, 300,000 computer specialists, and 150,000 medical doctors. In India, there are 10,000,000 teachers compared to 1,000,000 engineers and 50,000 medical doctors.

Given the considerable size of the teaching profession, its members can be expected to manifest wide diversity in their personal and social characteristics. Nevertheless, periodically, those concerned with quality of teaching raise the question, "who teaches?" with the implication that the profession is not attracting or retaining the right people. One or more of the following concerns tend to inspire this question:

First, in periods of rapid educational expansion, critics often worry that teachers are not like they used to be in some bygone "golden age," whether in terms of social origins, intellectual ability, class rank, gender, or quality of school attended. For most societies, the golden age proposition seems to fit the facts. But it needs to be accompanied by a second proposition: pupils also were more select in terms of these same characteristics. Thus, one not-so-startling conclusion of this paper is that the social characteristics of teachers mirror those of their pupils.

Second, in a context of emerging minority rights, advocates may assert that their subgroups, whether ethnic, religious, or social, are underrepresented in the teaching profession. This concern sometimes is answered through the institution of quota systems to bring about the desired aggregate balance of different groups, as Thompson points out in another chapter of this book, in Malawi, Kenya, and Sarawak, though such policies do not guarantee the intended balance at the school level.

Third, distinct from the legal rights of different subgroups is the concern for the ideal mix of teachers to maximize student learning: majority group and/or middle-class teachers may not be sensitive to the personality traits and other characteristics of minority group and/or working-class pupils, women may not be as effective in teaching science as men or men as effective in teaching language as women.

For these and other reasons, both educators and those concerned with education periodically ask who teaches. In what follows, after making some observations on the scarcity of useful data, I seek to summarize the available evidence. In reviewing this evidence, I am more interested in changes over time for particular societies (for which evidence is scanty), than for differences between societies at a common point in time. For most societies, I discern a common shift in the nature of teacher characteristics--toward increasing proportions of teachers that are female, toward teachers from families of lower socioeconomic status, and toward teachers that have undistinguished educational records--as the educational system expands and differentiates. Following my review of the available evidence, I offer a series of hypotheses to account for the typical shift in teacher characteristics. While I conclude that a "downward" shift in the characteristics of pupils is inevitable, it does not follow that the characteristics of teachers need go through a similar shift. The argument at this stage is preliminary, and hopefully will be improved through discussion and new information.

THE SCARCITY OF INFORMATION

The answer to "who teaches?"--a seemingly straightforward question--is frustrated by what Husen (1978) refers to as the "paucity of data." It is perhaps no accident that there is so little data; indeed, it can be plausibly argued that barriers are intentionally imposed on the collection of the appropriate information, and these barriers appear to rise higher with each passing year. For example, whereas the first round of International Association for the Evaluation of Educational Achievement (IEA) surveys asked extensive questions on teacher background (e.g., Comber and Keeves, 1973), the most recent surveys largely ignore this area.

The type and location of information that is available could be a subject of inquiry in its own right. For example, in the United Kingdom, schools are proud to note that some of their teachers are from Oxford or Cambridge. In the United States universities and high schools stress the educational attainment of their staff (percent masters, number of medical doctors). In Japan, while there once was extensive information on the social origins of teachers, this subject is now said to smack of discrimination: and hence is taboo. In contrast, data on teacher gender and discussions of the appropriate balance between sexes in a school or district are common, even in countries such as the United States and Japan, where the feminist movement has raised sensitivities about gender discrimination.

Four factors seem to influence the availability of information:

The Facts May Be Embarrassing

The objective trends to be discussed below are troubling to policy makers. In most societies, there are downward shifts in the social class origin of teachers, the proportion of male teachers, the average educational achievement of teachers, and the proportion of teachers educated in the "best" schools. These trends are a source of embarrassment to policy-makers. Suppressing reports of the trends averts their public discussion.

The Policy Implications of Shifts May Be Unclear

Studies, that have included "who" variables in analyses of school and student performance, have not produced compelling conclusions. Of 26 studies reviewed by Husen (1978, p. 15), pupils taught by males did better in 12 instances, by females in 9 instances, and there was no difference for the remaining cases. Men are not always better at math or social science teaching than women. Teachers from "good" homes do not obtain better results with their students than teachers from "common" homes. Insofar as these factors are important in predicting performance, they are so through interaction with a host of other variables. Of course, political leaders and communities often express concern for who teaches, and the schools are, therefore, under pressure to respond. But there is little evidence to suggest that their responses enhance the educational outcomes of pupils.

The Political Left May Object

In societies with progressive teachers unions, the appropriateness of the question is raised. The teachers perceive a dubious argument behind the issue of who teaches. That argument follows the following path:

1.   Who teaches is related to the quality of teaching.
2.   There has been a decline in the quality of those who teach.
3.   Hence, the quality of teaching has declined.

The progressive groups reject this "elitist" argument's unfounded assumption that who one is determines how one performs. They point to training variables as more critical in determining teacher performance. Thus, the question should not be who teaches but how teaching is done. For this reason, the teachers often boycott "who surveys" or at least those questions focusing on the "who" dimension.

The State Authorities May Object

We should also note that many of the new states, seeking to integrate diverse social, racial, and ethnic groups into a unified and loyal citizenry officially discourage discussion or analyses about "who," whether these be concerning who teaches, who goes to a university, who is wealthy, or whatever. In the United States, for example, questions concerning religious affiliation cannot be included in the national census or most other government surveys. Similarly, in Singapore, public reports of surveys usually do not include analyses by race or income group.

For all these reasons, information on who teaches is not as extensive as might be wished. Because I believe that characteristics of teachers are determined by long-term changes within societies, I am as much interested in historical as comparative data. By taking this orientation, it is also inappropriate to discuss only developing countries. For a few countries, the United States, Japan, and most European societies, there is reasonably reliable data over time for most of the social characteristics of interest. But only with respect to sex is there extensive data over time for most developing countries. Fortunately, even in the developing countries there is data on some of the characteristics for at least one point in time, so that by combining this data some profiles and trends can be determined.

THE EVIDENCE ON WHO TEACHES

GENDER

More evidence is available on the gender of teachers than any other "who" variable. On a comparative basis, the UNESCO statistical reports inform us for the following:

1.   At the primary level, there is great variation in the proportion of females, ranging, in 1980, from 9 percent in Yemen to 91 percent in Seychelles (UNESCO, 1980). In virtually all societies, where there is no prohibition against females assuming modern jobs, they constitute at least one third of all teachers. The female

proportion is highest in North and Latin America and lowest in Africa.

2.   At the secondary level, again there is much variation between societies in the proportion of female teachers. The pattern of variation closely follows that at the primary level, except for any given society the female proportion at the secondary level will typically be about 20 percentage points lower than at the primary level.

In general, the proportion of females tends to increase over time, which is parallel with the proportion of females receiving secondary and tertiary education. Teaching, because of its status, security, and short hours, is viewed as an appropriate occupation for educated women long before other modern sector jobs become accessible. In the United States, females were in the majority at the primary level before the Civil War. In Japan, they became a majority in the late thirties, as both prospective and active male teachers were recruited for the war effort.

Of course, there may be interruptions in the long-term trend, such as was the case in the United States after World War II, when the proportion of male teachers momentarily increased. Examination of comparative data suggests the trend toward increasing femaleness may progress until a threshold of 75 percent female at the primary level and 50 percent female at the secondary level is reached.

RURAL-URBAN DISTINCTIONS

It is difficult to develop generalizations on the place of birth of teachers both because of the lack of data and the differences in national definitions of rural and urban. However, for those countries where data is available, there usually is an urban bias in the teaching force in the early states of educational development correspondent with the urban bias in the location of schools and teacher education institutions. Over time, balance is achieved or even a slight rural bias emerges, especially in instances where policy-makers determine that rural-born teachers, because of such characteristics as simpler values and a more vigorous constitution, are more preferable. According to recent surveys, an urban bias is currently evident in the recruits to Indonesian teaching (Waskito and Cummings, 1981); balance was reported for the United States (Lortie, 1975, p. 35), and Germany (Pritchard, 1983, p. 342); and there is a rural bias among Japanese teaching recruits (Shimuzu, 1975, p. 230), and Irish teachers (Morgan and Dunn, 1981).

SOCIOECONOMIC BACKGROUND OF TEACHERS

As the labor market and other opportunities differ for men and women, discussion of socioeconomic background has to be broken down by sex. For men, once the modern economy reaches a sufficient stage of development, teaching loses its attractiveness in the eyes of males from privileged homes. Thus, among males, there is a disproportionate recruitment from farm and blue-collar homes. This shift is best documented in the Japanese case; in 1979, eleven years after the Meiji restoration, 80 percent of the male teachers were from the samurai class; by 1929 their proportion has declined to 9.5 percent (Karasawa, 1955, p. 86). A similar shift has been reported for the United States (Lortie, 1975, p. 34) and Indonesia (Beeby, 1979, p. 84; Waskito and Cummings, 1981, Table 3.10).

In contrast, during the early stages of industrial development, most women who take up teaching come from middle-class homes. While there is no clear indication yet, it is possible that the social origins of women may decline when sex discrimination declines for executive and managerial positions and in the established professions. At least that is the trend in the United States (Sykes, 1985).

Due to the higher educational requirements for high school teaching, the socioeconomic origins of high school teachers tend to be higher than for primary school teachers (Waskito and Cummings, 1981, Table 4.2).   This generalization seems to hold both for males and females.

ETHNICITY AND RELIGIOUS ORIENTATIONS

There is little evidence concerning the ethnicity and religious preference of teachers. However, in particular societies, certain subgroups are reputed for their interest in learning, such as the Jews in Europe and the United States, the Jordanians in the Middle East, or the Indians in Southeast Asia. Providing there is no ethnic or religious discrimination in the recruitment of teachers, these groups are likely to be overrepresented in the teaching profession. The likelihood of these groups being overrepresented in teaching is enhanced if they are minority groups that do not have a major influence in the political sphere and hence are barred from converting their educational credentials into top jobs in the mainstream of government service. Familiar examples of this condition would be the Indians in Malaysia and the Christians in Indonesia.

EDUCATIONAL LEVEL OF TEACHERS

UNESCO statistics (1984) indicate a wide variety in the number of years of education required of teachers; however, at the primary level the average is about 13 years and at the secondary level the average is about 16 years. In most developing societies, there has been a tendency progressively to upgrade the standards for teacher qualifications, resulting in a steady increase in the number of years of schooling expected for teachers (UNESCO, 1977, pp. 105-106). Husen et al. (1978, p. 22) observe, for the developing countries, that these increases in years of training yield strong dividends in student performance. In contrast with the pattern of increasing training requirements in the developing world, there has been no significant change in the educational level expected of American teachers since World War II, in spite of substantial changes for most other professions (Sykes, 1985, p. 265).

QUALITY OF EDUCATION OF TEACHERS

For those societies where data is available, a trend is evident of decline in average secondary school rank or in national college entrance examination scores for those who enter educational courses. And among those who take up teaching, the proportion from the best schools progressively declines (Waskito and Cummings, 1981; Boyer, 1983, p. 170). That this may not be inevitable is suggested by the high academic standing of Norwegian teachers (Rust, 1985) and the recent improvement in the relative academic quality of those entering teaching faculties in Japan.

TEACHING CAREER PROFILES

A final characteristic of note is the career history of those who teach. Inspection of the IEA surveys, which are the best source on teacher careers, indicates there is extensive variation between societies in both (a) the average years of experience of those who teach, and (b) the extent of mobility between different levels of the system. In general, greater mobility between school levels is possible when a system is relatively new and not highly bureaucratized. Average years of experience is a function of the relative absence of expansion of the teaching profession in a given society and of the relative attractiveness of teaching compared to other occupations to which teachers might move.

SUMMARY

For most of the variables, there is more data at one time across societies than at several times even for a few societies. Still it is my inclination to combine the data to formulate a series of historical generalizations as follows:

1.   The proportion of females among teachers increases until a threshold of 75 percent at the primary and 50 percent at the secondary level is reached.

2.   While teachers have been historically recruited from higher   status families, at least in the case of males, they increasingly come from farm and blue-collar backgrounds.

3.   Minority groups with strong educational traditions, such as the Jews in Europe and the United States, or the Christians in Asia, tend to be overrepresented in the teaching force.

4.   Over time, the number of years of training expected of teachers increases with a current international mode of 13 years for primary school teachers and 16 years for secondary level teachers.

5.   Over time, there is a decline in the relative status of the institutions that train teachers, or increasing proportions of those who teach come from lower status secondary and higher educational institutions.

6.   Over time, the academic achievement of those entering the teaching profession declines relative to those entering other professions.

7.   Over time, the average number of years of experience of those in the teaching profession appears to decline reflecting both (a) the increasing training demands and hence the later age of entry, and (b) the increasing frequency of outward mobility to other occupations and full-time commitment to home life. Thus, while the societal stock of teachers is large, shortages and problems of fit between training and specialization may be evident among those who teach.

Over the course of development, the school system experiences a dramatic shift in the social characteristics of the teaching profession. Schools experience increasing difficulty in recruiting the most able and ambitious members of society. And even among those first attracted to teaching, large numbers either seek educational jobs outside the classroom or leave the educational system altogether. Thus, even societies that develop a sizeable capacity for training teachers discover they have to keep at the task in order to replace those who move out of the profession in mid-career.   The above outlined shift in teacher characteristics is not encouraging for the leaders of school systems.

EXPLAINING THE SHIFT IN TEACHER CHARACTERISTICS

Several concurrent trends of social change seem to have a relation with the shift in teacher characteristics; economic development and the expansion of the modern employment sector, educational expansion and differentiation, the rising prominence of the centralized state, and the increasing complexity of political competition. As should be clear from the earlier literature on industrialization or the current debates surrounding educational expansion, there is no satisfactory theory of the relation between these different changes (Meyer and Hannah, 1980; Kaneko, 1985).

My assumption is that all of these changes are dynamically interrelated in a manner potentially reducible to a set of simultaneous equations. A number of studies have explored the relation of socioeconomic development to teacher supply and demand (Trow, 1967; OECD, 1971; Fuller, 1985). In Figure 1, I identify, in visual form, the relations between the key components of these changes that I think need to be highlighted in explaining the changes in teacher characteristics. In the paragraphs below I would like to outline in verbal form what seems to be involved.

THE BEGINNING

Prior to the changes noted above, most societies are predominantly agricultural, and education, especially beyond the primary level, is open to those few who seek learning to confirm their ascribed social status or to enter into a learned profession such as the clergy or the feudal and/or colonial bureaucracies. Most who seek education come from 'good' homes, and it is from this group that teachers also are selected. The women of good families are expected to become wives rather than enter the labor force.

FIGURE 1
Variables Influencing the Historical Shift in Teacher Characteristics

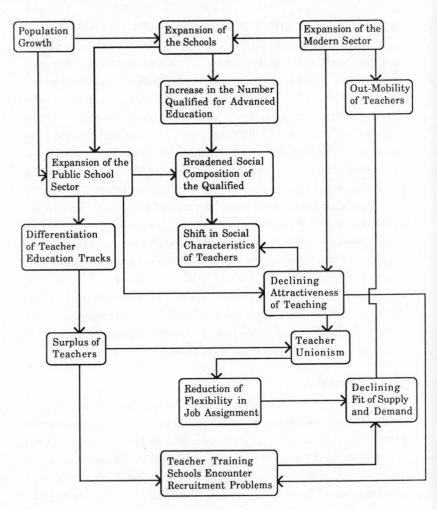

EXPANSION OF THE MODERN SECTOR

Initiating the dynamic changes that eventually affect the characteristics of teachers is the expansion of the modern sector (both absolutely and as a proportion of the total employment system), brought about through a combination of economic entrepreneurship and government planning. By virtue of this expansion, increasing numbers of jobs are created that require educational skills. Teaching positions initially are a significant proportion of those new jobs and are accorded awards equivalent to others requiring similar educational achievement. Teaching is sufficiently attractive that the best students consider a teaching career.

However, over time this may change. The number of modern sector jobs rapidly increases, and the productivity of most jobs also increases. Teaching productivity may not follow the same trend; teacher organizations and educational bureaucracies will tend to argue that the quality of education can be improved through lowering student-teacher ratios. To the extent their arguments prevail, teaching becomes more labor intensive; insofar as product-labor input ratios are used as a measure, teacher productivity may appear to decline (OECD, 1971, p. 155). Partly due to the relative decline in productivity and partly due to other changes to be discussed below, teaching's relative attractiveness may decline.

EXPANSION OF THE SCHOOL SYSTEM

In response to the increasing demand for educated people, the school system gradually expands. Primary education rapidly moves toward universal enrollment followed by secondary education (Trow, 1967). While children from high status homes will be most likely to attend schools, their numbers are limited. Following universal attendance by males, female attendance rates go up. Increasing proportions of school attenders will come from farm families, blue-collar and minority groups. With the expansion of education and in the absence of special regulations relating to teacher preparation, the numbers obtaining the basic educational background essential for teaching quickly exceeds the school system's demand for teachers. Among the school graduates will be increasing proportions of females, rural children and children of farm and blue-collar families.

Most of these school graduates aspire to jobs other than teaching, but the fact that large numbers have the basic qualifications weakens the bargaining position of individuals who actually seek teaching positions. Teachers, recognizing their vulnerability, may propose reforms so that teaching, like other knowledge occupations, acquires professional status. But the teachers' initiatives in this regard are likely to be weak and eventually co-opted by the state.

THE STATE'S CONTRIBUTION TO BUREAUCRATIZATION OF THE SYSTEM

The early stages of school expansion may be realized by private initiative, but at some point the state enters to insure opportunities in areas neglected by the private sector such as rural and isolated areas or in technical fields that require expensive educational facilities. The increasing prevalence of schools in rural areas also affects the attractiveness of teaching relative to other modern sector jobs that are predominantly located in the cities.

DIFFERENTIATION OF SCHOOLS AND REGULATION OF TEACHER CERTIFICATION

As the state becomes involved in the educational system, various rules begin to be introduced. Among these are regulations concerning the amount and type of training expected of teachers. Especially for primary teachers, these regulations are likely to include a number of courses in teacher training.

Special training programs may be established to provide these courses outside of the prevailing educational system, but in most societies the more common solution is to create special tracks at either the secondary or tertiary level for this purpose. Thus, teacher training becomes a distinctive component of the educational system separate from other educational experiences. The limited occupational opportunities associated with teacher training tend to restrict the pool of applicants willing to apply to this track. To some degree this liability may be offset by incentives such as scholarships or lower tuition for the students in teacher training. But incentives of this kind are most attractive to the able students, who cannot otherwise afford higher education, that is, those from lower-class families.

SURPLUS OF TEACHERS

The teacher training programs are established at a time when the educational system is expanding and on a scale aimed at meeting expanding future demands. Once established, these programs continue to recruit the number of students for which they have openings.

However, at some point the pace of school expansion will slow due either to the attainment of full primary and secondary enrollment rates or to a downturn in the size of the secondary school aged cohort. The demand for new teachers may continue for some time after school expansion slows as schools attempt to lower their student-teacher ratios.

However, at some point the demand for new teachers will slack off. But the established programs for teacher training with their fixed costs in buildings and staff will continue to produce the same number of teachers as in the past. A surplus in the number of qualified teachers will occur.

Teacher training systems have difficulty in accommodating to the surplus. A typical scenario sees the system allowing excess graduation for several years followed by a sharp cut in admissions. This scenario tends to repeat itself in what economists describe as a cobweb cycle.

The surplus is not likely to hold for all fields (or regions of a country). Special programs may be devised to fine-tune the system to adjust the fixed capacity so as to address these special situations. But there are obvious limits to the effectiveness of these adjustments. For example, it is difficult to convert a teacher training course in the social studies to a mathematics course.

DECLINING RELATIVE PAY

As the educational system expands under state auspices, education comes to absorb an increasing proportion of the state's budget and the national resources. The major item in educational expenditures is teacher salaries, and thus pressure mounts to curb this expenditure. Due to a surplus of teachers, it becomes feasible to limit the salaries paid to teachers, and they gradually fall behind salaries paid to other occupations requiring similar qualifications.

DECLINING ATTRACTIVENESS OF TEACHING

The various changes associated with the expansion of education inevitably result in the declining attractiveness of teaching (LaBelle, 1973, p. 101 ff.):

- The number of teachers increases so it no longer seems like a special job requiring exceptional training or qualities;
- An increasing number of teaching jobs are in rural areas and with children from ordinary homes who lack the skills and habits of children from "good homes";
- An increasing number of teaching jobs are in public schools and hence part of a large and faceless public system;
- The regulations on teacher certification tend to differentiate teacher training from other educational courses, thus limiting the occupational opportunities of those who select teaching;
- The regulations on teacher certification, as they require different levels and types of education for primary and secondary teachers, tend to restrict the possibility for upward mobility within the teaching ranks as from a primary teacher to a secondary level teacher;

- The numbers trained to teach exceed the number of positions and thus increase the probability that the time and money invested in teaching will not yield a satisfactory return;
- The relative salaries of teachers decline.

THE SHIFT IN THE CHARACTERISTICS OF TEACHERS

For all of the above reasons, teaching becomes less attractive to the most promising and ambitious young people, especially of the male sex. Thus, among males, there may be a tendency to recruit fewer with upper- and middle-class backgrounds and with outstanding academic records. Those males who enter the teaching profession will, with increasing frequency, look upon it as a stepping stone to a managerial position in the educational system.

And failing to achieve mobility in the educational system, many males may move out of education into other jobs in the modern sector that require related skills such as salesmen, office workers, or technicians. A recent OECD study observed that the relatively low training costs involved in teaching account both for the low pay status and the high leaving rates (OECD, 1971, p. 115). Outward mobility will be especially evident among those male teachers who have marketable skills, notably in areas such as science and mathematics, that are often scarce. Thus, despite an overall surplus of teachers, shortages may emerge in these fields.

On the other hand, to the extent employment opportunities for females are restricted in the modern sector, teaching may remain an attractive occupation for females. However, in far more instances than for males, females take up teaching with the idea of retiring after a few years to begin full-time homemaking. The extensive outward mobility and/or early retirement of both male and female teachers means that only a minority of those teaching achieve long years of experience.

UNIONISM AND THE STANDARDIZATION OF WORKING CONDITIONS

In reaction to the declining attractiveness of teaching, teachers may combine in associations to negotiate for better salaries and/or improved working conditions (World Confederation, 1972). In general, these groups achieve more of the latter than the former. Thus, the likely outcomes are lowered teaching hours per day, greater job security, more teacher voice in school management, and other such conditions. These improvements in teacher working conditions do not necessarily contribute to the improvement of education.

CONCLUSION

While the evidence is limited, we have found enough to suggest a dramatic shift in the characteristics of those who teach. In presenting this evidence and our explanation, we do not attempt to take a stand on the desirability or lack thereof of the shift we have described.

The processes we have described result in a gradual shift in the characteristics of teachers toward lower socioeconomic origins, more females, lower academic rank, and lower relative achievement. At the same time, the "average" characteristics of pupils are going through a parallel shift. In the case of pupils, this downward shift is an inevitable function of "filling the schools with the bottom half of the social cup." In the case of teachers, the downward shift has more complex causes. Still, it can be said that the rise of the common school is accompanied by the rise of the common teacher.

These trends have been worrisome to educational administrators, and occasionally reforms have been introduced to alter them. I am not aware of any systematic reviews of these efforts. In 1976, Japan introduced such a reform (including a 50 percent increase in teacher salaries), and it has had a dramatic effect of significantly upgrading the educational qualifications of those entering teaching schools and educational faculties (U.S.

Department of Education, 1987, pp. 19-20). But in the face of large government deficits, already by the mid-1980s the Japanese reform was waning. The Japanese story repeats the usual fate of reforms aimed at altering the characteristics of teachers. They are impressive but short-lived. Thus, there tends to be a cyclical pattern of these changes and hence to the characteristics of those entering the profession. This cyclical pattern leads to minor fluctuations in the long run trend for the characteristics of teachers to follow those of their pupils.

CHAPTER TWO

PRE-SERVICE TEACHER EDUCATION
IN DEVELOPING COUNTRIES

Zainal Ghani

INTRODUCTION

In this chapter we attempt to summarize a survey of the much varied programs of pre-service teacher education in 24 developing countries distributed roughly in four geographical regions: South Asia, Southeast Asia, Latin America (including Cuba), and Northern Africa (see Table 1). The data are based mainly on secondary source material, most of which is for the years 1984-85. These data have been supplemented by personal contacts with informants in a number of the countries included in the survey. The data on such elements as pre-service programs of study, types of courses required, and duration of the courses of study are readily available; however, data on such matters as admission procedures and teaching practices are difficult to identify and are therefore not complete.

Most of the discussion is descriptive, and intentionally so, because we wish to provide an overview of the kind of education pre-service primary and secondary teachers receive in the developing world. We shall engage in some comparative analysis in order to suggest general trends in pre-service teacher education. The basis of this comparison shall be the data collected by Gimeno and Iabanez (1981), which come from the mid-1970s, approximately one decade earlier than our data. We stress that there exist great regional and national variations and overall generalizations must be made with extreme caution.

A number of factors have been considered by scholars, who have attempted to compare teacher education programs around the world, including the "time" factor, the objectives of teacher education programs, the content of programs, instructional methods, and the experiential component of professional training. The one factor that is common to all nations is time. All systems specify the age of entrance, the duration of the program in hours, semesters, or years, and the minimum age of completion of the program. Time is also the fundamental classification variable of organizations such as the Organization for Economic Cooperation and Development (OECD, 1975), UNESCO (1980-88), and the Council of Europe (1970). Consequently, the first two sections of this paper shall focus on time. In the first section we shall deal with several time indicators related to primary teacher education and in the second section we shall consider the same time indicators as they are related to secondary teacher education. These indicators are: (a) the period of time required for entry to teacher education programs, (b) the duration of teacher education programs, (c) the age of students at the time they complete teacher education, and (d) the total number of years teachers are engaged in education in order to qualify to be teachers.

In the final section, we shall focus on several important qualitative aspects of the pre-service teacher education programs, including admission procedures, curriculum, teaching practice, and the probationary year.

Because Cummings has focused on "who teaches" in another chapter of this book, we have chosen not to deal with the socioeconomic and intellectual background of students. Suffice it to say that primary teachers usually come from lower-class backgrounds. In a few cases, elite families with low-achieving children may send them to teacher training institutions, but this is the exception. In the rural areas, where essentially everyone is poor, the teacher has usually been the reference for success. That is, teaching may represent a step toward upward mobility, and the brightest children from peasant families may gravitate toward the profession. At the secondary level, teaching continues to represent a status profession, although it is usually not equivalent to medicine, law, engineering, higher education positions, or business. Those students at the bottom of the higher education system usually end up as secondary teachers. Although these people represent the bottom of the elite, they remain, in most countries, in a high-status position.

PRIMARY TEACHER EDUCATION

The minimum requirements for primary teaching appear to be fairly uniform and standardized within most of the countries surveyed. Only 3 of the 24 countries surveyed have various types of programs within the country. All the others have a national standard that the candidate must meet, if a primary teacher candidate is fully certified. We must point out, however, that the demand for teachers is so great in most of the countries of the developing world, that the standards are not always maintained. It is not uncommon for half the teachers of a developing country in regions such as Africa to be unqualified (Greenland, 1983, p. 4). In fact, some countries maintain a policy of deliberately retarding the number of qualified teachers in order to avoid higher salary costs. The most extreme example of this is the territory of St. Vincent, in the Caribbean, where 70 percent of all teachers are unqualified, and a good percentage of these teachers are so poorly schooled that they do not even qualify to enter the teacher training schools where they could upgrade and qualify themselves (Poonwassie, 1987, p. 2). The important thing to keep in mind is that the so-called unqualified teacher will not have met the standards that are outlined in this chapter.

Our discussion is also confounded by the fact that where there are sufficient teachers, structural problems, as discussed by A.R. Thompson in another chapter of this book, create a situation that necessitates higher standards in some sections of many

Table 1

Primary Teacher Education in 24 Countries of the World in 1984/85

I.   Age at which primary education begins

II.   Years of general primary education

III. Years of secondary education before teacher training

IV.   Age at which teacher education begins

V.   Duration of teacher education course

VI.   Total number of years required for the education of primary teachers

VII. Age at which primary teacher education is completed

Country	I	II	III	IV	V	VI	VII
Afghanistan	7	4	4 + 2	17	1	11	18
Pakistan	5	5	3 + 2	15	2	12	17
India	6	5	3 + 3	17	2	13	19
Sri Lanka	5	5	5 + 2	18/19	2	16	21
Bangladesh	5	5	3+2	15	8 mo.	11	16
Nepal	6	3	4+3	16	1	11	17
Average years to		4.7	6.0	16.5			
Range in years		3-6	5-7	15-19			
Thailand i)	7	6	3+3	19	1	13	20
ii)	7	6	3+1	17	2	12	19
Malaysia	6	6	3+2	17	3	14	20
Singapore (1980)	6	6	3+2	16	2	12	18
Indonesia (1980)	6	6	3	15	3	12	18
Philippines (1981)	7	6	2+2	17	4	14	21
Average years		6	4.5	16.8			
Range in years		6	3-6	15-19			

Country	I	II	III	IV	V	VI	VII
Brazil (1987)	7	8	0	15	3/4	11	19
Chile	7	8	4	19	3	15	22
Cuba	6	6	3	15	4	13	19
Peru	6	6	3	15	2	12	18
Venezuela	7	6	3	16	2	12	19
Colombia	7	5	4	16	2	11	18
Average years			6.2	3.4		16.2	
Range in years			5-8	3-4		15-19	
Algeria i)	6	6	4	16	1	11	17
ii)	6	6	4	16	2	12	18
Ghana	6	6	3	15	4	13	19
Nigeria i)	6	6	-	12	4/5	10/11	6/17
ii)	6	6	-	12	2/3	8/9	14/15
iii)	6	6	3	15	2	11	17
Ivory Coast (1987)	6	6	4+3	19	2	15	21
Morocco	7	5	4+3	19	1	13	20
Kenya	6	7	2+2	17	2	13	19
Sierra Leone (1987)	6	7	3	16	3/4	13	19
Average years		6.1	4.8	15.7			
Range in years		6-7	3-7	12-19			

countries than the minimal requirements, if teachers hope to be hired. In Brazil, Venezuela, and Mexico, for example, long waiting lists exist for teaching positions in the major cities. These teachers are unwilling or unable to travel to the remote areas where teaching positions are always available, and so they are in competition with highly qualified people. In the wealthy Gallao area of Lima, Peru, for example, it is not uncommon to find engineers and scientists teaching at private academies offering highly academic courses to future university pupils. Of course, minimally qualified young people are not found in these schools.

There is great variation even in minimal requirements. Oliveros, in a somewhat dated study of Latin American primary teacher education programs, determines that the total number of general education and professional education hours required to become qualified, ranged from 7,750 in Brazil to 20,850 in Bolivia, with an average of 12,800 hours required in the 20 countries surveyed. Almost half of this time was spent in general primary schooling (47%) with about a quarter of the remaining time divided between general secondary schooling (28%) and professional schooling (25%) (Oliveros, 1975).

In our survey of 24 countries worldwide, we find the average primary teacher candidate engages in approximately ten years of general schooling, then enters the primary teacher education program at around 15.5 years of age, participates in a three year course of studies, and completes the program as a fully qualified primary school teacher about the age of 18.5 years.

GENERAL EDUCATION REQUIREMENTS

Even though the average primary teaching candidate has already engaged in approximately ten years of general schooling prior to entry into professional training, the variation in pre-entry requirements is enormous both quantitatively and qualitatively. The norm for most countries appears to becoming close to at least nine years of general schooling; however, pupils in the Ivory Coast must attend general secondary school for thirteen years, while young people in some parts of Nigeria are able to gain admission to a formal teacher education program after only six years of general schooling, while Brazil requires only eight years of primary schooling. All other countries in our survey require at least nine years of general schooling prior to admission to their teacher education program. Even so, there remains considerable variation, with young people in some countries attending school up to four years longer than the students in other countries.

If we consider the situation at the regional level, greater uniformity is usually observed within each region. Four of the six South Asian countries in our survey require a minimum of ten years of general education prior to admission to teacher training, while India (11 years) and Sri Lanka (12 years) are the exceptions. The extended general education requirement in Sri Lanka can be explained by the fact that young general secondary school leavers are formally qualified to enter directly into teaching, then they are expected to take additional training in an in-service capacity.

If we look at the Southeast Asia region, we find that three of the six countries in our survey also require ten years of general education, with Thailand (12 years), Malaysia (11 years), and Indonesia (9 years) deviating from the norm. Four of the six Latin American countries surveyed require nine years, while Brazil (8 years) and Chile (12 years) are deviant.

Only in Africa do we find a great deal of regional variability. As mentioned above, some parts of Nigeria require only six years of general primary schooling before entering a teacher training school; however, the Nigerian situation is a genuine exception and even it represents a definitional case. That is, even though a young twelve-year-old may enter a teacher education school in the northern Muslim area of the country, the first years of the pupil's program consist almost entirely of general secondary school studies.

Even in Nigeria most of the pupils take a nine-year general education program before entering teacher education. Ghana also requires nine years, while Algeria requires ten years, Kenya eleven, Morocco twelve, and the Ivory Coast thirteen. What this means is that some candidates have very limited general schooling while others have substantial schooling. Such variability in Africa is tempered by other variables. For example, while the Ivory Coast has exceptionally high requirements, its system is one that has changed very little since colonial times and its system remains highly elitist. That is, relatively high amounts of public funds go for education, but only about one third of the school age population is in school and approximately one third of the adult population is literate, so the policy is to use these funds to give extended education to a relatively small percentage of the population.

It would take us beyond the scope of this paper to deal with the content of the general education future teachers engage in prior to entrance into teacher education. Suffice it to observe that all countries require at least a primary education, lasting usually for six years. In addition, almost all countries require completion of the lower secondary school. All the countries in the Asian regions, except Indonesia, even require completion of the second stage of secondary schooling. In other words, Thailand, Malaysia, and Singapore all require approximately eleven years of general study prior to entrance into primary teacher education.

DURATION OF PRE-SERVICE PROGRAMS FOR PRIMARY TEACHERS

The average duration of pre-service primary teacher education programs is 2.35 years, if we consider all countries; however, the range is from one academic year in Bangladesh to five years in Nigeria. Such a range is very wide and reflects the variety of programs to be found for training primary school teachers in the developing world. It is important, however, to consider teacher education time in connection with the general education the young primary teacher education candidates receive, because there is, in many respects, an inverse relationship between the length of general schooling and teacher education. Whereas a young Nigerian student may enter teacher training after only six years of schooling, that person will probably remain in teacher education for five additional years before becoming fully qualified. In contrast, the Moroccan and Thai students, who attend general school for twelve years, must only engage in teacher education for one additional year to be fully qualified to teach.

We also find greater uniformity in programs when considering teacher education on a regional basis. Only in Africa do we find the full range in terms of program length (one to five years). In Latin America, the range is from two to four years, while in South Asia the range is from one to three years.

AGE AT COMPLETION OF PRIMARY TEACHER EDUCATION PROGRAMS

The mean age of young people who complete their pre-service teacher education program in the developing world in our survey is 18.5 years. Once again, however, tremendous variation in completion ages is found across the various countries. Whereas Nigerian students most often finish the program before they reach the age of 16 years, the average Chilean candidate is 24 years old upon completion. Similar variation is found in all regions, although the range is greatest in Africa and South Asia. It is also in these regions where the average age is from one to two years less than Latin America and Southeast Asia. In trying to explain this difference, some informants have speculated that the lower age could be indicative of the relatively high demand for primary teachers in these regions.

COMPARATIVE ASSESSMENT

Although it is unfair to compare the developing world with the developed world, recent trends in the developed world, particularly in Europe, might suggest the direction that professional training could be taking. We find three major recent trends in Europe. The first step European countries generally have taken has been to draw teacher credential candidates from those who have attained an academic grammar school education and who have passed a secondary school leaving examination that qualifies for higher education study. This was a major step because these schools have been highly elitist in the past, providing a very small percentage of the population access to this type of schooling. The second step taken has been to upgrade the teacher training institutions so that they have attained the status of institutions of higher learning with the right to confer a degree. The third step being taken, has been to integrate teacher education schools with other institutions so that they shift from "monotechnic" to "polytechnic" institutions. In other words, primary school teacher education is no longer always isolated from the rest of education, but it becomes a part of more general higher educational studies (Rust, 1984; Bruce, 1979).

From the data we have gathered, primary teacher education in the developing world has not yet begun to attain the three breakthroughs that have been taking place in Europe. Young primary teacher candidates are not yet drawn from those who have completed an academic upper secondary education program. In fact, most of them have not even engaged in upper secondary schooling prior to entrance into a teacher education program. Teacher education institutions have not attained a status as an institution of higher learning. In fact, primary teacher education remains, by and large, a secondary schooling activity. Because this is the case, teacher education is not being integrated into other higher education programs. Is there any movement in the direction suggested above? Because the UNESCO data from the mid-1970s represented the same time factors, it would be valuable to compare data (Gimeno & Ibanez, 1981). In fact, if the data are accurate, almost no movement is seen. In most of the countries surveyed the primary teacher candidates of the 1980s certainly take no more schooling to become certified than they did in the 1970s. The typical shift might be the addition of a single year of general . or professional training. Some dramatic shifts are being contemplated. In Indonesia, for example, where primary teacher education is a secondary school activity, it is quickly being transformed into a post-secondary schooling enterprise. Even there, however, it is unclear whether primary teacher training will be defined as a higher education activity.

SECONDARY TEACHER EDUCATION

In comparison to the pre-service programs for teachers of the primary schools, the programs for secondary teacher education seem to reflect even more variety, both between countries and within each individual country. This greater variety is due, in large measure, to the different types of programs available, the different types of secondary schooling requiring teachers, and also to the greater variety of institutions involved in secondary teacher education. In addition, tradition has often dictated that a university degree alone qualifies a person to be a subject matter teacher. In terms of professional preparation, secondary school teachers of the developing world are prepared in three main types of programs:

(a) Non-degree programs organized usually by colleges of education, (b) Concurrent degree programs, where students are offered a combination of academic and professional courses found usually in universities or other degree-granting institutions of higher learning, (c) Postgraduate programs, which are usually added after the student has completed the academic degree program.

GENERAL EDUCATION REQUIREMENTS

The great difference between the primary teacher candidate and the secondary teacher candidate is in terms of length of general education required. Comparing the data in Tables 1 and 2, we find that the average general education taken by a secondary teacher candidate is 12.5 years, compared with 10.1 years for the primary teacher candidate. This represents almost a two-and-one-half year difference. This difference is also accentuated by the fact that the

Table 2

Secondary Teacher Education in 24 Countries of the World in 1984/85

I.   Age at which primary education begins
II.   Years of general primary education
III.   Years of secondary education before teacher training
IV.   Age at which teacher education begins
V.   Duration of teacher education course
VI.   Total number of years required for the education of secondary teachers
VII.   Age at which secondary teacher education is completed

Country	I	II	III	IV	V	VI	VII
Afghanistan	7	4	4+2	17	4	14	21
Pakistan	5	5	3+2+2	17	3	15	20
India i)	6	5	3+4	18	4	16	22
ii)	6	5	3+4+4	22	1	17	23
Sri Lanka i)	6	6	5+2	19	3/4	16/17	22/23
ii)	6		5+2+3	22	1	17	23
Bangladesh	5	5	3+2+2+2	19	1	15	20
Nepal i)	6	3	4+3+2	18	2	14	20
ii)	6	3	4+3+4/6	20/22	1	15/17	21/23
Ave. where single program			12.4	18.5	2.6	14.7	
where lower level			12.3	18.3	3.0	15.3	
where upper level			15.0	21.3	1.0	16.3	
Range where single program			10-14	17-19	1-4	14-15	
where lower level			12-13	17-19	1-4	14-15	
where upper level			14-16	20-22	1	15-17	

Country	I	II	III	IV	V	VI	VII
Thailand i)	7	6	3+3	19	4	16	23
ii)	7	6	3+3+2	21	2	16	23
Malaysia i)	6	6	5+2	19	4	17	23
ii)	6	6	5+6+4	23	1	18	24
Singapore (1980)	6	6	4+2+3	21	1	16	22
Indonesia	6	6	3+3	18	5	17	23
Philippines (1981)	7	6	2+2	17	6	16	23
Ave. where single program			12.4	18.2	4.2	15.8	
where lower level			--	--	--	--	
where upper level			--	--	--	--	
Range where single program			11-16	18-19	4-6	15-17	
where lower level			--	--	--	--	
where upper level			--	--	--	--	
Brazil (1987)	7	8	3+3	21	1	15	22
Chile	7	8	4	19	5	17	24
Cuba	6	6	6	18	4/5	16/17	22/23
Peru	6	6	3+2+2	19	3	16	22
Venezuela	7	6	5/6	18/19	4	15/16	22/23
Colombia	7	5	4+2	18	4	15	22
Ave. where single program			12.4	18.2	4.2	15.8	
where lower level			--	--	--	--	
where upper level			--	--	--	--	
Range where single program			11-16	18-19	4-6	15-17	
where lower level			--	--	--	--	
where upper level			--	--	--	--	

Country	I	II	III	IV	V	VI	VII
Algeria	6	6	4+3	19	4	17	23
Ghana i)	6	6	3+2+3	19	3	16	22
ii)	6	6	5+2+3	22	1	17	23
Nigeria i)	6	6	5	17	3	14	20
ii)	6	6	5+2	19	3	16	22
iii)	6	6	5+2+3	22	1	17	23
Ivory Coast (1981)	6	6	4+3+3	22	1	17	23
Morocco i)	7	5	4+3	19	4	16	23
ii)	7	5	4+3+3	22	1	16	23
Kenya i)	6	7	2+2+2	19	1	14	20
ii)	6	7	2+2+2	19	3/4	16/17	22/23
Sierra Leone i)	6	7	5+4	21	0	16	22
(1987) ii)	6	7	5+1+3	21	0	16	22
iii)	6	7	5+3	20	1	16	22
Ave. where single program			14.5	21.5	2.5	17	
where lower level			12.8	19.0	2.8	15.5	
where upper level			15.0	21.3	1.8	16.8	
Range where single program			13-16	19-22	1-4	17	
where lower level			11-13	17-19	1-4	14-16	
where upper level			13-16	19-22	1-4	16-17	

general schools that secondary teacher candidates attend are usually not the same as those attended by the primary teacher candidate. Those destined to attend the university very often attend exclusive academic institutions that are usually sponsored by private groups, such as churches, so they charge tuition that prohibits the enrollment of those from poorer families.

The range of years required for entry into secondary teacher preparation programs is very wide, ranging from ten years for most secondary teachers in the Afghanistan and the Philippines to seventeen years in the program for upper secondary teachers of Malaysia.

About half the countries in our survey offer general education programs of a shorter duration for one type of program, than is expected in another type of program. The difference in expectation is usually related (1) to the level the teacher will teach, particularly whether it be a lower secondary post or an upper secondary post, or (2) to the subject matter the teacher will teach, particularly with regard to academic courses as opposed to more practical and nonacademic courses.

The higher-level teacher education programs may demand fourteen, fifteen, sixteen or even seventeen years of general education, while the more limited programs may require eleven, twelve, or thirteen years. Of course, a number of countries, particularly in Southeast Asia and Latin America, have but a single secondary teacher education format, appropriate for all secondary teachers. The minimum general education requirements are usually quite low in these countries, which typically have requirements of ten (Afghanistan, Philippines), eleven (Colombia), twelve (Chile, Cuba, Pakistan), or thirteen (Algeria) years. Singapore is the main exception to this observation in that it demands a minimum of fifteen years of general education of all secondary candidates.

DURATION OF PRE-SERVICE PROGRAMS FOR SECONDARY TEACHERS

The duration of the programs for secondary level teacher education averages about 3.2 years for the countries surveyed. This figure is somewhat misleading because the range of the programs is from one to six years. Just as is the case with primary teacher education, there is a general inverse relation between the duration of the general education programs and teacher education programs. In the seventeen-year program of Malaysia, for example, only one additional year is taken by the candidate to become fully qualified, while a student in the Philippines takes an additional six years of teacher education beyond the ten-year general education program. The Afghan student, who takes but ten years to qualify for entrance into secondary teacher education, must remain in that program another four years before becoming fully qualified.

In general, those candidates preparing for upper secondary school take an extended general education and a limited teacher preparation program. Seven of the nine countries in our survey, which have a two-level program, require only one year of teacher education for the upper-level candidates. The programs, which are of one year duration, are post-graduate courses similar to the British Post Graduate Certificate of Education (PGCE) courses. In fact, a large number of these programs have been modelled on the PGCE course. In some ways, the variation of duration of the programs found specifically in the South Asia, Southeast Asia, and Africa regions, is a clear manifestation of the various colonial influences. For example, in South Asia, there is still a strong English influence on the education structure of many countries. Likewise in Africa, the French and English influences remain enormous in some of the countries surveyed. In Southeast Asia, there are the added American and Dutch influences. In Latin America, quite a different colonial influence can be seen, coming mainly from Spain and Portugal, although United States influences are now substantial.

AGE OF COMPLETION

Secondary teacher candidates are generally rather mature by the time they complete their program of study. The mean age of our sample countries is 22.3 years, which amounts to an average of approximately 16 years of general and teacher education. This means that the typical secondary teacher candidate will have engaged in a significant amount of tertiary education. Because primary and general secondary education almost always consist of no more than 12 years, secondary teacher candidates will typically have taken at least four years of tertiary education.

The range of ages of those becoming fully certified is between 20 and 24 years. If we look at the regional level, we find the lowest graduating age of secondary teacher candidates to be from South Asia (19.8 years), while the highest average age is in Southeast Asia (23 years), although the range of ages across nations in that area of the world is rather large.

COMPARATIVE ANALYSIS

Three time measures are available. Not only do we have time data from our own sample, but the Gimeno and Ibanez data (1981, pp. 58-60), reflecting conditions in the mid-1970s, allow us to isolate almost all of the countries used in our study and also to isolate sample countries in the developed world for comparative purposes. We have chosen 15 European countries for this exercise. It is significant that the time averages of these three variables are almost identical. For example, if we calculate the average age of secondary candidates, when they complete teacher education training, we find the age of our current sample is 22.3 years, the age of our sample in the mid-1970s is also 22.3 years, and the age of those in Europe in the mid-1970s is 22.4 years. In other words, the length of training in the developing world has changed very little in the past decade, and it remains almost the same as the length of training in Western Europe.

Whereas primary teacher education in the developing world generally lags far behind the developed world, in terms of time, secondary teacher training is equivalent to the developed world. Clearly, the colonial legacy for the elites of the developing world remains such that those destined for teaching in the secondary schools are given enormous advantages, when compared with those training to be teachers in the primary schools.

If there is any insight about shifts that can be gained, it may be in the negative. Note that the time for training may even be slipping ever so slightly. Whereas secondary teacher candidates in the developing world were 22.4 years of age when completing their program in the mid-1970s, they are now 22.3 years of age. Such a shift is not significant, but it may suggest a tendency to begin reducing the time required for training as secondary schools are transformed from elite programs to mass programs.

ISSUES RELATED TO TEACHER EDUCATION

SELECTION CRITERIA FOR ADMISSION

The criteria used for selection to the pre-service programs in the various countries vary considerably both between and within countries. Most countries use more than one criterion for selection, and in some cases a combination of criteria are used. India, Sri Lanka, Nepal, Pakistan, Indonesia, and Malaysia, all use a combination of four different criteria in the selection process. We shall mention each of the criteria typically used.

First, the most common criteria is obviously the successful completion of the minimum required period of schooling which is usually associated with some type of certification, such as a secondary school certification or matriculation certificate. Such a requirement, of course is not expected of primary teacher candidates, whose teacher education program is usually a part of the upper secondary education system.

Second, a large number of countries, fifteen of the twenty-four countries in our survey, also require candidates to sit for some form of entrance examination.   These examinations usually have a scholastic achievement base, although, in some cases, they also test for general knowledge.

Third, personal interviews also seem to be a fairly common criterion used in conjunction with the above mentioned criteria.   It would seem that the main aims of these interviews are to judge the verbal fluency and the personality of the candidates, although personality attributes are usually determined from the next criterion.

Fourth, institutions where the student was previously located may be required to submit letters of reference for the candidates. These may point out the candidates academic qualifications, but the major purpose is usually to assess the   personal or "character" attributes of the candidates.

In addition to the above criteria, a few countries, such as the Philippines, Thailand, Nepal, and Indonesia, require some form of health certification from a physician.   In one case, the candidates are even required to submit a certificate of mental health.

These are the major criteria for selection, if we generalize to most countries of the developing world in our sample, although certain other information is required in selected countries.   In Malaysia, for example, an attitude test is currently being tested for use in the selection of primary and lower secondary school teacher candidates at the teacher training colleges.   In Ghana, an intelligence test is being used in conjunction with the entrance tests. Some countries also have an age limit for candidates.

CURRICULUM

In the survey of literature on pre-service education in the developing countries, details on the curriculum of the pre-service teacher education programs are very difficult to come by some information beginning to emerge (Hawes, 1982; Awour, 1982; Masota, 1984; UNESCO, 1975).   The surveys by Gimeno and Ibanez

(1981) and ILO/UNESCO (1975) also have not been able to provide sufficient information for an in-depth analysis of the curricula for pre-service education programs. My own survey material reflects these deficiencies, as I was able to gather detailed information on only eight of the twenty-four countries involved in my analysis.

ILO/UNESCO (1975) uses four main curriculum categories, which were adopted in this survey of programs. They are:

1.   General Education: This area includes academic study, as well as enrichment courses for personal development. The intention of these courses within the teacher education format is to broaden the teacher's general education and experience. Language development is particularly crucial in most countries.

2.   Specialized Subjects: This area of the curriculum is related to the specialized study of subjects beyond that taken for general education purposes. Teachers training to teach special subjects will engage in specialized training, so specialized training usually takes place at tertiary institutions, which expect students to concentrate in some subject field.

3.   Professional Studies: This area includes courses specifically related to the profession of teaching and includes methods courses but also foundations courses in educational psychology, history, sociology, or philosophy.

4.   Teaching Practice: This includes clinical experiences in the classroom, where the candidate acts in an apprentice-like capacity under the supervision of an experienced teacher.

Most of the countries surveyed indicated that their pre-service programs for primary teacher education contained courses which could be categorized in all four areas. However, the ratio of courses in each category is quite different. From Table 3, we find that in Singapore and Malaysia, students take a balanced program of courses across the three instructional areas with a relatively small portion of time given to teaching practice (15%). In contrast, Thai students devote approximately 40% of their time to teaching practice.

Table 3

Primary Teacher Education Curriculum

Country	General Educ.	Specialized Subjects	Professional Course	Teaching Practice	Co-Curriculum	Others
Afghanistan		59/81	41/19	41/19		Background Studies
Pakistan					Scout Master Training	
India		40%	40%	20%		
Sri Lanka		60%	40%	40%		
Thailand	58%	26%	12.6%	40%		
Malaysia	30%	35%	20%	15%	Compulsory Co-Curricular Activities	Language Proficiency Course
Philippines						Language Proficiency Course
Singapore	28%	36%	29%	15%		Language Proficiency Course

Country	General Educ.	Special-ized Subjects	Profes-sional Course	Teaching Practice	Co-Curric-ulum	Others
Ghana						Language Proficienc Course
Nigeria					Games and Physical	Language Proficienc
Ivory Coast						Guidance Practical/ Adviseme
Morocco	60%	30%	10%	10%		
Algeria						Leadershi
Colombia						Language Proficienc Course
Chile						Guidance Leadershi Supervisi
Cuba	44%	15%	18%	23%		

On the one hand, countries such as Afghanistan and Sri Lanka emphasize specialized subjects while neglecting general education/enrichment. On the other hand, Thailand and Morocco seem to emphasize general education. These countries do not neglect specialized courses but devote almost no time to professional courses. No countries require students to spend the majority of their time on professional courses, but the ratio difference is substantial. Up to 40% of the student's time is given to professional education in countries such as India, whereas only 10% of the time is devoted to professional education in Morocco.

In spite of these differences, a common feature of the primary teacher preparation curriculum can be detected. The proportion of academic studies, whether it be general or specialized, usually amounts to about 60% of the curriculum. The proportion of professional time, whether it be professional courses or practice teaching, amounts to about 40% of the curriculum.

In addition to the program of studies, several countries also require teacher candidates to follow different extra-curricular courses, such as participation in uniformed organizations, such as Boy Scouts, Red Cross, recreation clubs, community service, or games and physical training. These are seen, in these countries, as an essential part of the total professional development of the candidates, although all countries would view such participation with favor.

Two other curricular aspects are found in some countries. First, there is a requirement that students reach a certain language proficiency prior to becoming fully certified. Such an expectation obviously stems from the fact that schooling is grounded in language, whether it be a national language, foreign modern language, or classical language. Consequently, countries as diverse as Malaysia, the Philippines, Singapore, Ghana, Nigeria, and Colombia require language courses. In other words, such a proficiency requirement exists with at least one country from each of the four major regions which we have surveyed, except South Asia. Second, there is a requirement in Algeria, the Ivory Coast, and Chile that candidates engage in leadership courses, which provide training in spheres such as guidance, supervision, and management.

PRACTICE TEACHING

Because practice teaching is usually deemed to be the most important professional element (Gardner, 1979), we shall give special attention to it. It provides the opportunity for the students to observe and practice the skills for which they have been trained. It is also seen as the opportunity for the students to translate into practice what they have learned in theory. Of course, just as is the case in the developed world, the gap between theory and practice remains enormous and is one of the central issues in teacher education.

In this survey, certain aspects of teaching practice have been identified in at least thirteen primary and twelve secondary teacher education programs in our sample of countries. We inquire as to when it takes place in the program, the duration of teaching practice, the number of teaching practice sessions, where it takes place, and a few related issues.

When Teaching Practice Takes Place

Teaching practice sessions are usually held at the end of the professional course, either in the final year or in combination with intermediate years, both for primary and secondary teacher training. There are a small number of programs (two elementary and four secondary), where a continuous program of teaching practice is carried on throughout the professional part of the program. There are advantages and disadvantages to both formats. If practice teaching occurs toward the end of the program, the student ought to have a greater maturity and a greater knowledge of the theory on which teaching is based. However, if teaching occurs at the same time that theory is being learned, its relevance may more easily be seen, learned, and applied. Obviously, more countries have opted for the first of these approaches, but the potential of the latter might merit further exploration.

Number of Sessions per Program

Closely related to the above section, is the issue of the number of sessions the candidate engages in practice teaching. Of course, those engaged in continuous practice would not speak of sessions in the same manner as other programs. All but one of the noncontinuous primary programs expect the student to engage in two different student teaching sessions. Secondary programs, on the other hand, are likely to require but a single teaching practice session. The programs with single sessions are likely to be those post-graduate courses, although many of them also arrange for continuous teaching practice to take place.

Duration of Teaching Practice

There seems to be a wide range of options in terms of the length of teaching practice. A small number of primary and secondary programs require as little as four weeks of actual practice teaching, and a small number require as many as twenty or twenty-four weeks of practice teaching. The more typical arrangement, both for primary and secondary training, is for the candidate to experience twelve weeks of practice teaching.

Location of Teaching Practice

There seems to be a trend toward the use of schools which are closely associated with the training institutions, so that the practice sessions can be more easily related to the total teacher education experience. Such institutions may be laboratory schools (two countries use these for primary practice teaching, while one country uses them for secondary purposes) but the more common practice is to arrange for associated schools (seven countries use them for primary and seven for secondary teaching practice). These schools are not only open for clinical practice, but they provide demonstration lessons, participant observation, and pilot innovative teaching practices, instructional materials, and audio-visual equipment. Some teacher education programs also include practice sessions at the training institution itself, where such practices as micro-teaching, seminars, and discussion groups are conducted.

Other Aspects of Teaching Practice

One area of interest for teaching practice is the use of teacher-based supervision and/or evaluation. A large number of programs for primary teacher education, define the master teacher role to include supervision and evaluation of the candidates. Such a formal expectation is not made of most secondary teacher education programs, although the informal situation is probably fairly similar to that taking place in primary programs.

PROBATIONARY YEAR

Because of the enormous need for teachers in the developing world, little has been done, so far, in terms of supervising and monitoring progress of the teacher, once he/she leaves the training institution and enters the classroom. A few countries in our survey, Singapore and Malaysia, report that training institutions are taking on a new role, which involves monitoring and assessing the newly graduated teacher during the initial year of teaching. Such a practice ought to be beneficial both to the new teachers and to the training institutions themselves. This procedure will provide important feedback to the institutions about the effectiveness of their pre-service programs and the specific training dimensions that must be addressed if the new teacher is to be given the skills necessary to be successful in the classroom.

CONCLUDING REMARKS

From this brief survey of pre-service education in the developing countries, it can be seen that there is considerable variation in the structure of programs. There is greater variation in the programs for the preparation of secondary teachers than for primary teachers. These variations seem to be related, to some extent, to the influence of the former colonial masters. While the structure may differ greatly, the other aspects of pre-service education, such as the criteria for admission, the curriculum, and teaching practice, seem to be less varied.

CASE STUDY FOR CHAPTER TWO

TEACHER TRAINING IN VITORIA, BRAZIL

Jose Maria Coutinho

Brazilian educators are right now in the midst of a national movement to get out of a chaotic educational situation, in large measure because of the general economic crisis, engendered by a huge external debt of more than 110 billion dollars, which has turned attention away from education and other humane aspects of Brazilian life. Education has declined to the point that it now consumes less than 5 percent of the national budget and continues to be a privilege of the elites. Once it became clear that education is not a government priority, despite official declarations to the contrary, educators all over the country have, at times, been forced to stop teaching and confront directly the deterioration in the quality of education, particularly the quality of teaching. On the eve of a new constitution, which is being elaborated by recently elected congressmen, Brazilian educators discuss issues such as restructuring and democratizing the university, providing tuition-free education at all levels, financing the system, expanding secondary education, reducing repetition and the drop-out rate, eliminating illiteracy, improving the quality of teaching, etc. In many ways, these issues can be subsumed under the dual heading, "quality of teaching and social compromise." This paper describes comparatively two teacher training institutions, the students and teachers of those institutions, the strategies used in primary teacher preparation and the ways they differ from secondary teacher training.

CRISTINA AND ARNALDO: A PERSPECTIVE ON CLASS AND DEPENDENCY

Cristina Rodrigues has just begun her studies at the Teacher Training Institute located in Praia do Canto, an affluent urban upper-middle-class barrio of Vitoria, the capital city of the State of Espirito Santo. It may seem curious that the Institute is located in the elite district, because Cristina has a lower-class background. Her father is a factory worker and has only a primary education, while her mother dropped out of school after only three years of primary school. She is much like the other students at the Institute. She is nearing her sixteenth birthday, and enters an institution where 95 percent of all students are female. Over 80 percent of all students come from working class origins, most are sons and daughters of the large working group know as *boias-frias*, those who eat their food cold during working breaks. A small portion of her classmates represent the middle class, and that number is even growing slightly. Cristina must pay the equivalent of Cz15.00 (US$ .25) per month tuition, about which she has already heard many students complain. She will soon discover that she rarely has enough resources to purchase any books, and she will also find that the library is so outdated that the texts are not available. She has not been able to purchase her school uniform, which, fortunately for her, is optional (Rezende, 1987).

This situation stands in stark contrast to that of Arnaldo Gouveia, who is beginning his studies at the Pedagogic Center of the Federal University of Vitoria. Arnaldo's father is a lawyer, who, of course, possesses a university degree, as does Arnaldo's mother. Not only is Arnaldo continuing his education in an institution separate from Cristina, but his prior education was also taken in quite different places. In Brazil, all students are required to attend primary school; however, those of wealth rarely send their children to the public schools, which are really only for the masses.

Arnaldo did not attend public school, but he began his schooling in an eight-year private school run by a Catholic order

(Salesian Brothers).   Although the tuition at the school was only seven dollars a month, it remained so high that no children of the poor could afford to attend.   It was an excellent school.   All the teachers had university training, the children had textbooks for every subject, and the school possessed a library of more than 3,000 books. Even laboratories were available for the science courses.   In addition, the teachers were very demanding.

In contrast, Cristina spend her first eight years of schooling at Goiabeiras Public School, located in a poor section of the city.   She was not among the best of students and would have been considered vastly inferior by private school standards.   Though the school was rather large, having 800 pupils and poor in material resources, her teachers were, by and large, of high quality, when compared with primary teachers in the more remote areas of the country or the state.

Cristina was fortunate to have had fully certified teachers in each grade level.   This means that all of her teachers had attended a teacher training institute for at least three years following the eight-year primary school, and they had passed all requirements.   Not only had the teachers met these minimal requirements, but they were more mature and experienced than in the interior of the country. Even though a young person can theoretically enter teaching at the age of 17 or 18 years of age, none of Cristina's teachers were so young.   Places are not available for such young people in cities such as Vitoria, where there are long waiting lists for every available position.   Even so, the primary school was inadequate by any standard.   There is a saying in the town that the only assets in the school are "chalk and saliva."

There was no library in the school at the time Cristina attended, and there were also less than 100 textbooks for the 800 pupils.   Some improvement in this situation is taking place.   The Minister of Education had recently made great news by announcing that the average child will soon have two textbooks in school, which means that Cristina's school would have to increase its textbook supply by a factor of sixteen. Whereas Cristina had entered the Teacher Training Institute directly after her eight year general schooling, Arnaldo had entered general secondary school. Of course, he remained within the private sector, in a school also run by the Salesian Brothers. He remained there for three years and then faced the *Vestibular*, the University Entrance Examination. Because the school is one of the best in Vitoria, most of Arnaldo's classmates passed both exams and qualified for university studies. Arnaldo was not among the best of the students. In fact, he was among the lowest of those who qualified for advanced study. Upon entering the university, he attended a general program, which all students must take for one semester, then he concentrated on natural science (physics) for seven semesters. The best students would continue their studies in the field, but Arnaldo had already recognized that he was not suited to compete with them, so he had selected teaching as his career.

It would be inaccurate, however, to suggest that Arnaldo was not a capable student. Only 1.1 percent of an age-level in Brazil ever qualifies for university study. Consequently, he is, without question, one of the bright students, falling in the 98- 99 percentile of his age group, and he certainly falls in a different category of student from those entering primary teacher training.

THE TEACHER TRAINING SCHOOLS

The two teacher training schools of Vitoria are classified as being among the best in the State. The Primary Teacher Training Institute, named Instituto de Educacao Fernando Duarte Rabelo, is located in Praia do Canto, an affluent urban upper and middle class barrio. The Centro Pedagogico of the Federal University of Espirito Santo, is located in the suburb of Goiabeiras, a poor district. The size of the two centers is dissimilar. While the Instituto has 550 teacher training pupils, the Pedagogico has 700 students in all specializations. Although the location of the institutions suggests a corresponding socioeconomic background of the students, this is not the case.

The Institute does not have the reputation of being a rigorous institution, even though it is located in a high-middle-class area. Until very recently, it served mainly as a production mill for so-called *empregadas domesticas*, home maidens, who acted as baby sitters and house keepers. Their training was especially valued because they possessed some knowledge of psychology and had been initiated into the middle-class ideology and norms.   In spite of the fact that Institute personnel continue to complain about its deficiencies as a teacher training center, it is known generally for providing a model program for Vitoria.   However, it is not considered to be better than other types of secondary schools in the State, particularly those providing general education.   It is commonly believed that a "C" grade at the Institute remains equivalent to a "D" grade at the so-called scientific high schools.   While giving over 400 diplomas in its four specializations in 1986, it was only able to show eight University Entrance Exam passes, which is very low, considering the fact that schools like that attended by Arnaldo qualified most of their students.

Those involved in teacher education challenge such comparisons, because the Institute is not concerned with preparing students for the university.   It prepares middle-level professionals such as primary school teachers, administrative assistants, accountants, and secretaries.   And its graduates are actively recruited, more because they have received a general humanistic education, which is valued by the civil service sector, than because they have engaged in a rigorous academic experience.

The Teacher Training Institute is run by a principal assisted by a small office staff and a support staff of cooks, janitors, etc.   In addition there are five general coordinators, six educational supervisors, and three counselors but no subject-matter field coordinators.   Although dependency and clientelism permeate the nomination of an official in Brazil, usually the professional staff members of a training institute are professionally qualified.   The

Principal, Maria Ignez Rezende Freitas, has an undergraduate degree in school administration, sixteen years teaching experience, and almost four years experience as a principal of a small primary school. She is well prepared for this position and takes satisfaction in her ability to run the Institute.

The general training program prepares teachers who will be located in the first four grade levels of the primary school. If Cristina chooses to remain in the lower grades, she can complete her program within three years. Her course of studies will fall into three groups. First, she must complete a Common Core consisting of eight subjects. Second, she must study four other so-called Obligatory Subjects. Finally, she must study Professional Subjects, such as didactics, curriculum, and learning theory.

There are students taking specialties at her Institute other than primary teacher preparation. Some are preparing to be nursery school teachers (ages 2-4), some kindergarten teachers (ages 4-5), and some to engage in literacy training (ages 6 and above).

The type of instruction they receive is both theoretical and practical. Methodologies of teaching are varied, going from lectures to dialogue, from working groups to directed study or bibliographical research, from observations to actual practice teaching. Student evaluation is not rigorously defined and may include qualitative criteria such as participation in class discussions, self-assessment, but may also include quantitative criteria such as test results. Grades are given bimonthly. The students look at teacher training through different lenses. Not all of them are anticipating teaching and trying to understand its inherent responsibilities, being more interested in a quick entrance to the job market after school. Although the Institute does not promise much hope to enter the university, it does provide an avenue into occupational mobility through its four specializations.

Even though there are too many students in the classes and too few resources to develop the major part of the curriculum, the number of dropouts is minimal. Approximately 5 percent of the students drop out each year, although the number usually depends on the ability of students to find jobs unrelated to teaching. It is unlikely that Cristina could enter the classroom as a teacher before she becomes qualified. The number of unqualified teachers in the countryside remains higher than in the city, but Cristina would find some difficulty finding a teaching job anywhere, unless she becomes qualified. In fact, if she chooses to teach in the fifth or sixth grade levels, she must complete one additional year of study, or four years of study. Teachers in the seventh and eighth grade levels are mainly those who have taken a four-year university program in a subject matter field. In other words, Arnaldo could take a position of this kind when he finishes his program. He is more likely, however, to enter secondary school, which requires the same qualifications. In the State of Espirito Santo secondary teachers are trained at the three institutions of higher learning, including the Centro Pedagogico at the local Federal University.

Centro Pedagogico is a unit for teaching, research, and extension. It has three departments: Foundations of Education and Counseling, Administration and Supervision, as well as Didactics and Teaching Practice. It furnishes certificates in four areas of education: teaching, supervision, administration, and counseling. The University adopted, some fifteen years ago, the credit and semester system, based on the University of Houston model in the United States (Atcon, 1973). The general curricula of the Training Institute and the Pedagogico are similar in terms of the types of programs they offer, although they have typically been broadened or subdivided during undergraduate training, so that students take a plethora of specialized subjects before they are finished.

Most of the teachers at the Pedagogico hold a Masters degree, although some hold a Ph.D., and a small number hold an undergraduate degree or specialized diploma (Gianordoli, et al., 1987, p. 17). The advanced degrees were obtained either at highly regarded Brazilian institutions or universities in the U.S.A., England, France, Belgium, etc. The Pedagogico now offers a

Masters degree program in three areas: Administration, Educational Evaluation, and Social Development and Educational Processes.

An Interdepartmental Council functions, along with the Director of the Centro Pedagogico, as the administrative arm of the Center. The administrative units of all higher education are now being swept by democratic winds. Currently, the President of Brazil chooses the University President, who then chooses the Director of the Pedagogico and other centers. Each department elects its head for one year, and it is becoming commonplace that teachers, students, and other employees participate in some elections, although only teachers vote for the Council members. Competence, academic quality, efficiency, and social compromise are winds of democracy.

DEPENDENCY EXPLANATIONS

Cristina and Arnaldo typify the separation of the social classes, which continues to pervade Brazilian society, reflecting on the educational system. Incorporated by the internal structure of dependency via economic imperialism, Brazil and its educational system orbit around the capitalist system (Tavares, 1980), mediated by the national elite, the middle classes, military allies, and intellectual servants of the rich, both national and international. The Brazilian educational system, from colonial times, has transplanted foreign educational models, to which not all the population has gained access (Berger, 1976). Reproducing the ideology of the dominant classes, Brazilian education is structured in such a way that the masses are deprived and remain dependent on the elites.

Two interacting aspects of international capitalism, imperialism and dependency, have maintained Brazil's underdevelopment as a whole, and its development has been dependent on international financing through investments, loans, technology, and technical assistance. Her economy depends not only on the contraction and expansion of the United States economy but also on the interest rates fluctuating in the North American banks (Cardoso, 1980, 1973; Evans, 1979).

The Brazilian educational system has transplanted foreign educational models which historically have prevented certain groups from gaining access to schooling, which has led to conflicts between the cultures of the elites and the poor. Elementary schools suffer from the chronic disease of passing only 65.8 percent of the pupils from the first to the second grade level. These pupils soon drop out completely from the system, so that by the eighth-grade level approximately 80 of every 100 pupils has left the school system, and only 11 of every 1,000 pupils ever complete university study (IBGE, 1980).

The history of Brazilian education has, thus, represented a continuous struggle of the dependent masses to reach higher levels of schooling, while the elites have fought to retain their prerogatives as the dominant class. In recent years the situation has changed somewhat, in that the masses are expected to attend school. In theory and in Brazilian law, they are able to receive an eight-year basic education, and if they qualify, they are able to join the elite class. This seldom happens for the vast majority of Brazilians.

The teachers have come to play a significant broker role between the two social classes. The best of the lower classes rise and become primary teachers. The middle classes remain as the teachers of the elite schools. In this respect they tend to bridge the gap between the two classes. Today, the status of all teachers has been eroded by a continuous and galloping inflation, which has reduced teachers' buying power, not only in terms of their quality of life, but in terms of the quality of their teaching. Facing low salaries on one side and few resources for the schools on the other side, Brazilian teachers at all levels are perplexed as to where the economy, the politics, and education will go. Government measures to solve the problems of educators have proved to be ineffective. Having exhausted dialogue and all kinds of negotiations, teachers have resorted to slow-down tactics, strikes, and demonstrations.

Teachers in Brazil have confronted the government on several matters, mainly on the living conditions and school conditions. A more aware professional class is emerging and expresses concern about the kind of teaching and learning they are able to offer, taking into consideration the poor condition of the schools, of the pupils and the parents. Educators such as Paulo Freire, Marilena Chaui, Carlos Cuty, and Elizabeth Gama, located at the major Brazilian federal universities continually raise questions such as: "Who educates or trains who?" "How are teachers to be trained?" "Education is for whom and for what purposes?" "What is the role of teachers in cultural reproduction?" No resolution to these questions has yet been found.

WHAT SHOULD TEACHERS DO?

The Brazilian situation of dependency has contributed to a low investment in education, which has engendered a dual educational system. Education is simply not a government priority, because the best education remains the domain of the elites. In Espirito Santo, as in Brazil as a whole, it becomes burdensome for the public school teachers to teach undernourished children without being able to solve their problems at home. The children are so poor that the function of the schools is changing, so that teachers become responsible for feeding, caring for health, and even sleeping needs. They become preoccupied with the "salvation from poverty" of millions of school children, which shifts their philosophies, curricula, programs, and the entire academic climate of the schools. There is an ongoing discussion among Brazilian teachers about their functionalist and reproductive role as ideological agents and intellectual servants of the upper class. The teachers have become increasingly aware of their role in legitimizing and maintaining the status quo, including social inequalities and reflected in the 36 million abandoned or semi-abandoned street children, the so-called *pivetes*. Identifying with the general national working class, they have organized themselves in associations and unions, struggling for better education and better schools.

This awakening of the teachers endangers the humanistic curriculum and training they have received in school. However, it has awakened them to their general low status and the quality of life they experience as teachers. In spite of this, most continue to maintain the flame of humanistic and romantic ideals that they learned in school and teacher training.

CHAPTER THREE

EFFECTIVE IN-SERVICE PROGRAMS IN DEVELOPING COUNTRIES: A STUDY OF EXPERT OPINION

John H. M. Andrews
Ian E. Housego
David C. Thomas

INTRODUCTION

This study seeks to contribute to increasing the quality of teaching in developing countries by focusing on the in-service training of unqualified teachers. The target of unqualified teachers was selected because of the frequency with which educators from developing countries identify the large number of unqualified teachers as a crucial obstacle to any serious attempt to increase the overall quality of education. The percentages of unqualified primary teachers in 13 African countries range from 19% to 71%. By weighting the sizes of the teaching forces in these countries, this comes to an average of 46% unqualified teachers (Greenland, 1983, p. 4). Statistics from China show approximately 53% of the primary teachers unqualified in 1983 (Lo, 1984, p. 168). Thus, although there is a wide variation around the would, as many as half of the teachers in the developing countries typically are unqualified.

This situation arises usually because of the enormous political pressures in these countries, based on both economic and humanitarian concerns, to achieve universal education without delay. The urgency of achieving this goal frequently has led to the opening of schools staffed by the best people available, even though large numbers were unqualified.

The obvious remedy to this problem is the provision of in-service training (IST) for these unqualified teachers (note 1). Such programs have existed for many years and more are now being designed and implemented. The pace of development of such programs is, in fact, increasing as many countries turn their attention and resources from the tumult of expanding educational facilities to the challenge of increasing the quality of education. Thus, the question of what is most effective in the structure and practices of IST, particularly for unqualified teachers, has become one of considerable significance.

The literature, unfortunately, offers only modest help. Though a sizeable number of articles and books exist on the topic, most are anecdotal, usually authored by involved practitioners (Vivian, 1968; Ariyadasa, 1976; Ayot, 1983). Others, though reported by neutral observers, rarely present credible evaluation of the projects reported. Indeed, of 60 separate IST activities studied by Greenland in Africa (1983, p. 107), half claimed to have been formally evaluated, but in only six cases was there actual follow-up at the school level to judge effectiveness. In another particularly useful publication, Avalos and Haddad note:

. . . Given the number of inservice courses that have been organized in every country, some reviewers note the lack of studies on the effects of inservice training upon students

. . . There is also not much evidence of the effectiveness of different ways of organizing inservice training or methodologies used for this purpose (1981, p. 22).

The authors of the present study recognize the need for outcomes-based evaluation of different models of IST, but, in light of the present dearth of knowledge, believe that useful preliminary information can be obtained which may at least narrow the field for subsequent, project-specific research. In this study we obtained judgments about policies and practices of IST for unqualified teachers in developing countries from an international panel of nineteen nominated experts from the developed world (Australia, Canada, and the United Kingdom) and the developing world (Bangladesh, Barbados, Hong Kong, India, Kenya, Malaysia, Nigeria, and Singapore). This approach capitalizes on the experience of educators, who are internationally recognized for their expertise in teacher IST. Though subjective in nature, the confidentiality of responses and the broad base of the study are expected to minimize spurious effects and maximize thoughtful professional judgment.

The panel members were invited to respond to a field-tested questionnaire composed of questions derived from a taxonomy of possible characteristics of IST programs, constructed from an extensive review of the literature (note 2). Questions were generated under the following categories: (1) the most appropriate approach to operational control of IST programs, (2) the best use of money available in relation to program costs, (3) the best approaches to the motivation of unqualified teachers to become and remain involved in IST programs, (4) the most cost-effective methods for the delivery of IST programs, (5) program content emphasis (subject matter vs. pedagogy), and (6) the best means to ensure that the training is, in fact, implemented in the performance of those who took part in IST programs.

The questionnaire was focused on the six areas. It also sought perception about the degree to which one is able to generalize from the opinions of the respondents with respect to (1) all developing countries as opposed to one or a few, and (2) the continuing education of fully qualified teachers as opposed to unqualified teachers. Originally, it was felt that rural and urban differences would be so great that generalizations across the two spheres would be misleading; however, no significant differences were found on any question (using Chi-square, p .05), so our conclusions were usually drawn from the combined rural/urban frequencies.

In responding to the questionnaire, panel members were asked to reflect on their own real experience with in-service training in developing countries. In other words, they were asked for their opinions about what they consider "best practice from a realistic perspective as opposed to an unrealistic ideal perspective."

Field trial validation of the questionnaire was undertaken with the cooperation of five graduate students, most from developing countries, who responded to the questions and then commented on their appropriateness and clarity. As a result, a number of changes were made. An amended questionnaire was then administered to three other graduate students from developing countries. Their reaction to the questionnaire raised no further concerns.

THE RESULTS

In our discussion of results, we shall view conclusions drawn from our own survey results in the context of the literature. In the main body of the questionnaire, our panel of specialists was asked to make some judgment about fifteen program characteristics. At the conclusion of this section, they were then asked to rate, on a five point scale with five designated as "most important," the importance of each program characteristic in influencing the effectiveness of an IST program. From Table 1 we find the highest six program characteristics were ranked in the following order: 1. Ensuring that the IST is Implemented in Practice; 2. Motivation of Participants; 3. Program Content Emphasis; 4. Control of Program; 5. Best Use of Available Funds; and 6. Best Methods of Delivery of Program.

In what follows, we look more closely at each of these items, in order of their importance, as well as at a few characteristics of lesser importance.

ENSURING THAT THE IST IS IMPLEMENTED IN PRACTICE

The literature describing actual practice in IST programs leads one to believe that attempts at integration of the acquired learning into the actual teaching job are limited. Authors frequently deplore this program deficiency. For example, Vivian says:

Table 1
Relative Importance of Program Characteristics

Characteristic	Item No.	Rating of Importance					Ave.	Rank
		1	2	3	4	5		
Ensuring implementation	13	0	0	0	9	23	4.72	1
Motivation	3	0	0	6	7	17	4.37	2
Content emphasis	10	0	6	0	10	16	4.13	3
Program control	1	0	0	13	5	16	4.08	4
Best use of $	2	4	3	5	8	6	3.35	5
Method of delivery	4	2	8	8	5	6	3.17	6

In many primary level teachers, there is an urgent need for effective follow-through if these courses are to bear much lasting fruit. This, however, might well be said of the very large majority of in-service courses. It is a point which will, one hopes, be given very careful thought in future planning (1969, pp. 44-45).

In spite of the lack of attention implementation activities have received, the panel has placed it at the top of the list in terms of its relative importance for good practice. The panel also rated alternative approaches to implementation, including provision for a continuing study group for those who had an IST program, coordination of IST programs with regular supervision processes, provision for travelling consultants to visit the teachers, and providing IST to groups of teachers who work together so that natural interaction will reinforce the experiences. Our panel members rated all four approaches as being important.

MOTIVATION OF PARTICIPANTS

Those who plan or deliver IST programs must address the question of how to get unqualified teachers caught up in in-service training activities and how to keep them interested. Previous research often suggests that the most effective motivators of unqualified teachers in developing countries are extrinsic in nature. Greenland, for example, reports a survey of teachers, which shows that, of reasons given for dropping out of an in-service program: "the absence of a new qualification and salary increase received the highest number of votes with 62 percent either strongly agreeing or agreeing" (1983, p. 111).

Our study confirms this finding. The desire for self-improvement was well down the list, while the two most important factors were found to be increased salary and ministry certification, nominated by 84% of our panel. The next two most important items, university credentials and career enhancement within education, were also extrinsic motivators.

PROGRAM CONTENT EMPHASIS

Traditionally, the curriculum of IST has been directed toward improvement of academic or subject matter skills to the exclusion of skills for the improvement of teaching (Lo, 1984, p. 166). This has been particularly so for unqualified primary teachers, because minimum qualification has often been set at the level of secondary school completion with little or no specific pedagogical training. It seems likely that the predominance of concern for training in subject matter has prevailed because, at marginally low levels of both, the substance of teaching looms over the form in importance. Especially is this so in a context where traditional rote learning methods are accepted. Teachers merely carry on a set of well-known procedures.

When rote learning methods are challenged, however, it might be expected that methodology of teaching in more complex forms would become an increasingly important part of IST for the unqualified teachers. This is, in fact, the overwhelming judgment of the experts surveyed. Only 3 of the 19 panel members reflected the traditional view of exclusive subject matter emphasis, while 13 (rural) and 12 (urban) votes were cast to recognize the need for a combination of content and pedagogy.

It is important to determine what type of pedagogical and content emphasis should be given in an IST program. Panel members responded to eight pedagogical options selected from the literature. They typically indicated an average of three of these eight options, and as can be seen from Table 2, the most important items, each checked by more than half the panel members, had to do with developing skills for teaching the existing curriculum, for meaningful rather than rote learning, for positive attitudes to lifelong learning, and for participating in curriculum development. Items such as developing methods for character development, for supporting national purposes, for teaching community development and for teaching new curriculum, were not considered as important by most of the panel members. Taken together with the previously noted emphasis on including methodology in IST, this becomes a strong expression of the need to move away from the traditional teaching methods in order to make teaching more effective.

It is important to note that subject matter teaching remains significant, though combined with pedagogical concerns. We derived four subject matter items from the literature, including: (1) general upgrading of the teachers' knowledge and understanding of areas related to the school curriculum, (2) knowledge relevant to new curriculum, (3) knowledge required to participate in local curriculum development, and (4) knowledge required to further national goals and development. By far the most important emphasis was the first, a general upgrading in areas related to the school curriculum. This view, no doubt, is in response to the low

Table 2
Most Important Emphases for Teaching Methods

	Rural*	Urban*	Combined
Methods for helping teachers acquire specific skills for teaching the *existing curriculum*	12	13	25
Helping teachers aquire methods for teaching for *meaningful rather than rote* learning	12	12	24
Helping teachers aquire methods for developing in pupils a positive attitude to *lifelong learning*	11	11	22
Methods for helping teachers engage in *curriculum development* activities	9	10	19
Methods for helping teachers acquire specific skills for teaching *new curriculum*	7	9	16
Helping teachers acquire methods for teaching *community development* knowledge and skills	7	6	11
Helping teachers acquire methods for supporting *national purposes*	4	5	9
Methods for the *character development* of the teacher	2	2	4

*None of the differences between rural and urban are significant at the .05 level.

level of educational background of many of the unqualified teachers. The support for the other three alternatives was less than half of the respondents for each.

In summary, the advice of the experts seems quite clear in rejecting the traditional emphasis on subject matter in favor of a combination of subject matter and pedagogy. The panel stresses the kinds of pedagogy, which will enable teachers to break away from traditional classroom practices and to present subject matter relevant to the present curriculum. Other kinds of subject matter, such as that related to new curriculum, curriculum development, and national purposes, may be important but are not the first essential for unqualified teachers.

CONTROL OF PROGRAM

Previous studies indicate that, whether IST has to do with initial teacher preparation or with preparing practicing teachers for new roles, operating responsibility and decision-making authority in practice rests largely with the ministry of education and the central government (Greenland, 1983; Ariyadasa, 1976; Vivian, 1968). When it comes to the professional aspects of programs (particularly the choice of course content, teaching methods, and assessment of procedures), these studies report that control is typically delegated to educational institutions with the expertise to do the job.

This study finds judgments about best practice to be consistent with that view of control. By far, the greatest preference for program control was for the teachers college, followed by the ministry of education and the university, with a minority preference for the regional school system, special institute, and local school system. The substantially higher preference for the teachers college than for the ministry of education, suggests, however, that many panel members prefer the college to have considerable autonomy from the ministry.

BEST USE OF AVAILABLE FUNDS

A question that IST planners must face is how best to allocate scarce funds to enable practicing teachers to take part in IST activities. Is the best option to put money into released time from teaching in order to enable teachers to engage in IST or should funds be directed at program costs other than released time? The literature available to us did not deal with this issue directly. The ratings of our panel members suggest that expert opinion is not in favor of allocating finances for released time only. Instead, the panel members favor the allocation of funds toward released time in balance with other program costs. There was fairly strong sentiment, however, that funds should go to program costs exclusively and not to released time.

BEST METHODS OF DELIVERY OF PROGRAM

The literature summarized by Greenland (1983) and Dove (1981) indicates that most successful IST programs have been those which stress formal, planned instruction, usually in the lecture format. More informal approaches, while appearing to be enticing, did not prove to be successful. The exception noted was clinical supervision, and its success depended upon the amount of professional expertise already acquired or displayed by the participants. Another exception is the report of Lo (1984) favoring the principle of self-reliance as stressed in self-study and nonformal approaches. Here the skills of experienced, presumably competent, teachers were critical in assisting their less experienced, and less competent, colleagues.

In the present study, expert opinion favors almost equally six different approaches: (1) school based programs, (2) individual consultations with supervisors or other experts, (3) teachers' centers, (4) central IST facilities, (5) observation of excellent teachers, (6) inter-visitations.

Only one of these preferred approaches is usually associated with the lecture method. With that exception, all approaches would locate the IST program right in the actual school or in the local area.

Distance education and nonformal approaches receive little support. The frequent impression conveyed by the literature that distance education is the method of the future is not strongly supported by the expert opinion here. Not surprisingly, however, opinion more strongly favors distance approaches for rural than for urban areas, but even for rural use distance learning is surpassed by the three top approaches listed above.

Certain of the basic types of programs referred to in this final section may be implemented in different ways, so the panel was asked for opinions about the effectiveness of some of these options.

SCHOOL-BASED PROGRAMS

Several issues within this kind of program were addressed: when the programs should be held, who should control them, and the degree of formality they should have. Panel members overwhelmingly favored released time during the school hours, rather than during vacation periods or after school hours. The strength of support for released time has not been encountered in the literature. Thompson (1984, p. 8) does state that ". . . all initial training [in Sri Lanka] is effectively inservice," and to the extent that this is true of other countries, the importance of released time during the regular school hours does not come as a surprise. On-the-job training is recommended by Eddy (1981, p. 66) from experience with the Canadian Training Awards II programs in the Leeward and Windward Islands though in the somewhat different context of one-to-one apprenticeships or attachments. It should be noted that this finding about the importance of released time should be interpreted in view of the previously expressed preference for allocation of funds to a balance of released time and program expenses.

There is no strong agreement about the responsibility for program control among those respondents who favored school-based

IST programs. Their recommendations were fairly equally distributed among teachers, headteachers, and outside officials. Though teachers did lead the list of the three groups, if the issue is seen as teachers vs. authority figures (combining heads with outside officials), the preference was clearly for the latter. Some experts checked more than one possibility, suggesting, no doubt, that program control should be in the form of a partnership. This view is supported in Edelfelt's discussion of in-service policy in Indonesia (1985, p. 48), where he suggests the importance of cooperative coordination of in-service.

Careful planning was emphasized by almost all of the respondents who favored school-based IST programs, when queried about program approach. An equal number of respondents opted for planned and formal programs as opposed to planned and informal arrangements or arrangements to be negotiated in advance. Comments written in the questionnaire indicate that the term "formal" did not meet with the approval of many respondents, though "planned" did seem to be considered essential.

INDIVIDUAL CONSULTATIONS WITH SUPERVISORS OR OTHER EXPERTS

Those respondents who stressed consultations with supervisors or other experts strongly favored the clinical supervision model as opposed to micro-teaching, simulation, and competency-based analysis of teaching. The marked emphasis upon this form of individual consultation reinforces the reports and recommendations of Dove to the World Bank (1981, p. 183), where she summarizes IST as ". . . a massive, intensive, and prolonged training and retraining programme, beginning with the teacher trainers themselves and gradually extending to the teachers" (1981, p. 183). There were few, if any, marked differences in recommendations concerning cost-effective individual approaches for rural and urban settings.

TEACHERS' CENTERS

Within the teachers' center approach, a number of options are available: when teachers should participate, who should control the program, and the amount of planning in the program. In terms of when activities should take place, we suggested three options: released school time, after school, and vacation periods. No option received overwhelming support, though released time headed the list. This option was particularly strong for urban areas, though even this difference was not statistically significant at p .05.

As for program control in the teachers' center, opinion strongly favored teacher control. This finding is in interesting contrast to the preference for control by authority figures in school-based programs and presumably reflects the tradition of teachers' centers.

As to the amount of planning in the program, it was quite clear that planned and formal programs were deemed more important than spontaneous and informal programs. Written comments once again confirm that even informal programs ought to be planned.

CENTRAL IST FACILITIES

For central programs, such as at a teachers college, panel members were asked to indicate the best way for teachers to participate and the degree of planning and formality felt to be appropriate. Among the options were the possibility for residential vacation programs, college staff traveling to local areas, or residential short courses with substitutes covering the teachers' responsibilities. Residential vacation programs received the strongest support, though almost as strong was support expressed for staff members to travel to local areas. These two possibilities could, of course, be combined so that residential courses would be followed up by local visits. Such an arrangement would give effect to the strongly expressed need for effective implementation provisions mentioned at the beginning of our study. The system of decentralized university or college centers connected by "landlines" to universities in Queensland, described by Kitchen (1969, pp. 38-41) is one model which would combine these approaches.

As in the other options, noted above, planned and formal emphases were strongly preferred over spontaneous and informal approaches.

DISTANCE EDUCATION

With regard to the effectiveness of different media and the form that programs would take, the panel members who believed distance education to be effective, considering both cost and quality, strongly favored print correspondence courses over broadcast television, radio, video tapes, audio tapes, and satellite television. In fact, this medium was heavily favored by all panel members, including those who did not see distance education as an important cost-effective form.

The emphasis on correspondence courses is consistent with the views of Grenholm (1975, p. 5) and Erdos (1975, p. 21), who emphasize the necessity of some physical action to stimulate activity and change. Erdos points out that the choice of medium must be related to the circumstances in which both the institution and its students must work and stresses that ". . . teaching by correspondence and administering correspondence education are essentially activities which are 'learning by doing'" (p. 57). Clearly, the more advanced technologies, such as television, do not appear to be considered superior to the more traditional print approaches, which usually require more extensive written responses by participants. As in earlier general recommendations, all forms of distance education were recommended more for rural settings than for urban ones, though these differences remain not statistically significant.

Methodological recommendations, by those who favored distance education, strongly supported formal courses as opposed to informal learning by teachers or learning from courses directed toward pupils. Once again, this sentiment is consistent with the emphasis on formal instruction found in other sections of the current survey. Naturally, the favored medium, print correspondence courses, lends itself to formal rather than informal instruction, but support for planning and even formality in all kinds of programs has been apparent. Absence of much support for the more advanced media may reflect traditionalist approaches to IST. Yet, in view of the modern views expressed on other topics, it seems more likely to be a judgment that the more advanced media have yet not proven to be competitive with print sources. Unfortunately, it is not known what the panel considers the potential of the newer media to be.

GENERALIZING TO QUALIFIED TEACHERS

Although in this study we chose to focus on unqualified teachers, we tried to determine how much the panel experts felt their opinions could be generalized to programs for qualified teachers. If the two groups have quite distinct needs, the indication would be that separate kinds of programs would be required. If not, the same kind of program might well be adapted to both purposes.

Very few of the panel members see the differences between the two groups as substantial, but the largest number see some program aspects to be the same and others to be different. Respondents are not asked what the differences would be, but one might speculate on such differences as not restricting subject matter content to that required by the present curriculum.

GENERALIZING ACROSS COUNTRIES

Basic to the present study and many others is the presumption that it is meaningful to generalize about developing countries as a group. Some experts argue that social processes like education are so strongly determined by cultural factors that generalizations even within a multi-cultural country may not be meaningful. The views of the expert panel on this crucial issue were sought as relating to the validity of this and similar studies.

The results are displayed in Table 3. Perhaps surprisingly, none of the experts took the "uniqueness" position described above. The most common reply was that results apply fairly generally across the different developing countries. It is important to note the qualifier "fairly" as a recognition that some differences may arise from culture, geography, economics, religion, etc. Those who said they "cannot say" often commented that they did not feel their experiences covered enough countries to make a full generalization. Fortunately for the growing number of studies which make such generalizations, the validity of this basic assumption seems vindicated by the present, widely experienced group.

SUMMARY OF FINDINGS AND CONCLUSION

Judgments of nineteen internationally known experts from eleven countries around the world were expressed regarding the best practice in different aspects of in-service training for unqualified teachers. We have summarized the results by developing a profile of best IST practice.

PROFILE OF BEST PRACTICE

This profile comprises those IST characteristics which were supported by half or more of the panel of experts.

* The most important of all characteristics of the effective IST program is that it includes provisions for ensuring implementation in the classroom of the acquired learning, through the following devices: (a) a continuing study group is provided for those with similar IST experiences; (b) the IST program is coordinated with the regular supervision of teachers; (c) provision is made for travelling consultants to visit teachers.

* The IST program provides motivation for participants by ensuring increased salary.

* The curriculum of the IST program provides a balance of pedagogy and subject matter as opposed to exclusive emphasis on one or the other.

Table 3
Generalizability Across Countries

	Rural	Urban	Combined
Results apply fairly generally	9	12	21
Different countries are quite unique	0	0	0
Cannot Say	6	5	12
Other	1*	1	2

N = 19

*Comment added was that results apply generally in much of the world but less so in Asia.

---

* The pedagogical component of the training contains four elements: (a) methods for helping teachers acquire specific skills for teaching the existing curriculum; (b) methods for teaching meaningful rather than rote learning; (c) methods for developing in pupils a positive attitude to lifelong learning; (d) methods for helping teachers engage in curriculum development.

* The subject matter component of the training provides general upgrading in areas related to the school curriculum.

* The teachers college should have operating responsibility for the program.

* In organizational form, the program should be school-based.

* Participation should be enabled through released time.

* The school-based program should be controlled jointly by teachers, outside officials, and principals.

* The program should be planned and formal in nature.

ORGANIZATIONAL MODELS

Strong support emerged for three organizational models.

School-Based Model

This model had the strongest support and would have its support substantially increased when combined with the following particular in-school activities: (a) individual consultation between the teacher and supervisor or other experts, especially with emphasis on clinical supervision; (b) observation of excellent teachers; (c) inter-visitation.

Local Teachers' Center Model

The second model, in terms of panel support was the teachers' center.   The best practices for the teachers' center model are: (a) participation through released time, as opposed to after school and in vacation periods; (b) control by teachers, as opposed to officials; (c) programs which are planned and formal, as opposed to spontaneous and informal.

Centralized Teachers College Model

The characteristics of the third most popular model are: (a) use for residential vacation programs; (b) program should be planned and formal.

Models with Weak Support

The distance education model was supported by less than a quarter of the experts and those who did support it strongly preferred print over other media. Nonformal approaches were supported by even fewer panel members. Respondents were not asked about the future potential of these or other models, but they made no written comments about their potential.

CAPACITY TO GENERALIZE

A.   Few experts felt that opinions expressed about programs for unqualified teachers would be substantially different from opinions about qualified teachers.

B.   As to capacity to generalize across developing countries, most of those with an opinion said results apply fairly generally. No one said that different countries are so unique that some generalizations cannot be made.

CONCLUSION

1.   The three most promising models for IST are quite clearly school based the local teachers' center and the central teachers college models.

2.   Some experts see these models as complementary in contributing particular strengths to an overall comprehensive program. Others see one or two as valuable and the remainder as unsupportable. Hence, to some extent they are competitive. Further evaluative study of these three models is strongly recommended.

3.   Further work in developing cost-effective distance education programs should, no doubt, be encouraged.

NOTES

Note 1:   Some people choose to distinguish between programs for unqualified teachers and qualified teachers by calling programs for the unqualified "on-service training," and programs for the qualified "in-service training." See, for example, Edelfeld, 1985. We choose not the make such a distinction in this study.

Note 2:   The taxonomy, the questionnaire, and specific statistical results are available on request from John Andrews, Faculty of Education, University of British Columbia, Vancouver, British Columbia, Canada.

CASE STUDY FOR CHAPTER THREE

THE CIANJUR PROJECT

Roy Gardner

INTRODUCTION

BEGINNINGS

In Indonesia during the 1970s, major strides were made to improve the quality of primary education. Despite considerable difficulties caused by the size of the education system spread over a vast area in a relatively poor country, a new curriculum was issued in 1975 and new textbooks were designed, produced, and distributed for the four main subjects: Language, Mathematics, Science, and Social Studies. In addition, in-service training was organized for all primary school teachers. Despite these efforts, it was conceded that the overall improvement in classroom instruction and learning had been far less than expected. Research on primary school achievement in 1976 showed that in certain classrooms all the children were doing well, while in other classrooms having children of similar backgrounds, the children were performing at a lower level. In other words, certain teachers were better able to bring about high achievement. It was decided that classroom interactions and management had perhaps greater importance as determinants of quality than other variables surveyed (Hawes, 1982, pp. 1-5). These conclusions led to the acceptance of the need to establish new patterns of classroom behavior and to provide the teachers with the necessary support to bring about the changes. Thus, in 1979 an experimental project was launched with the cooperation of the

Directorate of Primary and Secondary Education and the National Educational R&D Center, with the support of the British Council and the University of London Institute of Education.

The project was located at Cianjur district and became known as the Cianjur Project. It was conceived as an Action Research Project, and it had an initial life of five years, after which it was evaluated by the R&D Center. Replication projects were initiated in West Lombok in 1985 and North Sumatra in 1986. The Cianjur approach has been so successful that it has become official policy, and discussions are taking place on its dissemination nationally.

Cianjur district was chosen because of its close proximity to Jakarta, about three hours driving time, and hence its accessibility for the R&D Center staff, as well as because its Governor and Director of Education were highly committed to educational innovation. In order to provide for the collection of data on the operation of the project so that wider dissemination might be based on a full understanding of the factors involved, it was decided to work in three sub-disticts: one in the town, one in a rural area near the town, and one in a remote area of the district. The sub-districts chosen were Cianjur Kota, Cugenang, and Pagelaran. In each sub-district a number of schools were selected: 86 in Cianjur, 42 in Cugenang, and 73 in Pagelaran, a total of 201.

The schools were selected so as to form clusters with one school taking the lead in each cluster. At the lead school, a room was provided for teachers meetings and as a resource room. In addition, within each sub-district, a Teachers' Center was established and equipped with tables and chairs. Within each cluster of schools the teachers were organized into Teachers' Clubs, and Club meetings were organized on a regular basis during school hours. At the Club meetings activities were organized to help the teachers and included demonstrations, practical work sessions, and the discussion of problems. In addition, for the headteachers and the inspectors, other clubs were arranged, although no special accommodation was provided. For operational purposes the Project did not provide for quantities of materials and equipment, and the only expenditure of note was for the construction of the additional rooms for the teachers at the head school and for the Teachers' Centers. The Project was designed essentially as a low-cost undertaking with a view to the wider context of dissemination throughout Indonesia.

PROJECT DESIGN

Included in the design of the Project was provision for training which was considered to be necessary at three levels. The first level was for personnel from the R&D Center and the IKIP (a tertiary institution for training secondary teachers) of Bandung, who were sent for training at the University of London Institute of Education. The purpose of this training was to develop new styles of teaching specific methods in the four main subjects, and to look closely at supervision techniques. The second level of training was at the district level for the staff of the participating schools including the headteachers and the inspectors responsible for the schools. This second tier training took the form of an education seminar held at a selected location in or near Cianjur district. The third level of training took place at the classroom and school-level and was organized by the headteachers and inspectors and through the Teachers' Club meetings. The second and third levels of training involved all the participating staff and deserve special attention.

The organization of the second level seminars struck new ground in in-service training in Indonesia. The traditional pattern of lecturing, with an emphasis on content, was replaced by one which depended more on small group activities and a practical approach to training. The stress was placed on the translation of the new methodologies in subject teaching to the classroom, bearing in mind the realities of the schools. The participants chose one school subject and spent the majority of their time looking closely at how to teach the curriculum and in devising suitable teaching aids. In addition, the teachers gave careful thought to the organization of their classrooms so as to create more interesting and encouraging environments. The headteachers and inspectors joined in the subject work as full participating members, but then additional sessions on supervision and staff development were also held. These were also of a practical nature and guidelines for supervision were produced. The active participation of all in the seminars demanded a change of attitude on behalf of those who had attended education seminars before. The participants responded enthusiastically to the new approach and worked long hours in order to cover as much as they could during the limited period of the seminars, which usually lasted two weeks. The University of London Institute of Education, through the British Council, provided consultant assistance in the four subject areas. There was, however, no expatriate presence throughout the year and the only expatriate inputs each year were to the London-based course, to the in-country seminars and through a Project consultant, who visited each sub-district for approximately one month.

The third level of training also required the adoption of new attitudes to in-service training. The attendance at the Teachers' Clubs became a regular feature despite the teachers receiving no additional payment from the government to cover their expenses. Some grants were made by the Parent Associations. Additionally, the teachers had to accept that the headteachers had a responsibility for, and a role in, the supervision of what went on in the classrooms. This demanded the development of new attitudes of professional cooperation in the school and an appreciation on all sides of the relative roles of the headteachers and class teachers. The inspectors also were identified as having a major role to play in the professional development of the teaching staff. The potential contribution of the inspectors to qualitative improvement was emphasized at the education seminars with the hope that this would lead to the inspectors having a more positive impact on classroom behaviors.

The Cianjur Project was based on two major thrusts. First, to change what happened in the classroom, and second, to introduce a change from supervision and inspection to support. At the start of the Project the classes were organized along traditional lines with the children sitting in rows facing the front, with the teacher dominating the work which was taken largely from the textbooks. Little opportunity was taken to look for learning experiences outside the classroom. The routine of the classes changed little from day to day, with the minimum of interaction between the teacher and the children or among the children. The rooms generally were dull and uninteresting. The Cianjur Project sought to bring about dramatic changes in the classrooms and to make the children active participants in the lessons that were organized. The classrooms were rearranged to introduce groups and the lessons were to be centered around a variety of learning activities, which were intended to provide opportunities to explore topics being covered and to reach conclusions. Interaction between the children and the teachers was encouraged. An emphasis was placed on stimulating the production of work and the results were displayed. A heavy reliance was placed upon the use of environment. The stress on activity methods led to the adoption of CARA BELAJAR SISWA AKTIF (student active learning) as the label of the Project.

GOVERNANCE

The Project does not have a management cell or a project implementation unit. Leadership in the Project is given by the R&D Center, which oversees the planning for educational seminars and overseas training. Within the R&D Center, the Project falls under the Curriculum Office. Funds for R&D staff to make necessary journeys to the Project areas are provided out of the R&D budget. Coordination of development within the Project is provided for by agreement between the appropriate Directorates within the Ministry of Education and Culture, who meet from time to time as required. The Minister of Education has overall responsibility for decisions about the development of the Project. With the R&D Center, a number of staff participate as tutors in the organization of education seminars, but all concerned have many other jobs to do.

At the provincial level, the management of the Project is the responsibility of the Director of Education, who arranges for in-service training the provides the appropriate funds for seminars, courses, materials, and capital improvement.

SUPPORT

From its inception, the Project has received only very limited support from outside Indonesia. The costs of overseas training and the travel costs and fees for overseas consultants have been met by the British Council. All local costs have been met from in-country sources. The costs of the education seminars were provided originally by the R&D Center. The costs are now divided between a number of offices--the province and the Directorate of Primary and Secondary Education meet the local costs of the participants. The R&D Center provides the services and meets the costs of the R&D staff, who conduct the courses. Overseas staff costs are divided between the British Council and the R&D Center. At the local level small sums have been allocated to schools for materials. Some additional sums are paid by the Parents Associations and the Teachers Cooperatives.

EVALUATION

The Project has undergone one major evaluation. In 1984 the Indonesian government engaged in an in-country assessment under the direction of the Indonesian National R & D Center, located in Jakarta, as part of the Action Research Project. That evaluation was so successful that the government decided to expand its activities beyond Cianjur to other parts of the country. Consequently, it has undertaken replication projects in West Lombok and North Sumatra and has plans to expand the project throughout the country. In addition, some teacher training institutions are also adapting their programs to conform with project ideals.

There has been no formal evaluation of the Project carried out by agencies external to Indonesia, although a small scale research program has been initiated in the Cianjur region which includes non-Indonesians.

CHANGE ANALYSIS

OVERCOMING GENERAL CONSTRAINTS

The main factors hindering the adoption and development of student active learning were the formal teaching approaches in the classroom, the entrenched attitudes of the teachers, children, and parents to formal teaching, and the general poverty of the classroom environment. To this must be added the conservative nature of the primary teachers colleges. A major factor was the attitude of the inspectors, who were dealing mainly with administrative matters and carrying out annual assessments of the teachers. Finally, there was little in-service training for teachers; once they were trained in a formal mode the teachers received little help and support throughout their careers.

The first step in overcoming these barriers was to replace inspection and criticism with the concepts of supervision and support and to persuade the headteachers that they had a role in supervision, at least to the extent of commenting upon and offering advice on the conduct of lessons. The second major step was to establish the concept of active learning, which proved easier than expected. By adopting a strategy of making the annual seminars, organized by the R&D Center and Cianjur, mainly practical and basing the work directly on the current curriculum, the participants were forced to think about the meaning of activities in the classroom. Initially, many activities merely kept the children busy but gradually the educational value of particular activities became the most important consideration and a reassessment of lesson structure could go ahead.

A further major constraint was the 1975 curriculum, with its highly detailed and carefully defined lesson-by-lesson program, confining teaching to 30- and 40-minute slots and making lesson preparation based on activities more difficult. It also made integration across the curriculum difficult. Initially, no attempt was made to encourage integrated work although some did develop naturally out of the work in hand. Little could be done about the curriculum but some leeway was given by the Director of Education at the District level, who allowed teachers within the Project schools in Cianjur to diverge from the curriculum to some extent. However, it must be borne in mind that at the end of class six there is a national attainment test on which selection to the lower secondary school (SMP) is based; too great a divergence from the curriculum could lead to difficulties for the children.

NEED FOR COORDINATED TRAINING AND MONITORING

A serious constraint on the Project in Cianjur was the lack of coordinated training and monitoring between the annual courses. Attempts to create new posts of subject inspectors for primary schools linked solely to the Project failed because of administrative barriers and hence the encouragement of development at the school level was left to the inspectors who spent little time in schools and to the heads who were unsure of their role and the contribution they could make. There was also no provision for the R&D Center to participate in monitoring. Finally, apart from notes issued during seminars, the teachers had no documents on which to base their discussions and thinking. It was not until 1983 that small handbooks were produced, and these were not distributed until 1985.

Thus, from the initial seminars in 1980, there was slow growth until 1982. Only after that did the Cianjur Project begin to develop rapidly. A further reason for this slow development may be found in the selection of people to attend the annual seminars. No clearly worked out plan for attendance was drawn up, and each year's participants have been made up of some of those who have attended in the past and some who have not. A plan to have each participant attend at least two consecutive courses, so that an integrated program could be provided, was not established. In addition, the schools from which the participants were drawn provided another basis for concern. The large number of participating schools suggested a need for some strategy for concentration and internal dissemination in order to establish the project fully within areas. This approach was not adopted and participants ranged over the whole of the Project area with the consequent thin spread of ideas.

DISSEMINATION STRATEGY

NATIONAL DISSEMINATION
The Project is now set for national dissemination, and already there are requests for participation from several provinces. In addition, there are a number of small-scale initiatives which have been started in different parts of Indonesia. Currently, the expectation is that there will be an increased demand to participate, and it may well be that the government will have to consider measures to keep demands within bounds so as to ensure that quality is maintained through a full understanding of the requirements of student active learning. The number of people interested in seeing the system in operation in the schools is considerable and in 1986, Cianjur received over 8000 visitors.

ORGANIZATION OF REPLICATION ACTIVITIES
The replication of the student active learning model in new provinces will be organized by the provincial head of Education and Culture, through a coordinating committee at the provincial level. To ensure that a fully integrated plan for the introduction of the model is worked out, provinces may be required to submit a development plan. Such a plan would have to indicate the strategy for introduction, which would state the training schedules to be used, the physical plant to be made available, and the financial resources to be provided.

In 1986, a new program to introduce a revised primary curriculum was started with the organization of a short in-service course for 400 master trainers from all over Indonesia. The in-service course focussed on the Cianjur model, which had been introduced into the new curriculum. The function of the master trainers is to train headteachers and teachers throughout Indonesia through a cascade system with one sub-district in every district. It is hoped that the integration of the provincially based projects and master trainer program will bring about significant changes at the primary level.

The success of student active learning depends very much upon the support given to the teachers. A major component of the support system is the Teachers' Club, and the very regular attendance by teachers at the Teachers' Clubs suggests that these activities are valued highly by the teachers. This use of the Clubs has been unique in the history of educational development in Indonesia and clearly the concentration on issues relevant to the daily organization of the classrooms and lessons is something which is considered to be worthwhile by all concerned.   The idea of the Teachers' Club being one which moves from school to school within the clusters has also found acceptance and has led in Cianjur to the erosion of the leadership of the lead school in the cluster, with a consequent leveling of standards within the clusters.

Still another support notion is that not only that inspectors and heads constitute a part of the support system but that teachers themselves must be full and participating members of the support program. This approach should lead to more cooperative attitudes between teachers, headteachers, and inspectors and facilitate the move from traditional teaching to student active learning.

The successful spread of the model depends entirely upon a full appreciation by all of not only what student active learning means in terms of actual classroom practice and in teacher support systems but also in terms of the resources which are needed to establish and maintain the model. While these resources are not great, they are not insignificant, and in the current financial climate it may be that education authorities may seek to slow down development. This, indeed, may be to the good. A slower spread of the Cianjur model may lead to a greater understanding of the system and its demands upon all concerned and a higher level of practice in the long run.

CHAPTER FOUR

PARTICIPATORY APPROACHES TO
IN-SERVICE TEACHER TRAINING

Sheldon Shaeffer

INTRODUCTION

As a result of the contemporary pressures on teachers and on teacher training institutions, a number of quite different approaches to training have been developed in recent years. Most still emphasize, in different combinations and proportions, a mixture of content and skills training and of college lectures and teaching practice. The literature is filled with descriptions of planned or on-going training courses, of varying length and depth, most of which share one characteristic: the trainee as the "empty vessel."

Such training is top-down and prescriptive, the implication being that teachers are deficient in some particular knowledge and skills, that trainers and administrators understand better and more wisely the teaching process, and that therefore certain teacher-proof lessons must be transmitted to new and practicing teachers. Lanier (1984, pp. 21-22) calls this mere "teacher training" rather than "professional teacher education," because it is all form and no substance, focuses on practical know-how, and has no faith in teachers' judgments.

The major debate in the literature concerns the relative emphasis in training placed on academic improvement in a particular subject area or on practical skills in teaching, in other words, on what to put into the empty vessel. The most characteristic example of this debate contrasts the teaching of new skills to the inculcation of a new conception of teaching, what Avalos (1985) calls the "skill development" and the "model" approaches. The former concentrates on changes in discrete teaching behaviors (questioning the use of time, lesson planning), the latter on a "thorough restructuring of the trainee's conception of teaching on the basis of epistemological, psychological, and sociological considerations" (1985, p. 294). This leads to models based on various learning theories (such as behaviorism), humanistic theories (phenomenology), sociological approaches (discourse analysis), curriculum theory (mastery learning), or empirical research (direct instruction). Whatever the specific side chosen in this debate, proponents assume that the body of knowledge related to it must be transmitted from tutors to teachers. This often leads to programs based solely on lectures, tutorials, and demonstration lessons. It also leads to an over-emphasis on evaluating the success of training programs only in terms of "skill formation, cost, and implementability" (Haddad, 1985, p. 51). Quite a different approach is represented by what might be called participatory teacher training.

PARTICIPATORY TEACHER TRAINING

Characteristics

Participatory teacher training is not a clearly defined approach, but it has a number of general characteristics, some of which overlap with other, more traditional approaches. First, and above all, the teacher plays an active role in the training process and is therefore not a passive recipient of others' accumulated knowledge about methods and content. The teacher becomes a participant in decisions regarding the needs to which training must respond, what problems must be resolved, and what skills and knowledge must be transmitted. The teacher becomes an agent rather than an object of change, the assumption being that the "most effective learning occurs when the learner is treated as a constructor of his or her own knowledge and given the opportunity to share responsibility for the selection, prosecution, and evaluation of the tasks through which knowledge and competence are required" (Wells and Chang, 1986, p. 1).

Second, as a result of participation, training becomes self-directed and the teacher self-taught. The autonomous nature of the teacher in the classroom is recognized in the training itself as he or she is encouraged to assess problems and design and experiment with appropriate solutions. Russell states the argument clearly: "ONLY TEACHERS CAN TEACH THEMSELVES TO TEACH" (1985, p. 4). In one teacher training program in India, for example, trainees teach themselves child psychology by observing children at play and work (Goad, 1984).

Third, training is based on reflection and introspection. The teacher's needs, problems, status, roles, etc., are not presented by outside observers or experts (supervisors and trainers) but are defined, examined, and analyzed by the teachers themselves. Such reflection-in-action (Schon, 1983) is meant to lead to greater self-awareness where teachers learn to seek explanations for, and possible solutions to, their problems by looking into their own situation and practice. This is similar to Elliot's "self-monitoring," the "process by which one becomes aware of one's situation and one's own role as an agent in it" (1976/77, p. 5). Teachers, in other words, have skills, beliefs, and styles of their own, which are not valueless; they possess a certain "craft knowledge" worth further assessment and analysis. They "know a great deal about teaching, and when given the time to reflect on their practice, they can bring about positive change in their classrooms" (Eaker & Huffman, 1980, p. 3).

Fourth, participatory training bases teacher introspection on the actual, concrete experiences of working with children in classrooms and schools. Generalities or universals are not examined, as is so often the case in college-based training, but the particular situation faced every day. In some cases this situation may go beyond the school to include local, community-related activities and wider critiques of the nature of the education system itself (Vera, 1982, pp. 4-7).

Finally, though based ultimately on individual refection, autonomy, and action, participatory training is often structured by the group.   Teachers collectively examine and analyze their experiences, assisted by trainers working more as facilitators and resource persons rather than experts, and so cooperate in solving problems and learning from each other. Hunt has called this a "persons-in-relation" approach wherein a group or network of teachers is responsible for planning its own in-service activities (Hunt, n.d.).

In essence, the *process* of learning and of change becomes as important as the *product*, and the personal development of the teacher as important as the improvement of professional skills. Training becomes an integral and permanent part of teaching.

The outcomes expected from participatory teacher training relate closely to its characteristics. The teacher who learns to be actively in control of his or her own learning becomes empowered, self-confident, self-reliant, a more active agent of change (Goad, 1984, p. 143). A more autonomous teacher takes more responsibility for what is learned and what is taught, not only at the moment but throughout a professional life. Greater teacher "autonomy in decisions regarding the learning and teaching process furthers their sense of responsibility in regard to their development" (Vera, 1982, p. 3). Teachers better able to reflect on their own particular situation, problems and roles modify their frames of reference *vis-a-vis* the educational process and become more sensitive to the myriad factors affecting their school experiences and actual needs. This leads to real skills, be they lesson construction, materials development, or more appropriate methods. And cooperative learning leads to more cooperative, perhaps even more democratic, attitudes, so that teachers may prove more willing to fight against the isolation and atomization which the self-contained classroom so often imposes.

Out of all this is meant to come a more motivated, "professional" teacher, who is more open to new ideas, more innovative in trying out new methods. And through participatory training in which the teacher becomes an active, autonomous learner with new knowledge based on real experience and collective effort, teachers should also learn the kind of alternative learning processes which they themselves will practice in the classroom. Thus, those trained to be teachers "should participate actively in their own training and should experience the kind of education which they themselves will practice" (Goad, 1984, p. 121). "When teachers themselves experience this mode of learning, they are more likely to be convinced of the need to implement it in their own classrooms" (Wells & Chang, 1986, p. 1). Avalos and Haddad also found evidence that more participatory training methods (e.g., microteaching, role-playing, interaction analysis) "appeared consistently effective in promoting changes in teaching techniques" (1981, p. 33).

METHODS OF PARTICIPATORY TEACHER TRAINING

A wide variety of methods and approaches on how to achieve such objectives is discussed in the literature. Few of these explicitly recognize something called "participatory" training. But in reviewing literature on examples of such training, a few basic categories of approaches and methods emerge. These include cooperative learning aimed at curriculum development, reflective self-instruction, training by simulation and situation, and the teacher as researcher. While these methods may be used as well in pre-service education, the discussion which follows focuses more on their use in in-service training, the premise being that experienced teachers will bring to such training a basic knowledge of educational theory and practice and considerable experience in classroom life.

Cooperative Learning

In this approach to participatory teacher training, teachers and trainees work together to establish needs, identify problems, suggest and evaluate possible solutions, and, in so doing, develop new curricula, syllabuses, methods, or texts. Such an approach has been labeled the "curriculum development" approach to teacher training (Greenland, 1983). It is meant to produce new products (materials, methods, skills), greater skill in using the products, and, because of the participatory process involved, a greater sense of responsibility and efficacy. It invariably focuses on practical problem-solving and permits teachers to learn from each other's experiences and to participate in training as they construct curricula, organize syllabuses, and write material.

What is important here is that teachers are not merely placed on the occasional subject panel to comment on the readability and validity of new content, are not taken out of their classrooms on full-time secondment to a curriculum development institution, or are not set down in a classroom to be told about the newest variety of mathematics curriculum written in the metropole. Rather, they themselves are involved in curriculum development and change as practicing teachers--and trusted to do so--because of the recognition that curriculum change is a daily occurrence in schools as teachers adapt to the problems which confront them. Two rather different approaches to cooperative learning will be discussed here: teachers' centers and teacher workshops. Teachers' centers are usually places (model schools, district offices, training colleges), where practicing teachers come for guidance, training, and information. Most are quite traditional in orientation, with experts on hand to provide more or less formal courses on new curricula, texts, and equipment and to handle specific problems of individual teachers. Others, however, can be more participatory with teachers meeting in small groups, becoming actively involved in discussing classroom experiences, proposing and experimenting with new methods, and writing locally based materials. (See the 1978 CERI studies for detailed reviews of such centers in the developed world.) Teachers are brought into contact with other teachers; through such contact and cooperative work, isolation may be overcome and self-regard and commitment increased.

The most commonly described centers have perhaps been the Teacher Advisory Centres in Kenya, where teachers are expected to cooperate to develop their own instructional material and familiarize themselves with new course books in the local setting (Greenland, 1983; Haddad, 1985, pp. 59-60; Ayot, 1983). Similar projects have been described in Botswana (Molomo, 1983) and Nepal (Young, 1985). Another curriculum-related approach includes more informal teacher clubs, clusters, or workshops. These may be completely school focused, where most or all teachers of a school meet to define needs and experiment with solutions in relation to that school's particular policies and context. Teacher clusters in Thailand and School Learning Action Cells in the Philippines reflect this approach (APEID, 1985, pp. 18-25). The expectation behind such activities is two fold: the development of new and appropriate teaching practices and the encouragement of more cooperative and innovative attitudes within the school. These clusters or workshops may also be established across schools; e.g., from among particularly interested teachers in a given district. The Cianjur project in Indonesia does this (Hawes, 1982), and, to some extent, so does the Pakistan-German Basic Education project (Bude, 1985). One principle of such projects is that teachers develop new methods, try them out in classrooms, and then report back to the group on their success.

A particularly interesting version of the teacher workshop is one developed through a network of research/action centers in Latin America. First begun in Chile and then adapted in Argentina, Uruguay, and Bolivia, these workshops begin with the assumption that in order to transform the performance of teachers in the classroom, it is necessary to assist them to better understand the authoritarian and dogmatic role they currently play within the educational system and towards their students. Teacher training becomes not a series of discrete courses but rather a "permanent critical analysis of teaching practices and a permanent process of innovation and improvement" (Vera, 1982, p. 16).

Teachers are grouped in workshops, usually from several schools, in order to develop the ability: (1) to analyze critically their own teaching practice in order to facilitate the development of more participatory and research-oriented forms of learning and teaching; (2) to work in a group; (3) to do research and experiment within their own learning and teaching setting; and (4) to analyze the factors which influence social change (Vera, p. 21). With the help of a facilitator, but largely through collective effort, teachers critically analyze the role assigned to them by the government, the role they enact in class, and the role which they actually desire to play.

Though methods vary, teachers are generally observed by peers in classrooms or observe themselves through video tapes; they write about, discuss, and use role-plays of daily incidents, in order to analyze their assigned and enacted roles; they carry out a small piece of scientific research; they develop new and simple materials for teaching; and they try out new approaches in the classroom. The most important part of this process, perhaps, is the stimulation of the "teachers' awareness of the context in which they teach" (Avalos, 1985, p. 295). They also analyze extensively their own ability to work within the alternative, collective, non-authoritarian and non-dogmatic style of the workshop and then transfer this style to the classroom.

Of course, collaborative programs can go beyond the school into the community. A project in Bangladesh attempted to focus many training experiences of both teachers and their students to the village (Duncan & Löfstedt, 1982), and Dove has proposed a "rural challenge model" of teacher training which is field based, structured by teams, and involves the local community in the training of local teachers (1982). The Bunumbu project in Sierra Leone is often cited as an example of such work.

The important aspect of all of these projects is that the training is meant generally to be field-based, in the school and community, and to be collaborative among teachers, trainers, students, the community, and even administrators. Such an approach, Dove argues, revolutionizes teacher training, because "teamwork involving all who work in or on behalf of the school becomes essential to the coherence, meaning, and efficiency of the program" (1982, p. 25).

REFLECTIVE SELF-INSTRUCTION

This approach is based on self-instruction, often through some form of distance education (radio, correspondence courses, self-instructional modules, etc.), and is participatory when it encourages a learner to become autonomous, self-reliant, and active in learning and then to reflect on this learning. Such programs as radio courses which simply give new information to practicing teachers are not participatory because they are merely re-filling the vessel with modern technologies.

One form of self-instruction includes manuals, modules, and guides. These might be used as part of a more formal group course or by individual teachers. One example of this is the Teacher Preparation Packages developed by five Southeast Asian countries in a project coordinated by the SEAMEO Centre for Innovation and Technology (INNOTECH) in the Philippines (Tugade & Winarno, 1986). The content of these packages, devoted to "non-traditional" teaching, varied by country, from lesson planning in Indonesia to TEFL in the Philippines and mathematics in Malaysia. Teachers were heavily involved in the design and testing of these modules, and in those countries where they are still much in use (Thailand and Singapore), they require the teacher to take responsibility for systematically reading, reviewing, and correcting the lesson presented. Only in Thailand, however, are some of the modules designed specifically for use in small groups; it is perhaps no coincidence that Thailand has had the greatest success with these packages. Another project that used modules as part of a more integrated training method was the Universal Primary Education project in Bangladesh, where the school-based cluster training of teachers, designed to increase their motivation and involve them in group activities, as well as improve their performance, was complemented by modules which covered real-life situations (Basu, 1985). Both this and the INNOTECH project require the active reflection of teachers in regard to their own practice.

Various distance education methods can also fit this category of reflective self-instruction. Correspondence courses, study guides, radio and television lessons, etc., have all been used in this regard, some more reflective than others. These focus largely on upgrading teachers in basic knowledge and specific skills and often complement residential courses. The ZINTEC course in Simbabwe did this through correspondence courses (Sibanda, 1983), a Tanzanian project through radio and cassette programs (Chale, 1983), and a Kenyan project through radio, cassette, study guides, and textbooks. In the Ivory Coast, a distance education process of "auto-formation" encouraged groups of teachers to organize their own learning and seek responses to particular problems (Goad, 1984).

TRAINING BY "SIMULATION AND SITUATION"

By "simulation and situation" we mean training which is grounded in concrete, school-based situations but which also simulates these in ways which compel the trainees to become active participants in the situations. Role-playing is an example, where teachers play out roles as students, administrators, or teachers (Vera, 1982). Case studies of particular problems or critical incidents are another. Micro-teaching is appropriate as well if it is used not merely to fine-tune teachers in some pre-determined skill or toward some ideal image of a good teacher but rather to encourage teachers to reflect introspectively and actively on their performance in a particular situation. Many of the projects discussed above use these techniques.

THE TEACHER AS RESEARCHER

The fourth, and perhaps most participatory of all such approaches, is research itself--the teacher is the researcher. Many aspects of participatory teacher training come together in this process: action, autonomy, self-direction, reflection on concrete reality, even collaboration in some cases. But how does the action of research relate to the process of teaching? An International Bureau of Education (IBE) study has one response, quoting from Slastenin:

> Educational activity is creative by its very nature. In attempting to solve the countless recurring and new educational problems that arise, a teacher, like any research worker, arranges his activity in accordance with the general rules of heuristic investigation. . . . (He) hopes for by comparison with the initial data, analyses the available resources for checking his initial hypothesis and achieving the desired result, works out the actual process to be used in teaching and puts it into effect, evaluates the data obtained, and defines what must be the next stage (IBE, 1979, pp. 6-7).

Training in the methods of research, because of its similarity to the process of teaching, helps the teacher more systematically structure and focus his/her work.

Wells and Chang have another position. Teachers, they believe, "already have a practical theory of teaching; without such a theory, they could not make the many decisions . . . required of them on any day in the classroom." But these are:

> . . . implicit and unconscious . . . not easily amenable to self-determined evaluation and improvement. If teachers learn to make sensitive observations of their children's behavior, they will be led to make their theories of learning and teaching more explicit and so available for . . . critical examination . . . (which) may thus lead to teachers questioning their theories of

instruction and modifying their classroom practices (1986, p. 2).

Beeby perhaps puts it best: research by teachers would help to make teacher training more realistic, sensitize teachers to the need for changing some routine practices, and make them more professional (1977-78, p. 11).

There are various ways in which teachers can be involved in research. They can be consumers and experimenters, testing research findings in terms of classroom applicability (Eaker & Huffman, 1980). More easily, at least in the developing world where research results are not readily available, they can become researchers themselves. They can learn to observe others and then become able to observe and monitor their own practice and so improve their teaching continuously throughout their career (Brophy, 1979). They can learn to test their children, not only to check knowledge but to diagnose problems (Gardner, 1979, p. 185). And they can learn to examine the outcomes--both intended and unanticipated--of their work.

Does this need to be terribly sophisticated research? Aarons tells of a project in Papua New Guinea, where she helped teachers and elementary school children collect data on what the children ate at home and at school. This research led to community and school action projects to improve local diets (Aarons, 1981). In another case in Portugal, teachers did simple research on the causes of high repetition rates (Pedro, 1984).

To the extent that teachers are doing this research in partnership with trained researchers, we can talk of genuinely collaborative research: the teacher as active partner rather than passive informant. Such collaboration is of benefit to the professional researcher, combining the firsthand experience of the insider-practitioner with the theoretical and methodological skills of the outsider-observer (Wells & Chang, 1986; Shalaway & Lanier, 1978; Florio & Walsh, 1978).

Such collaboration can occur in various ways. It can be the informal sharing of results from earlier research (Florio-Ruane & Dobarich, 1984) or of the observation of children, the more formal meeting of collaborators to explore the implications of their observations and experiences, and the more systematic exploration of a particular problem (Wells & Chang, 1986). The second and third of these approaches are particularly important.

Teachers can be encouraged and trained to explore the methods and results of their teaching. To the extent that this is done in collaboration with a researcher equally in pursuit of understanding, rather than a trainer who already claims to understand, it recognizes the teacher as a reflective being and involves the teacher as an active researcher.

The Institute for Research on Teaching (IRT) in Michigan developed a project where:

> . . . classroom observations, video-tapes, and project meetings were used to facilitate the teachers' relections. In conjunction with weekly observations, three teachers and six researchers exchanged journal entries about the observations. Teachers gained insight into their practice by viewing video-tapes of the classrooms and further defined the project's goals in team and group meetings (Eaker & Huffman, 1980).

An excellent example of research on teaching in the developing world is a project carried out in Kenya over the past four years, which brought together a small group of secondary school teachers with a university lecturer to examine teaching problems, discuss teaching roles, analyze teacher motivation and performance, and experiment with different teaching methods.

> Teacher participation in research in this study was envisaged at four levels. First, teachers were expected to get involved in planning and undertaking some of the logistical aspects of the research project such as collecting data from students in their classes, rating the

quality of their own lessons, making themselves available for preactive teaching interviews and other more general interviews. Second, the teachers were expected to participate in seminars where they would meet with teachers from other schools and undertake reflective discussions concerning two main issues: the factors within their school environment which might affect their work; and their own teaching practices as observed from video and audio recordings of their lessons. Third, the teachers were expected to identify areas within their practice which they felt they needed to improve and, using both their own ideas as well as suggestions from their colleagues generated during the seminar discussions, implement observable instructional techniques designed to work towards improving selected teaching strategies. Lastly, the research participating teachers were expected to share their experiences about participation in the research with a larger audience of teachers with a view to encouraging other teachers to develop channels of dialogue among themselves in order to share experiences that might result in improving the quality of their practice (Namuddu, 1986, p. vii).

Audio and video tapes were used to record teaching practices, and extensive interviews with the teachers and others in the school were undertaken to clarify the context in which the teaching occurred. All of this became data and then proper grist for the mill of small meetings of the teachers-researchers. Discussions were frank and wide-ranging; points of view clarified, attacked, and defended; behaviors (even seemingly unimportant ones) dissected and explained; and alternative methods tried out (Namuddu, 1986). Namuddu concludes that:

. . . the processes of learning together which the teachers and myself attempted were in themselves a

learning experience. Certainly, the procedures that led
the teachers to identify needed change in their own
instructional strategies revealed to them the nature of
their "live" work. The video tape was a particularly
powerful aid in getting teachers (to) see and hear what a
teacher "is normally saved from"--his own teaching--
thus precipitating the desire to make some changes and
the efforts to change. . . . These efforts were very useful
and worth the effort and the high financial and psychic
cost, perhaps even more important than the change in
instructional strategies that we observed and were told
about, since it wrought overall changes among the nine
teachers, particularly in the way they perceived
themselves as teachers, as professionals and as
participants in the dynamic societies of the school and
the nation's educational systems as well as in the
cultural life of Kenya (1986, pp. 122-23).

More systematic exploration of particular predetermined
problems can also be done: the causes of repetition, the diets of
children, the problems of reading or writing. An example of this is a
project carried out at Milton Margai Teachers Training College in
Sierra Leone, where a dozen lecturers are paired with an equal
number of secondary school teachers to explore collaboratively a
range of problems ranging from the teaching of local art to dropping
out of the teaching profession (Wright, 1985). In one particular case,
teachers were trained for a new integrated science program in a
traditional "cookbook" style. This was generally considered a failure.
During later training more collaborative in nature, teachers and
researchers outlined, elaborated, and analyzed a wide range of
problems and worked out solutions to some of them (Wright, personal
communication). One further example occurred in Lesotho, where
five development studies teachers worked with a university
researcher in describing and analyzing classroom practice.
Awareness of classroom processes was sharpened, and the teachers

gained insight into learning problems, added to their repertoire of skills and strategies, and increased their confidence and morale (Stuart, 1986).

Beeby urges that such collaboration go even further, to bring together on a common task all the individuals and agencies in a particular area whose job it is to keep education "alive and growing," to investigate local problems, and "then to ensure that there is a way for their considered findings and conclusions to get through to those who make national policy" (Beeby, 1977/78, p. 11).

What might one expect to come out of the teacher as researcher? Wells and Chang believe "they become informed professionals whose decisions are grounded in more accurate understanding of the different variables that may be operating in particular learning and teaching situations;" they develop, in other words, a "theory-in-use" (1986, p. 11). The IRT project concludes:

> Seeing their practice through outsiders' eyes, the teachers became aware of possibilities beyond the district curriculum and the established models of teaching and classroom structure. Changes occurred in how they redefined the task of teaching. Challenging what they once had perceived as constraints, they were able to seek answers and solutions to teaching dilemmas that were informed by their professional knowledge (1986, p. 3).

CONSTRAINTS TO PARTICIPATORY TRAINING METHODS

Participatory methods are already being used, often unconsciously, by teacher trainers throughout the world. Such use, however, is usually sporadic, atheoretical, and unevaluated. More should be attempted. But many problems remain before such methods become common in the developing world.

First, it is clear that this kind of training is labor- and time-consuming. Small-group work, reflection, discussion, self-learning, action research, none of these are particularly fast, efficient, or inexpensive processes. Where hundreds if not thousands of teachers need to be trained quickly in a new syllabus or a new method, these methods will not work. Also, not all teachers are willing. Many are uncomfortable with group dynamics, self-analysis, and consciousness-raising. Others, especially in the poorest parts of the developing world, simply don't have the time or energy required, and their salary levels may rarely motivate them to experiment with new and often complex methods.

Second, government bureaucracies, ministries of education included, are frequently rigid in their own right and constrained by serious structural and financial problems. Teacher training institutions are burdened by the same problems and are dominated by staff more comfortable with traditional training processes. Schools, and the administrators and inspectors who control them, are often unsympathetic to change.

It can be argued as well that the kind of school-focused, self-actualizing, empowering nature of participatory training may, in fact, be based on a Northern or Western premise that teachers are and should be professionally autonomous and that schools have and should have a well-established climate of professional attitudes in which teacher initiatives are expected and encouraged. In many societies, in fact, they are expected to be part of, and subservient to, a much larger system, with its own particular goals, mores, and norms (Greenland, 1983; Bude & Greenland, 1983). In such places, new initiatives are not particularly welcome. The result in Chile, for example, has been a focus on more receptive private school systems and on working with individual schools rather than the government bureaucracy. Another problem is that such training can often stop at raised consciousness only, at newly felt efficiency, at higher motivation. They may not provide enough content, methods, and direction to help teachers deal with "the effects of poor material conditions of teaching, of pupil learning difficulties, and of an often miserable wage structure" (Avalos, 1985, p. 297). Nor do they always move beyond attitude change into providing clear-cut evidence about their benefits to the children to whom they are directed. And even if they did lead to changes in individual teachers, one cannot guarantee that these teachers will be able to practice them in a system based on different assumptions or transfer them to a regular school setting, especially if the school itself does not provide a "culture of mutually reinforcing expectations and activities" (Haddad, 1985, p. 47).

But these constraints should not stop the attempt to make teacher training more participatory. Teaching is now more than ever before a complex, difficult task. And even more innovations are being developed to make the teacher training systems better able to prepare qualified teachers. The World Bank's recent review of its experience in teacher training mentions a few of these: distance teaching, "ripple" or "echo" systems, mobile tutor teams, resource facilities, etc., these all to "provide teachers with continuous input and to help central education staff develop materials that respond to teachers' needs" (Haddad, 1985, p. 48).

The problem with this, as Greenland concludes, is that the teachers he studied "wanted to be more involved in the courses they were taking. They were offended at being subjected all the time to lecturers and at being treated as if they were school leaver trainees" (1983, p. 110). Thus, the use of more participatory approaches, whatever structure of training is created, should be increased. Colleges can slant "their training curricula to the acquisition by future teachers of abilities enabling them to participate in active research and in the utilization of the results of research" (IBE, 1979, p. 17). As Avalos suggests:

> . . . more importance should be given to schemes that
> (a) concentrate on the nature of the change process . . . ,
> (b) allow teachers to examine reflectively their experience and the constraints they must endure, and
> (c) enable teachers to receive information and assistance as they plan, over a period of time, the course of their practice. In other words, what is needed is attention to the training process in its relation to teacher awareness and willingness to change, as well as in its relation to the

provision of information. Such information is valuable only if it is represented as alternatives for choice and not as prescriptions. Its purpose should be to aid teachers in deciding what to use in order to structure their practice for the benefit of pupils (1983, p. 297).

In this way teachers may, indeed, learn that teaching is a lifelong learning process, requiring action, self-awareness, autonomy, collective learning skills, and problem-solving skills. As they do so they will become "'agents' of change rather than simply 'patients'" and will come to recognize that their professional development is "an ongoing process of active observing of and listening to children, and of interpreting what they see and hear. . . . Teachers begin to learn from their students, seeing them to be the most important resource for their continuing growth as professionals" (Wells & Chang, 1986, pp. 12-13).

FURTHER AREAS OF RESEARCH AND DISCUSSION

The above discussion leaves many questions unanswered. Several of the examples used to illustrate various aspects of participatory teacher training were based on project descriptions written at the commencement of the innovation rather than on evaluations written at the end. It is now clear that some of the examples cited, such as the Kenyan Teacher Advisory Centres, have not achieved their original goals and that many of the constraints mentioned above did, in the end, seriously weaken the effort. They were too ambitious, too simplistic, perhaps too dependent on the experimental nature of the project itself. Whatever the reason for their failure, many of the "data" available about these projects are now out of date and suspect.

So two kinds of further exploration appear necessary. The first are studies into the participatory process itself. Now more and more commonly touted as an alternative to "traditional" development processes, whether it be in teacher training, rural development, or primary health care, both this process itself and the increasingly cautionary reactions to it are in danger of becoming fads. More systematic research into participation, what it can and cannot do, in what circumstances, and in what way, is therefore needed.

In regard to participatory teacher training itself, more (and more extensive) descriptions and evaluations of various projects are necessary, both of those once regarded as exemplars of the approach and of those more recent in development. These might be case studies of on-going activities, some of which are already available as project reports (Wright, 1985; Namuddu, 1986; Vera, 1982), but not yet as systematic assessments. Others might be actual experiments contrasting participatory training with other approaches in terms both of process and outcomes.

The need for such studies of purely participatory projects should not obviate the importance now of encouraging more participatory approaches within traditional teacher training, both pre-service and in-service. Many of the characteristics of these approaches are paid lip-service to within such training and could be more seriously and effectively carried out. At least some of the goals of participatory teacher training might therefore be achieved in the short-run while the more complex and still obscure nature of the process as a whole is further studied.

CASE STUDY FOR CHAPTER FOUR

EDUCATORS' WORKSHOPS IN CHILE: PARTICIPATIVE PROFESSIONAL DEVELOPMENT

Rodrigo Vera

INTRODUCTION

Educators' Workshops in Chile have been developed by one of the key research institutions in the field of education in Latin America. The *Programa Interdisciplinario de Investigaciones en Educacion* (PIIE) is now a non-profit research center, but during its first years of operation it was located as a unit of the Catholic University of Chile. Between 1971 and 1973, its work became central to the efforts of the government to reform the national system of education. However, in 1977, PIIE was removed from the university as a result of the intervention in Chilean universities by the military government. The institute was forced to operate independently, with the protection of the Catholic Church and support from such funding agents as the International Development Research Centre in Canada. Experimentation in Educators' Workshops began in 1981 with two workshops for primary school teachers which ran for seven months. In 1983-85, there were two workshops for primary teachers and one for junior secondary teachers. This latter experiment ran for two years and participants were trained as workshop coordinators. A supervisory workshop is currently in progress to monitor the work of the coordinators. The research done in these experiments facilitated the gathering of knowledge leading to the implementation of workshops on a large-scale basis.

Educators' workshops are based on a number of guiding ideas of professionalization, group formation, and autonomous learning. First, they attempt to provide an opportunity for research by the participants themselves leading to critical reflection on their own teaching practice and the real situation in their schools. Second, they attempt to serve as an opportunity for research and learning about how to learn in small groups, which differs from the methods which predominate in the school system. Third, they attempt to provide an opportunity for professional development, for teachers to learn how to learn spontaneously, analyzing problems in the teaching practice of the participants and connected with the group experience they are undergoing.

Present political conditions in Chile make it impossible to adopt this type of professional development nationally. Despite this, however, the style of professional development through workshops has spread throughout the country. We shall elaborate on the guiding ideas of the workshops.

TECHNOCRATIZATION - PROFESSIONALIZATION OF THE TEACHER'S ROLE

Studies of institutionalized teaching practice in the school system of Chile generally portray teachers as rigidly and uniformly applying a sequence of content prescribed by the administration of their school, almost all teachers using similar and traditional teaching methods. In this framework, the teaching role in Chile can be characterized as "technical" rather than "professional" and serving the implementation of curriculum which is technical in style. Seen in this light, the Educators' Workshops are a form of professional development designed to convert the role of teachers from technician to professional. They provide training to enable teachers to adapt and recreate the curriculum constantly so that it leads to the achievement of the intended learning objectives. This involves a better understanding of teaching learning processes and of the heterogeneity of the problems which necessarily derive therefrom.

To achieve this, the Workshops place research into the pedagogical practice of the participants as central to professional development. The purpose is to make their teaching practice come to depend upon methods and ways of thinking which they can autonomously evaluate and correct on a continuous basis. It is not our purpose to have each teacher become a professional educational researcher, but rather, that individually and in groups they can expand their capacity for critical thought about their practice as the essential condition for transformation towards more efficient and democratic forms of teaching-learning.

ATOMIZATION/GROUP FORMATION OF THE TEACHER'S ROLE

The role of teachers is also defined by the kind of working relationships among teachers in a school. Studies of teaching practice confirm that, in general, teachers carry out their functions in a state of extensive isolation, and the Workshops are a way of reorganizing teaching in schools, or in related establishments, so that the atomized work of teachers becomes interactive and group oriented. We base this on the supposition that group work sets a climate in which responsibilities are shared, the supervisory system is collectively "socialized," and ways of cooperation and mutual stimulation are sought.

As Educators' Workshops become a form of organization of the work of teachers, they also become a way in which there can be professional development directly coupled with the needs of teaching practice. In this light Workshops represent an alternative for overcoming the narrow parallelism between technical training and practice and a way of rendering permanent professional development as an integral part of the day's work for teachers.

DEPENDENT AND AUTONOMOUS WAYS OF LEARNING AND THE ROLE OF TEACHERS

Among the basic options which define the role of teachers are the ways of learning they demonstrate in dealing with students. In speaking of "ways of learning," one is referring to the extent of the involvement of learners, or the degree to which their thoughts, feelings, and actions are involved in the process of learning. One can thus speak of ways of learning dependent upon an authority which emits judgments about truth and value which must be learned in a predetermined manner, or of more autonomous ways of learning in which such judgments have to be constructed by the students themselves as they participate in the learning situations.

Studies indicate that teachers generally favor dependent ways of learning. They demand that students memorize content and do not encourage sustained training in thought, independent research, and judgment based on the experience of the students themselves.

The Workshops try to provide a situation for spontaneous learning by drawing on the experiences of the teachers and on their capability for systematic thought. It is research into their own practice which constitutes the central point, coupled with a group situation for confronting their own conflicts. The purpose is to develop their capacity for thought as the necessary precondition for learning to understand their own experience. Our notion is that as teachers acquire independent modes of learning, they will be able to set up learning situations for their students, which, in turn, encourage the internalization of autonomous modes of learning. As teachers learn to understand their own experience, they will encourage similar patterns of learning for their students. We also believe that as students acquire autonomous ways of learning from appropriate methods of instruction, the rate of successful learning will rise above that available from traditional methods of instruction.

THE EVOLUTION OF WORKSHOP EXPERIMENTS

The Workshops have now gone on for many years, and during that time we have tried a variety of methods. In the course of our work, three major stages can be perceived.

PERIOD OF RESEARCH INTO THE SITUATIONAL PROBLEMS OF SCHOOLS

In the first stage, participants were charged to investigate the educational and social realities which were likely to affect the instruction and learning processes in the school system. We introduced them to the research tradition that now characterizes the modern world and some of the conceptual and methodological tools that researchers possess. We then explored ways that research could be used to understand one's environment. Teachers were expected to learn about the cultural status of students, their habits, needs and interests. The high dropout rate, poor levels of achievement, and disciplinary and behavioral problems all constituted research concerns.

Teachers also learned about the communities in which their schools were located and set up contacts with social organizations and families of their students. The problems investigated included unemployment, family income, the illiteracy rate, rates of malnutrition, health conditions, environmental hygiene, housing conditions, etc. Generally, rigorous social science research methods and techniques were used, especially from sociology.

Some group dynamics techniques were also used, but at this stage we lacked any theory to understand the origins of conflict within the group, so the main orientation was on researching the schools and the environment. We felt that as teachers learned how to do research they would be able to introduce it into their teaching activities.

PERIOD OF RESEARCH INTO BIASES

During this phase, participants were charged with investigating the reality of the explanations they themselves gave to the problems of poor achievement and unruly behavior. We assumed that as teachers managed to understand the problems in new ways, they would be able to work out alternative answers to those they were currently applying.

The theoretical and epistemological basis for "protagonistic" research (self-examination) has developed from the cumulative experience of a succession of Workshops. We attempt to convert a particular event or action into an object of knowledge that helps explain the beliefs, emotions, and rationales which are involved in teaching practice. These are then interpreted to determine what personal, institutional, and social factors help influence the action being examined. Alternatives are formulated to support alternative teaching methods.

Protagonistic research begins with the confrontation of the teacher of a problem in his daily practice. At this stage the problems selected are those the teachers consider to be most urgently in need of solution. The group helps the actor reconstruct an episode in such a way that it can be viewed objectively. In the process of reconstruction attempts are made to explicate the beliefs, emotions, and rationalizations involved in the episode and to observe it without bringing in value judgments and avoiding premature interpretation.

In succeeding phases, we try to reconstruct the episode from internal and external perspectives, formulate hypotheses which can be validated, make a critical analysis of the rationalization employed, and suggest alternative ways of handling the episode. The research method used in the phase is based on the methods and technologies of sociology, anthropology, and psychology. For example, one group of teachers started from the notion that the low achievement of students was directly associated with the destruction of family life. Another group attributed it to the use made by students of their free time, particularly the number of hours they spent watching TV. In most cases the biases and hypotheses were not validated, requiring the group to start investigating other aspects of the problem.

The outcome of this phase was that teachers began to question the way in which teachers viewed the problems facing them. If teachers are to modify their practice, they would have to adopt a questioning attitude and not allow their attitudes to become stereotyped.

"PROTAGONISTIC" RESEARCH PERIOD

During this period the participants were expected to investigate their own practice. They discovered, interpreted, and criticized the terms of reference on which their actions were based. At the same time, the coordinator worked with the group as the source of investigation of his own practice. In this respect the coordinator attempted to indicate the obstacles encountered by groups and help them become, as a group, an instrument for learning and interpretation.

In this context, the group dealt with the methodology of protagonistic research, the interpretation of group phenomena, learning theory, the analysis of school reality and the theory of professional development. The three kinds of research taken on by the participants during the Workshops effectively made teachers reflect upon their practice and modify it towards more effective and democratic methods of instruction. As for group learning, we reached the stage of being able to propose more coherent goals.

It was during this phase that the greatest productivity was seen. Protagonistic research demonstrated that it was a powerful tool for investigation of the degree of subjectivity brought by teachers to problems involved in the daily performance of their tasks. The research reports drawn up by the participants could be circulated as scientific research and contribute to the reflections of other teachers upon their practice. Also, the epistemology, theory, and method of protagonistic research turned out to be an important option for educational research, which by concentrating on specific cases, can contribute generalizable terms of reference applicable to cases other than the immediate objectives of this research. Lastly, protagonistic research showed that it was a useful way to help teachers handle the recurring problems in their practice and attempt to resolve them in novel ways.

CHAPTER FIVE

MAKING THE BEST USE OF TEACHERS: DEPLOYMENT ISSUES

A. R. Thompson

INTRODUCTION

The argument of this paper is that while much attention has been given to staff training, relatively little has been given to the effective deployment of staff in education systems. Yet, improved deployment patterns and procedures may not only reduce waste of valuable resources but also positively contribute to the ongoing improvement of the staff and of the education we offer our children (see also Thompson, 1984).

The discussion of deployment will deal with four main aspects: the authority structure, the staffing structure, allocation to post procedures and criteria, and support services. The illustrations provided are drawn from a survey of some twenty countries, mainly in Africa and Southeast Asia. Since few practices have been rigorously evaluated, this paper should be regarded as offering questions rather than conclusions, an agenda for research rather than for action.

AUTHORITY STRUCTURE ISSUES

Here we are concerned with the decision making and accountability structures within which education staff will be called upon to work. A deployment policy which is inconsistent with the authority structure is unlikely to be successful. The basic assumption of all the education systems surveyed is that management and administration should be conducted through a bureaucratic pattern of organization, which is usually highly centralized. That is, direction and control are exercised through a hierarchical range of offices. Education staff of whatever grade are appointed to posts within this hierarchy and are expected to fulfil specified roles within this machine, according to a manner and style of operation which has been predetermined.

Whatever their theoretical strengths in terms of managing education within an overall national development plan, the practical weaknesses of centralized bureaucratic structures have become generally evident in recent years. In particular, the following weaknesses have been identified:

a. Such systems are designed for continuity and are less able to cope with the demands for change.

b. Responsibility for education is commonly shared between several ministries and departments of government: lines of responsibility are consequently complicated, coordination of action in the field is often inhibited, and multiple cadres of staff, often with different terms of service and modes of operation, are created.

c. There has been a predominance of power-coercive strategies in the management of innovation which have proved to be inadequate for institutionalizing change in education systems, which consist of administrators, teachers, and pupils, who are concerned with their own interests and who possess considerable power to resist changes decreed from higher levels.

d. Communication has tended to be nondirectional, top-down, from remote senior levels lacking the competence or perception to make the small scale and local adjustments necessary if broad policy directives are to be applied relevantly and effectively at the school level.

e. Lower management has neither the authority nor the competence to make local adjustments, nor are they able to cope with the increasing complexity of educational expansion.

f. Decision making, except in routine matters which can be dealt with according to the book, tends to be referred upward through the bureaucracy to higher levels, which become congested and diverted from broader policy concerns.

g. System needs tend to take precedence over the individual needs of education staff, leading to low morale. Professionalism of staff tends to be assumed to be of the craftsman and para-professional variety, with the consequent failure to mobilize and make effective use of the experience and knowledge of the local staff.

There are good reasons for retaining a high degree of central direction and control in an enterprise, which is viewed as central to national development and which consumes high proportions of the limited resources usually available to national governments. It is interesting to note that, in recent years, many governments have sought to modify their centralized bureaucratic structures and procedures in order to make management more sensitive, efficient, less costly, and more satisfying to staff. The 1971 Kenyan Commission of Enquiry into the Public Service was early in this field, arguing for the need to change the traditional conception of the Civil Service as "the transmitter of impulses received from the cabinet" into one in which it was "a creative force constantly reappraising the problems confronting society and enabling it to solve them by designing new solutions" (Republic of Kenya, 1971, p. 3). In general, these reforms have involved deconcentration, devolution, and delegation in varying patterns, and there is growing acceptance of the necessity of allowing decision making in some areas to be undertaken at the institutional level in order to achieve local adaptation of policies and to promote greater commitment and more professional attitudes among staff.

It is clearly understood that changes in the managerial structure will not, in themselves, overcome current weaknesses and certainly will not overcome shortages of competent personnel. Indeed, such policies will place even greater demands upon staff at all levels of the system. The expectation is not so much that decentralization will release abilities and energies which have previously been constrained as that it offers the opportunity for staff to develop these abilities on the job and the hope that increased opportunities will help to generate the motivation and professionalism among staff at all levels upon which managerial efficiency depends.

For such opportunities to be real rather than illusory, active staff development measures will have to be pursued, and deployment of staff will need to ensure that individuals are placed where they are most needed and can maximize their contribution. Staff must be given a genuine opportunity to develop the new skills they will need, notably those of decision making and problem solving, and to learn to use them. Deployment assumes a new and greater importance in this new context.

It is not assumed that every country will adopt decentralized management, and indeed it may be asserted that most will retain a high degree of central control and direction. But whichever system is to be adopted, we need to consider how we may make better use of our existing stock of skill and expertise and facilitate its improvement on a continuing basis. The staffing structures, procedures, and support services which we now proceed to discuss may well demand review but such a review can only be undertaken in the light of the authority structure and any shifts in that structure which are contemplated.

STAFFING STRUCTURE ISSUES

The staffing structure is the matrix of posts and positions into which staff are recruited and within which they must function. Here we will be concerned with the categorization of staff, the incentives and reward structures associated with the various categories, and the opportunities for lateral and vertical mobility within the profession. We also touch on the extent to which these structures affect the morale and self-concept of staff, opportunities for self-development and self-realization, and a climate of quality seeking within the system.

There is remarkable variety in the structures of education staffing in the countries under review. Evaluation of these structures is almost nonexistent, although a limited amount of information is available in Harris' survey of sixteen countries. The very existence of diverse structures suggests that no consensus exists or perhaps has been sought about the way in which an education service ought to be organized. Some differences may be accounted for by local historical and cultural factors, while others may stem from the authority structure, but it does not appear that the major differences can be clearly attributed to the uniqueness of local situations. Consequently, there would seem to be considerable potential for comparative analysis of current staffing procedures.

It is common practice for Ministries of Education to be composed of two divisions, an administrative division, which is responsible for general management, financial control, and personnel, and a professional division, which is responsible for curriculum, examinations, and supervision of the day to day work of the schools. The logic of such a separation of functions appears to be superficial, born of administrative convenience rather than professional purpose. This is particularly apparent where the administrative division occupies a dominant position, which is common, and where professional experience in education is not required for appointment to the administrative division and to the most senior official positions within the Ministry. In consequence, staffing allocations are likely to be made from administrative rather than professional considerations. Some of the practices which result from this will be examined in the following section.

It is common for different categories of education to be separately administered, such as primary education, secondary education, teacher education, curriculum development, inspection, and so on. Most illogical of all is the existence of technical education as a separate category. Given the dominance of vertical lines of communication and the importance of protocol, interdepartmental communication is inhibited, imposing an organizational and psychological frame upon the system which does not accord with the professional realities of education, in which change in any one branch is likely to require change in several others. While the standard pattern of organization is probably good enough for servicing and maintaining existing educational practices, it is profoundly defective in coming to terms with the demands of change.

Allied to these considerations is the custom for "professional" staff themselves to be compartmentalized into teaching staff and administrators. A hierarchy of esteem, influence and reward has usually developed, which places teaching staff at the bottom of the heap and the administrators at the top.

Personnel functions are commonly delegated to a Teaching Service Commission, which selects, appoints, allocates to a post, transfers between posts, pays, promotes, and disciplines education staff. However, there is considerable variation. For example, in some Nigerian states, secondary-level teachers are placed under the general Civil Service Commission. In Zambia, all primary and secondary staff are under the Teaching Service Commission, but teaching staff in technical institutions are under the Civil Service Commission. It may be wondered how far such distinctions between categories of staff and the involvement of Civil Service Commissions with education staff may inhibit the creation of career structures better suited to the needs of teachers. How far will linking teachers with civil service scales of salary create satisfaction in teachers through parity with other civil servants, and how far will it generate dysfunctional attitudes and inhibit the development of career structures appropriate to the nature of the teaching profession, the staffing of which is structurally very different from that of most other branches of the civil service?

In several countries an organizational distinction is made between teachers and professional administrators. In Zambia, for example, the teaching staff fall under the Teaching Service Commission, but education officers, inspectors, planning and clerical staff come under the Public Service Commission. A similar system was employed in Ghana until 1974, when the Ghana Education Service was established to bring together members of the then-nongraduate teaching service and of the then-graduate education branch of the civil service together with all those other kinds of staff employed by the Ministry of Education in accounting, secretarial, general administrative roles, and all support staff paid for from public funds (Williams, 1974). The clear intention was to achieve three things: first, to offer all teachers the same conditions of service and a common career structure; second, to facilitate interchange of staff between administrative and teaching posts; and third, to give all concerned with education a greater measure of autonomy in the management of their profession. Sadly, the political and economic circumstances of Ghana have adversely affected the development of the Education Service, but the principles then established may merit consideration elsewhere.

Some countries, such as Malaysia, have a structure of career grades not dissimilar to the Ghanaian grade arrangements, whereby all posts within a particular grade carry the same salary scale. In principle, this should lead to equity between different kinds of work and greater flexibility in the utilization of staff. On the other hand, grading of posts and the requirement of certain levels of qualification for entry to particular grades may lead to senior posts in the higher grades being filled by highly qualified but inexperienced and unproven staff to the exclusion of experienced and proven, but less well qualified staff trapped in the lower grades.

If grade to grade promotion is determined by qualifications rather than performance, there is some danger that the energy of the ambitious teacher will be diverted from his teaching duties to private study for examinations. Provision of overlapping salary scales between grades, as in Malaysia and Nigeria, may ameliorate the position somewhat and enable, for a time, some experienced staff in a lower grade to earn a higher salary than the less experienced staff in the higher grade. Nevertheless, there are obvious implications for staff competence and morale here.

More commonly, there is no grade system at all, but academic qualifications are thought appropriate and necessary for certain levels and kinds of post. Often this is highly systematized, as in The Gambia, where teachers need a Primary Teachers Certificate to teach in secondary technical schools and to fill certain junior administrative posts and degrees to teach in high schools and tertiary level institutions and to fill senior administrative posts. In Nigeria, it is not uncommon to meet a secondary school teacher who first spent five years training to be a Grade II primary teacher, followed by three years training for the Nigeria Certificate in Education, in order to teach in junior secondary schools, followed by three years study for a degree to qualify to teach in senior secondary schools. We must be very sure of our categorization of posts and of the necessity of entry qualifications to impose such a burden and such a distraction upon our staff. Since in Nigeria the demands of educational expansion have resulted in considerable relaxation of the system, so that, in practice, teachers may be teaching classes higher than those for which they are technically qualified, an opportunity exists to examine how far such qualificationism is really necessary. The somewhat exceptional arrangements in Nigeria, where a Grade II teacher may be awarded "honorary" Grade I status and in Kenya, where nongraduate S1 teachers may be awarded "approved teacher" status, affording them similar prospects to graduate teachers, might also be examined.

Where teachers with different grades, designations, and qualifications are working side by side and doing the same work, it might be imagined that this would open up opportunities for staff to be promoted and assume higher responsibilities irrespective of their qualifications. In practice, however, it may not, and this may create real dissatisfaction among the less well qualified. In Malawi, diploma teachers are reported to be very unhappy at receiving lower salaries than graduates doing the same work. Under a post grading system, they would be eligible for the same salary.

ALLOCATION TO POST PROCEDURES AND CRITERIA

Here we are concerned with how far posting and promotion procedures take account of individual qualities of staff members, how far they ensure the best utilization of staffing skills and qualities available and affect motivation for self-improvement.

POLICY ISSUES

It is a common complaint that attempts to achieve greater equity in education have been undermined by gross disparities in the quality of schooling, notably between urban and rural areas and between more and less developed regions within countries. It might have been expected, therefore, that rigorous staffing policies to ensure greater equity would have been pursued. It is, however, not clear that this has been done, not merely because of the inevitable logistical problems caused by rapid expansion and limited administrative capacity, but because the need for such policies has not been adequately grasped. These issues relate both to the staffing of individual schools and the system as a whole.

Research findings reported by Husen et al. (1978) and Avalos (1979) suggest that the training, experience, qualifications, age, and sex of teachers may be significantly related to their performance, though in different ways, according to subject and level of class taught. Perhaps because these findings are as yet insufficiently conclusive to form the basis of staffing policy, and because basic shortages of teachers are so acute, no countries surveyed appear to have considered defining ideal school staffing proportions in terms of such characteristics.

The question of the use made of female teachers is notably contentious and culturally sensitive. Full and effective use of female teachers is often impeded by the use of single sex schools, and the notion that female teachers should normally teach in the girls' schools. The practice of coeducation may facilitate more flexible use of female teachers and improve their status and career prospects. Some problems will remain, however, notably rigidities created by cultural objections to posting young unmarried women to isolated stations and by the humane custom of seeking to post the increasing numbers of married women in the profession to their husbands' places of employment. This latter policy may have the significant advantage of helping to relieve staff housing problems which are often acute but tend to lead to an undue concentration of women teachers in urban areas, since they will commonly marry salary earning men there.

Since trained and experienced teachers are usually in short supply, particular attention needs to be paid to the means whereby we obtain the best value from their services. The question of whether such teachers conventionally employed with the more able and senior classes might not be more effectively utilized in the less able and junior classes is by no means the most important or vital aspect of this question.

In many countries, where qualified teachers are relatively scarce, it is customary for them to occupy the senior posts in the school, notably those of head, deputy head, or head of department. In these posts they are likely to do less teaching than their less well qualified colleagues, yet their administrative role may well consist largely of routine trivia which could be equally well dealt with by less well-qualified staff. Nor has it been usual for those administrative roles to include other than nominal supervision and support of less well-qualified colleagues. Delegation of duties and the assumption of professional support roles will not necessarily increase the direct impact they may have upon pupils but may lead to better use of their time and expertise.

Team teaching approaches may create greater opportunity for the better qualified, more able and experienced teachers both to contribute to the training of their colleagues and to make a greater direct impact upon pupils than through a conventional timetable in which teachers work in isolation, with whole classes being consigned to the ministrations of less able teachers. Team teaching may also permit variation in class sizes, allying the benefits of access to a specialist and expert teacher in the large group situation to those of individualized attention in a small group situation where even the less well-qualified teachers may have some hope of success.

An imaginative attempt to make maximum use of qualified teachers through larger class size is to be seen in Project Impact Schools in the Philippines. Here each instructional supervisor is responsible for approximately 100 pupils. Actual instruction is largely conducted by older pupils under a version of the monitorial system and through specially prepared self-instructional materials. A further important feature of this approach is the employment of parents and members of the community as ancillary staff, performing limited support and supervision roles, liberating the instructional supervisor for more significant tasks (SEAMEO, 1980b).

This particular model may not be generally acceptable; however, it is not the model but the principle to which attention is being drawn. The use of paraprofessional ancillary staff has commonly been opposed by the teaching profession as representing dilution of the profession and a threat to status. Properly used, such a system may, in fact, enhance status as well as efficiency, and the principle which is employed in limited ways through the use of parents in nursery and infant classes and of laboratory technicians in secondary and tertiary institutions appears well worthy of imaginative consideration for more general application. A scheme for utilizing aboriginal teachers' aides for aboriginal children in Australia was designed primarily to compensate for high rates of turnover among the qualified teacher staff, but it provided a valuable bonus in their understanding of pupil culture and language. Consequently, the project was reviewed to place greater emphasis on the contribution such aides might make to curriculum development and staff training (Valadian & Randall, 1980).

The use of self-instructional materials, also embraced by Project Impact, has been widely canvassed. Husen et al. (1978, p. 44) maintain that the use of suitably programmed teaching materials may enable untrained teachers to substitute for trained teachers. Experiments with radio and television to compensate for teacher deficiencies are showing increasing promise.

A further way forward may be to seek to extend the impact of qualified and experienced staff beyond the boundaries of a single school, particularly those whose subject expertise is in short supply. The convention whereby each school is individually staffed and expected to be sufficient unto itself is long overdue for re-examination. In some countries peripatetic teachers have been used, but it is rare to find teachers of high-status subjects so employed.

A better approach may be that of school clusters employed in Thailand, the Philippines and Sri Lanka. In Thailand, clusters of five to ten primary schools have functioned as a means of sharing scarce material and human resources since 1960 and have become integral parts of the decentralized administrative system since 1980. Core schools host educational resource centers developed and operated jointly by all the schools in the cluster and the clusters become the focus of all school improvement activities.

The Sri Lanka model is more recent and the school clusters, in addition to being larger, include both primary and secondary schools. Again the expertise of qualified and specialist teachers is shared between schools, and in-service training is organized by the cluster. The Learning Action Cells, in the Philippines, exist at school, district, and regional levels and are the channel for school self-appraisal and staff development. Principals also receive leadership and management training at the district and regional levels.

Evaluation studies are reported to confirm the effectiveness of the organizational patterns in these three countries (ACEID, 1984, pp. 13-17; Kaewdang, 1983; Wanasinghe, 1983). Similar patterns of operation are in use in the Nepal pilot project on education and rural development and, for staff in Bophuthatswana, the Cianjur project in Indonesia, and in the designation of resource teachers and of resource teacher coordinators for school zones in Zambia.

The value of clustering, where schools are small, may be particularly great. Small schools possessing perhaps only three or four staff members are particularly disadvantaged, since any poor, inexperienced, or underqualified members of staff will have a "disproportionately adverse impact upon pupils, and, if teacher turnover is high, small schools are disproportionately destabilized" (Dove, 1985, p. 4). Professional isolation is likely to undermine the morale of teachers working in difficult circumstances and to restrict their participation in the staff development activities they may so badly need. The difficulty is that such schools are more common at the primary level and in rural areas. Consequently, it is not easy to resolve these problems by adopting a minimum school size policy or a cluster strategy. This should not mean, however, that such strategies may not be adopted where they are appropriate.

An alternative strategy may be for schools in a particular locality to develop specializations. In The Gambia, one of the most acute problems is the shortage of qualified staff in certain key subject areas. In consequence, there has evolved a degree of specialization in Banjul high schools, whereby one school concentrates on pure sciences, another on pure and applied mathematics, yet others in commercial studies and economics. Such specialization, if applied to lower classes, might result in damaging restriction of the combinations of subjects which students may study but may be of particular value in senior classes where the curriculum involves specialization.

Tanzania, since the early 1970s, has adopted the principle of specialized biases for all its secondary schools, which are categorized as agricultural, technical, commercial, or home economics. There are, however, difficulties in reconciling subject specialization with close community links, which are also sought in many countries, particularly in Africa. The full benefits of such a system may require its application within local clusters of schools rather than at the national level.

A major issue confronting many countries is that of staffing rural schools, particularly in disadvantaged regions. Such schools often suffer from isolation, are often less well equipped than urban schools and suffer more from the problem of adapting educational content and methodology to the cultural and social environment. Teachers find themselves and their families disadvantaged in terms of access to educational opportunities, libraries, transport, and other such facilities. Consequently, qualified and experienced teachers are reluctant to move to stay in such schools. What staffing policies are applied to overcome the problem?

Dove has analyzed the factors affecting teacher attitudes and hypothesizes that economic factors may be the most crucial in attracting teachers to particular postings, but that the socio-cultural environment may be crucial in retaining them in the post (1985, p. 10). She suggests that compulsion or bonding methods "built into the system a high rate of teacher turnover, encouraging them to seek early transfer." Where incentives are used, such as salary loading, hardship and disturbance allowances, accommodation, travel concessions, accelerated promotion, study leave, all of which are in use in various countries, these need to be very strong to be effective. Even so, if they are associated with compulsion, they are likely to be diluted in their effects. Dove concludes that such measures based upon the rural deficit approach, represent a short-term solution of doubtful effectiveness, rather than a long-term strategy, which she maintains should be based upon a rural challenge approach.

The needs of rural and disadvantaged areas are such that it is necessary to create a cadre of able and experienced teachers willing to spend much of their careers in such areas so as to develop real expertise, and Dove argues that the main focus of such an approach should be upon the special training and preparation of these teachers. Such specialized training may well be necessary, but, even assuming that appropriate training is possible, one may doubt its effect unless associated with positive discrimination in terms of facilities, materials, support services, accommodation, and career progression. In addition, as Dove again suggests, measures must be taken to select the right type of teacher for training and deployment to the rural schools.

One particular aspect of this is the effort to recruit teachers from minority groups and disadvantaged areas, which may well necessitate relaxation of entry criteria but be compensated by possession of real understanding of the communities, their language, culture, and problems. It appears, however, that while many countries make special efforts to recruit teachers of shortage subjects and in specialist fields such as special education, efforts to recruit from minority groups are considerably more rare, though there have been examples, as in Iran and Thailand. Sometimes a quota system is employed, as in Kenya and Sarwak, for admission to teacher training. Malawi's Education Plan 1973-80 sought to ensure that every tribal group was represented at all levels of government to correct the imbalance left by colonialism. It is unclear, however, whether such policies are associated with a deployment policy whereby minority group teachers are posted to their own communities. We should not, of course, assume that teachers from a particular group and region will wish to return to their own areas, and the need to create national unity in some countries may demand that teachers be deployed to regions other than their own.

The problems associated with rapid staff turnover apply to all branches and levels of education services. It may dissipate specialist expertise in, for example, teacher training or inspection and undermine attempts to develop balanced staffing within schools and to build up cadres of experience and competence. Staff turnover may also encourage hierarchical and non-participatory styles of school management and isolating teaching styles. It may also be argued that too stable a staff may lead to stagnation, particularly in disadvantaged schools; however, Dove concludes that the "benefits of stability are, on the whole, likely to outweigh those of the variety created by a rapid turnover of teachers" (Dove, 1985, p. 11). In few countries has any policy in these matters been arrived at, let alone implemented, and even basic data concerning the average duration of service in particular posts or rates of transfer are not available.

There is, of course, a strong case for the use of job rotation to broaden and update the experience of staff. The case for interchange of posts between inspectors and teacher educators has been made frequently. A particular form of rotation may enable certain teachers to move from grade to grade with a particular class and facilitate the structuring of subject content over more than one year to provide for individual differences. Once again, however, there is little evidence that such policies are being pursued consistently in most of the countries surveyed.

A less well-understood issue presents itself at this point. In recent years much has been made of the principle that staff should receive in-service training before being required to assume posts for which their previous training and experience have not qualified them. While, indeed, there is a strong case for this, there is a basic problem of finding staff qualified by real experience to train others. Education systems are changing rapidly in structure, management style, curriculum content, and methodology, and consequently in crucial areas where expertise may simply not exist, training might become formal and theoretical or irrelevant.

It may be argued that to cope with many of the new demands being made of education systems, staff will, for some time at least, have to learn by doing. Deployment policies may, therefore, have to be reviewed, with allocation to post no longer assuming capacity but presenting a challenge and an opportunity to develop the necessary capacity. The importance of support services in this respect will be discussed later. However, it is clear that such an approach assumes that education staff will be given considerable discretion to develop their own patterns and styles of working. They must be regarded as fully functioning professionals. This set of circumstances constitutes the main argument against the notion of education staff, particularly at the school level, being regarded as technicians or paraprofessionals and has considerable implications for the authority structure discussed earlier (see Thompson & Greenland, 1983).

STAFFING PROCEDURES

The central issues here are the following: who decides who will serve where, what criteria are taken into consideration, and what procedures are used? The underlying question is which procedures are most likely to reconcile system needs with staff needs and the potential to ensure the most satisfactory utilization of staff? In general, posting of staff is undertaken by administrative personnel acting in accordance with system needs often interpreted mechanistically. In some countries, allocation to post is determined by only two sets of consideration, the qualifications of the staff member and the number and nature of vacant posts. Thereafter, the postings may be constrained by marital status in respect of female teachers and availability of accommodation, which has become a determining factor in some Nigerian states resulting in teachers being posted to their home areas where they may share family accommodation. In general, it may be argued that where teacher shortage exists, centralized and directive postings tend to meet the immediate needs of schools but inhibit more sensitive and sophisticated strategies.

The development of strategies, which take adequate account of individual qualities and preferences, appears to be inhibited not merely by the limited capacity of the administrative unit but by the common practice whereby those agencies responsible for teacher training, teacher employment, teacher deployment, and teacher supervision, function largely in isolation from each other. Consequently, training staff and supervisors, who may well possess a detailed knowledge of the personalities and capacities of teachers, are not consulted by agencies which send teachers to post.

Responsibility for postings is sometimes delegated. In most countries, allocations are commonly made by the appropriate service commission, sometimes directly to schools and units but often to regions or provinces following which regional or provincial authorities deploy staff to schools. Different procedures may be followed in respect to different categories of staff. Generally, the procedures for employing and deploying primary school teachers are different from and more directive than those for secondary school teachers. Such differentials may well be justified by reasons of administrative convenience and the pressure of numbers but are nevertheless liable to involve the creation of advantage and disadvantage, leading to professional dissatisfaction and discontent. High rates of staff turnover may well reflect not merely the existence of dissatisfaction but the capacity of ordinary teachers to manipulate the system informally.

How far are postings made after consulting the wishes of staff? It is common for the teachers' contract of service to require them to serve anywhere in the country where their services are needed, but in some cases teachers may express a preference for service or apply for transfer to a preferred area. In some countries vacancies are advertised and so teachers have the opportunity of volunteering to serve in specific posts. Some countries, such as Swaziland, St. Lucia, and Papua New Guinea, advertise all posts, though this appears to be a luxury more possible in small countries. Other countries advertise only secondary posts, as in The Gambia and Sierra Leone, or senior posts, as in Zambia and Sri Lanka.

The practice noted above of staged deployment, whereby teachers may be allocated to a region and thereafter to schools by regional authorities, offers some prospect of taking teachers' regional preferences into account and of local needs being matched with personal qualities. Admittedly, these prospects are bound to be limited except where vacancies exceed supply. Nevertheless, both the practice of advertisement and that of staged deployment are worthy of consideration for at least some categories of post in countries which at present do not use them.

PROMOTION PROCEDURES

In education, the vast majority of staff must be engaged in teaching duties. Management positions are relatively few in number, and promotion to such positions usually removes staff from work for which they have been trained and which may not necessarily be suited to their tastes or capacities. The procedure of removing staff from the classroom associates promotion and seniority with non-teaching tasks and downgrades the central task of the education enterprise.

Efforts to create opportunities for promotion within the classroom, which might raise the status of teaching and encourage competent staff to remain in the classroom, have tended to take the form of salary increments. This practice tends to degenerate into automatic salary progression, save in extreme disciplinary cases, and consequently fails to motivate teachers to exceed the norm. In some countries, there have been efforts to establish merit awards and honors and to create posts of special responsibility within schools, as in the case of Botswana. Commonly, such posts are linked with non-teaching duties, and we need to ask whether posts of a more professional nature can be created, which will offer enhanced status with real responsibility for improving the quality of teaching and learning. Such posts are easier to establish in larger schools, and this may involve discrimination against teachers in small and rural schools, encouraging teachers to transfer away from the very schools where their services are most needed. Perhaps the adoption of school clusters and school based in-service teacher education may offer greater opportunities for the creation of posts of genuine professional responsibility.

There will remain out of classroom and out of school posts which should not be denied to teachers and for which professional experience may well be desirable. If promotion to such posts is to motivate teachers to improve their classroom performance, the promotion criteria used must include performance. It appears, however, that promotion is engaged in by administrative procedures, which take account of formal qualifications and length of service. Appraisal of performance may well be resisted by teachers fearing corrupt practice. Nevertheless, appraisal procedures are in use in a number of countries. In Papua New Guinea, teachers may apply every two years if they wish to be considered for promotion and those who apply are then visited by inspectors. In many countries, a system of annual appraisal operates but teachers typically regard this as a mere formality.

In few countries the career and promotion structure is sufficiently systematized so that staff may be informed of the criteria necessary to be eligible for certain kinds of promotion or career specialization. For a time in Papua New Guinea, staff were made aware of the criteria and the means, usually in-service courses, which they could make use of to qualify for promotion. Selection for promotion was then made from the ranks of those who had so qualified. More commonly, the procedure is to select for promotion and then train, which offers no guarantee that the trainee will be willing or able to perform well, either in training or in post. In Ghana, a third procedure is used, whereby training leading to promotion to posts is advertised, and selection is then made from those applying. This helps to guarantee the willingness of staff to assume posts and perhaps limits the field for more convenient appraisal of staff, but it may still leave training as a formality.

In-service teacher education commonly suffers from this lack of system in that most courses, whether compulsory or voluntary, are not clearly related to the career structure and carry no clear career credit. Consequently, teachers may not be strongly motivated to take advantage of them. Admittedly, if all in-service teacher education were associated with career progression under current career structures, teachers might well be induced to undertake training for counter-productive reasons. Nevertheless, some closer linking of some in-service training with career progression might well represent an advance on current procedures in a number of countries.

A further aspect of this notion of more systematic selection for promotion lies in the idea of training grades and posts. In some countries, for example, the post of deputy head of a school is viewed as a training post within which experience may be gained and skills learned which will confer eligibility for promotion to headship. Rarely, however, are active steps taken to enable deputy heads to learn on the job. In most countries there is no clear conception of training grades, and in few does it extend beyond preparation for institutional headship.

Associated with this concept of preparation is the idea of induction. Prior training may well be of value but still leave the new officer ill prepared for the assumption of new responsibilities. Many countries have schemes whereby teachers serve for a probationary period before being confirmed as recognized teachers. However, there is a strong case for applying the notion of probation with systematic support and appraisal to more senior posts also in order that the incidence of "promotion to the level of incompetence" be reduced. In Singapore heads of schools are subject to mandatory external appraisal every two to four years and may be relieved of their headships and redeployed to teaching duties.

SUPPORT SERVICES

Support services here are taken to include all agencies and services which provide opportunity to education staff, enabling training and experience to be effectively utilized, professional attitudes to be encouraged, and staff development to be facilitated. Such services are too numerous in the countries surveyed for a comprehensive description and discussion to be offered here, but a number of important issues may be noted.

Most basic of such services is the provision of adequate and appropriate facilities, materials, and equipment. Some writers stress the emphasis which should be placed upon the improvement of the availability and quality of teaching/learning materials as distinct from the quality of the teachers and the introduction of a changed pedagogy (Heyneman, 1984, p. 295; Heyneman, Farrell, & Sepulveda-Stuardo, 1978). Most would probably argue that the two should proceed hand in hand. In one small country, Bophuthatswana, a most interesting Primary Education Improvement project is being pursued with the firm intention of closely linking the retraining of the teacher with the physical improvement of that teacher's classroom environment, a direct link which is often lost sight of in larger scale "transformational" approaches (Holderness, 1986).

The Bophuthatswana project is notable for being largely managed by circuit teams consisting mainly of primary school heads and teachers. It is more common for staff development activities to be organized by the central authority, perhaps through the "cascade" approach to in-service training, as in the PKG project of Indonesia, but there is currently much discussion of the desirability of involving practitioners in the planning conduct of in-service activities on some variant of the school-based model. What is plain, however, is that if local administrative and teaching staff are to be called upon to assume greater responsibility, not merely for the routine activities but for their substantial improvement, staff will need all the support which can be made available to them. They cannot pull themselves up by their own boot straps if they do not possess boots. While it is not argued that the provision of adequate support services will guarantee that teachers and others will develop and display the necessary professional skills and attitudes, it may perhaps be the case that without them such professional development is unlikely to occur.

Again, while many countries may point to the existence of certain kinds of support services, it is not so much their mere existence as the manner of their operation which we have to question. A "service" provided to staff may, under certain circumstances, create undesirable dependence upon the providers of the service, rather than generate creative autonomous attitudes and capacities. It may tend to pauperize rather than professionalize staff. As Streat comments, ". . . many forms of professional support have negative roots--they can be subtly or even overtly coercive-- 'cajoling the laggards'" (1981, p. 2).

The most widespread and standard form of support service is that offered by the inspectorates which, however, have rarely been sufficiently well staffed or equipped to supervise the large numbers of schools for which they are responsible. Moreover, in recent years, the attempt to reorient inspectorates towards a support role has been bedeviled by the necessity of their retaining a directive, inspectorial, disciplinary function, which has impeded the development of relationships with teachers built upon trust and cooperation. Too often, this support role has been interpreted as simply the provision of in-service courses and of problem solving interventions. The development of school based staff development activities with inspectors acting as consultants assisting teachers to develop the capacity to solve their own problems, as recent theory of innovation indicates to be desirable, has rarely been attempted. The mode of operation of the Hong Kong Advisory Inspectorate, whereby a well-staffed inspectorate works in a geographically manageable education system, largely through the medium of well-equipped teachers' centers, is perhaps closest to a professional support service of any of the countries surveyed. At the other extreme, the Penelik system of Indonesia, wherein the inspectors serve essentially administrative functions, has left a gap in the country's professional support services.

While this gap may be filled by other agencies, their functions are generally so narrowly specific that their support role may be a temporary expedient. In other cases, this role may be subordinated to other functions to which the agency gives higher priority, and support is often limited to the provision of in-service training for individual members of staff at central locations, a procedure which has been recognized to provide very inadequate support to the professional development of the whole staff of an institution. Often, there is no clear coordination of the activities of various agencies, and instances of duplication and of conflict are not hard to find.

One notable and common weakness of this support provision is the limited participation of teachers' colleges where, in theory, the main body of expertise in the field of staff development has been assembled. For many years, the argument has been advanced that teachers' colleges should not confine themselves to the initial preparation of teachers but should seek to follow their products into the schools. Thereby, it is argued, initial and in-service training may be more effectively integrated within a career-long professional development continuum, and colleges themselves may benefit from improved feedback from the schools they serve. Colleges, it has been argued, should be staffed and equipped to serve as resource and support service centers for schools in their region. Indeed, UNESCO has funded a number of developments of this kind, most notably in the IPAR of Cameroon and at Bunumbu in Sierra Leone, the second of which is now to be replicated in all teachers' colleges in that country. Although some interesting examples can be cited, generally, it appears that colleges are struggling to cope with their initial training task and have neither the capacity nor the desire to take on wider tasks. Unless they are staffed and equipped for this purpose, experience suggests that in-service and school support activities will inevitably be subordinated to their primary task of initial training.

Attention should be drawn to a further but sadly defunct innovative attempt to harness the expertise of the teacher training institution for ongoing support to schools. In the Experimental project run by the Institute of Education in Singapore, tutors were nominated to serve as consultants to specific schools, which could call upon their services as and when they wished (Cheong Lum Peng, 1976). The potential of such a scheme for promoting school based development, leaving the initiative largely with the schools themselves, appears to merit further experiment.

The development of teachers' or resource centers continues in many countries, and experience suggests a number of lessons, which may be worthy of note. There is some danger that, because of their cost, countries may resort to the establishment of a few major and prestigious centers, which, no matter how well staffed and equipped, then face the problem of distance from most of the schools. The Resource Centres of Malaysia and Nigeria, for example, now confront this difficulty. A tendency may be noted for such major centers to become in-service training centers, drawing teachers into occasional, course-based activities, which are conceptually and geographically remote from the schools and incapable of supporting whole-staff development. On the other hand, small local centers may not possess the credibility to have a major impact upon local schools. Even the promising school cluster approach, whereby each cluster will create its own resource center, reflecting its own views and priorities, will have inevitable limitations, unless structurally linked to major resource centers and/or colleges.

Perhaps the most disappointing feature of support services for staff who claim to belong to a profession is the limited extent of the contribution made by professional organizations. Since employers will seek to meet the needs of the system and may neglect the personal and professional needs of individual teachers, it might have been expected that professional organizations would have stepped in to fill the gap. And since any group claiming to be a profession ought to seek participation by members of the group in decisions affecting its activities, it might have been expected that such organizations would have seen it as a primary task to involve their members in self-directed professional development activities of other agencies. Even when they do participate, because they tend to be organized nationally, their activities and resources are rarely accessible to the teachers in greatest need. There has been only an occasional attempt to complement such national activities with local activities and effective local branch organization.

CONCLUSION

In this paper, the author has attempted to draw into current debate a large number of issues which he considers to be of the highest significance, but which he believes have been neglected. The intention was not to prescribe solutions or "best procedures," but to define an agenda for further inquiry. It is extremely unlikely that any one country will wish or be able to support research in all the areas indicated. Priorities will be defined nationally and will differ from country to country. It is argued, however, that there is a wealth of experience around the world to be called upon and that far greater efforts need to be devoted both to the investigation of current practice and to the international dissemination of findings.

SECTION TWO

CLASSROOM CONTEXTS AND INSTRUCTION

CHAPTER SIX

THE QUALITY OF EDUCATION
AND THE WORKING CONDITIONS OF TEACHERS

Paul Hurst
Val D. Rust

Efforts to improve the quality and efficiency of education around the world are often seriously undermined by the pay, status and self-esteem, and the conditions of service of teachers. Like all international generalizations about education, there are numerous exceptions to the general statements which we shall make. There are over 30 million teachers throughout the world living and working under enormously varied conditions (ILO/UNESCO, 1984); however, all of them are affected in crucial and direct ways by the conditions under which they serve.

In this chapter, we shall consider crucial factors which are related to most of the teachers in the developing world and their working environments. We shall then outline a theoretical model of how teachers react to innovations and reforms aimed at improving educational effectiveness and efficiency. This model is based on previous research which involved testing in both low-income developing educational systems and rich, industrialized ones (Hurst, 1983). Finally, the paper attempts to show how the first set of factors impinges on the second. That is, we shall consider how teachers' pay, status and self-esteem, and conditions of work in the developing world influence their response to innovation and attempts to improve the educational process.

TEACHERS' PAY

Although teachers' pay is probably the most serious element in the entire equation affecting the quality of education in the developing world, very meagre comparative data exists regarding the realities surrounding it.   At first glance, this may seem difficult to understand, but as we probe more deeply into the issue, the complexity of the problems surrounding comparative analysis of salaries becomes evident.

The most direct type of analysis would be to compare incomes of teachers with each other, and indeed, a few attempts have been made to collect information on pay in various countries (WCOTP, 1962; WCOTP, 1964), but these are of little value for comparative purposes, because exchange rates shift regularly, distorting comparisons.   Even if exchange rates were rather stable, direct or implicit comparison of average levels of teachers' pay and overall income across economies is not always helpful.   On the one hand, income differences within certain countries are often larger than income differences between countries.   In Brazil, for example, it has been determined that women teachers earn less than one half as much as men teachers, and the average income of teachers in Sao Paulo is six times as much as teachers in Maranhao and Piaui. If we combine these factors, we find that the average male teacher in Sao Paulo earns more than ten times as much as the average female teacher in Maranhao and Piaui (Birdsall & Fox, 1985, p. 538).

On the other hand, context factors often play a much larger role than simple income in determining relative advantages of income.   For example, in 1975 the average salary of government school teachers in Bangladesh was about $29 a month or about $300 a year (Dove, 1982a, p. 19).   The shocking injustice of this reported wage, when compared with teachers in other countries, is readily apparent.   At that time the average beginning American teacher's salary of $12,000 a year was over 50 times as great as the average teachers salary in Bangladesh (ILO, 1978).   The Bangladesh teacher's salary, taken out of context, is shocking and borders on unreality, but put in context, it represents 3.5 times the average income of $90 a year in that country, which is one of the poorest in the world. It also does not account for the fact that the salary is paid on a regular basis in a country that, in many respects, still lacks a money market economy. In addition, the teachers typically supplement their salary with income and resources from privately owned small farms or businesses (Dove, 1982a, p. 19). Another example might be the salary of a beginning primary teacher in Indonesia in 1985, which approximated $30 a month, including cost of living payments, but in that country a large number of teachers maintain two or three teaching positions, which at least allows them to cover basic costs.

When taken out of context, even the highest salaries in most developing countries are difficult to appreciate, when compared with the developed world. In Sri Lanka, the Educational Service recently announced that the highest annual salary was little more than $1500. It would be absurd to explain such salaries on some world-wide scale, because they simply highlight the obvious: teachers in the developing world are poorly paid.

More meaningful comparative schemes have been suggested and even attempted. It might be more appropriate to compare the level of pay of teachers with an indicator such as a cost-of-living index, which would give some idea of the relative purchasing power of the level of pay. This has its own problems, because even where such indices exist and are kept up to date, they often refer to different "baskets" of goods and services. For example, in one country water may be an expensive good, while in another country it represents no expense at all. Residents of some areas may devote much of their income to food, while in other areas food is readily available and inexpensive. In some areas heat and warm clothing represent major budgetary items, while in other areas they represent little expense. If feasible, however, this approach would give some idea of how well or badly teachers are paid relative to each other (i.e., in different systems and at different grades) in terms of rough purchasing power equivalents. The major drawback of this approach is that it does not indicate how well or how badly teachers are paid relative to comparable compatriots.

Generally speaking, the most obvious comparable group are officers in the public administration services, holding equivalent qualifications. Some comparative data does exist regarding this approach. In 1983, for example, the ILO/UNESCO conducted a survey of a number of countries to determine if teacher salaries compared with civil servants having comparable qualifications. An important finding of this survey was the fact that in two thirds of the countries surveyed, teachers' salaries were comparable or better than other public servants, while in one third of the countries the teachers were rather poorly paid compared with civil servants (ILO/UNESCO, 1983).

One problem with this approach at comparison is that civil servants are not always the occupational reference group with which teachers often seem inclined to compare themselves, or more strictly speaking, to whose pay, status, and conditions they aspire. Teachers often tend to aspire to the condition of the professional occupations, such as doctors, lawyers, and accountants. In this regard, they are generally a long way from realizing such aspirations, and indeed, in the poorer countries the disparities are so great that such ambitions are not widely entertained. Where levels of teachers' pay are particularly depressing, it is more common to hear teachers comparing themselves (unfavorably) with farmers, secretaries, and even building laborers.

Still another way in which teacher salaries have been compared has been to contrast them with other sectors of the work world. Zymelman and DeStefano (1988) have compared primary teacher salaries in Sub-Saharan Countries with occupations such as stenographers/typists and auto-mechanics, finding that in only two of eight countries do teacher salaries exceed those of stenographers/typists, although in six of eight countries they exceed those of auto-mechanics.

In the late 1970s, the International Labour Office engaged in a novel experiment in international comparison of what teachers earn (ILO, 1978). The ILO chose to compare "earnings of teachers with those of a relatively large occupational category within the modern sector of the national economy which, by reason of its size and relative stability and homogeneity, offers a reference basis against which the position of other occupational groups may be assessed" (ILO, 1978, p. 76). The category they selected was the workers in the manufacturing industry, because they make up a substantial proportion of the labor force in all countries.

In Table 1, we have outlined the beginning and highest salaries of primary and secondary teachers in six developing countries included in the survey. Certain general observations are immediately clear. Primary teachers' salaries, even at the highest levels, do not exceed the lowest salaries of secondary teachers. Further, there are extremely large variations in the salaries, relative to the manufacturing industry. The primary teacher in Syria never achieves parity with those in industry, whereas the beginning primary teacher in Nigeria exceeds the average industrial worker's salary many times over.

Some data are available on salary shifts over time, but the information is simply too meager to draw conclusions (ILO, 1978; ILO/UNESCO, 1983), except that little progress is being made in most instances.

Still another means of comparative analysis would be to assess attitudes people have about teaching. The overwhelming impression one receives is that teachers around the world, for the most part, perceive themselves to be poorly paid and disadvantaged when compared with people having similar qualifications and, often, with blue-collar workers. In Malta, a recent survey showed that 57% of teachers were "highly dissatisfied" with their pay.

The cause of this state of affairs is not far to seek. Education is in most economies either the largest or second largest sector of public spending, often costing more than defence. There have been cases

TABLE 1

The Ratio of Beginning and Highest Salaries of Primary
and Secondary Teachers in Six Developing Countries
in 1974, Compared with the Average Salaries in the
Manufacturing Sector of the Country

	Primary teachers		Secondary teachers	
	Low	High	Low	High
Mali	113	210	293	537
Philippines	99	131	127	155
Sri Lanka	100	185	191	292
Syrian Arab Rep.	85	99	135	
Zambia	65	135	216	426
Nigeria (1976)	250	400	400	600

where 30% and even 40% of recurrent public expenditure has been
allocated to education, although somewhat smaller expenditures are
the norm (Faure, 1972, p. 43). For example, Senegal devoted 22.4% of
its national budget to education in 1982/83, Swaziland 23.7%, and
Niger 18% (*Encyclopedia Britannica*, 1985). Even these lower
percentages far exceed those in most developed world budgets.
Generally, about 90% of educational expenditure goes for teachers'
pay. It is a highly labor intensive sector. With the massive recent
expansion of educational enrollments, particularly at primary level,
there has been a concomitant expansion of the teaching force, to the
point where serious strain has been put on public finances.
Although class sizes have risen, public policy has generally been to
avoid very large classes (partly because it is not usually feasible to
accommodate them). The consequent pressure on governments to
hold teachers' pay in check has been immense.

The consequences have been serious. The better teachers have tended to leave service for more attractive occupations leaving only the less capable teachers to care for the children. An obvious route open to teachers would be to organize and struggle collectively for better pay and conditions. In certain instances they have organized but in some areas their efforts only drain their energies while giving them few benefits. In some countries of Latin America, teachers' associations claim a long and distinguished history (Oliveros, 1975a). The British Guiana Teachers' Association was first organized in 1884, and the Argentine Primary Teachers' Association has also existed for three quarters of a century (WCOTP, 1964). Teachers throughout Latin America constitute a vital force for broad social change. They recognize that little can be done given the structural and ideological constraints that exist in their countries and they work actively to better general political conditions.

In certain instances teachers' associations even go so far as to strike. In Brazil during 1987, teachers in certain states went on strike, forcing the government to provide salary concessions, raising the average salary of teachers from the equivalent of $100 to $150 a month. This is remarkable when put in context of the entire third world, because teachers rarely think of themselves as militant and labor union oriented. In fact, it is illegal to strike in many countries, and in most instances teachers think of themselves as members of a "caring" profession that places the general welfare above personal considerations.

The public also looks upon teachers, nurses, and doctors in such a way that militant action inevitably attracts a good deal of public opprobrium and may be counterproductive in that the consequent public backlash enables governments to settle disputes with teachers on harsh terms. Moreover, striking often cuts across the self-image of teachers and divides them against each other. School principals in particular are caught between the authorities, the teachers favoring strikes, and those opposing them and have often been as much victims in countries where teachers' strikes have occurred as the children themselves.

Poor pay leads to teachers' energies being dissipated on second jobs and moonlighting, and inevitably many of those who can find alternative employment will take it. In countries where migration to find work is common (e.g., Lesotho, Sri Lanka, Jordan) teachers form a significant proportion of emigrants, with a consequent loss to the economy which trained them, which is unlikely to be balanced by remittances. Recruitment to the teaching force can be depressed by poor pay, and better-paid opportunities attract holders of language ability. Recruits to teaching are in consequence, underqualified, of poor calibre and poorly motivated. In Malaysia, for example, as in a number of other countries, entrance requirements for teacher training have been lowered in some instances, while there are vacant places on other courses. The problem of poor pay is compounded by the attenuated career structure common in educational systems, imposed partly by the need to economize on salaries, which in turn leads to a demoralizing lack of promotion prospects.

In the past twenty years, the International Labour Office has worked closely with UNESCO in studying ways to improve the deplorable condition of teachers. From the beginning of their joint work, the improvement of their economic status has held the top priority in these efforts (Edman, 1968, p. 22). This has not changed, and in the last major report published on the status of teachers, the joint recommendations of the ILO and UNESCO once again emphasized that "particular importance should be attached to salary," if their status is to be enhanced (ILO/UNESCO, 1984, p. 42). Status is also contingent on the type of working conditions teachers are subjected to, and in the next section we shall consider what these conditions are in the developing world.

WORKING CONDITIONS

Not only do teachers in the developing world usually face adverse economic conditions, but the kinds of conditions they work in are at times almost overwhelming. Fortunately, ethnographic work is going on that allows us to gain a fuller picture of these conditions. The case of Maria, taken from the 1987 field notes of another contributor in this book, Jose Maria Coutinho, exemplifies the kinds of insights we are beginning to gain about the life of teachers.

Maria is a primary school teacher in an urban center of Brazil. Her salary, which is near the minimum a qualified teacher earns in the country, amounts to the equivalent of about $50.00 a month, although that figure is difficult to calculate, because inflation is so high. Although she is only 21 years of age, she is already losing her teeth, because she has no funds to pay for medical and dental care. Fortunately, she has not experienced any serious medical problems, but the provisions for her health care are vague and seldom insure adequate treatment. One of her great hopes is that she will fall in love and marry someone who has a better situation in life than she, but she is aware of the fact that many women teachers remain single and poor, and many who do marry find themselves alone with children to care for when their husbands leave them.

Maria finds great pleasure in coming to school, even though life there is very hard. She wears the same dress almost every day and her sandals give little protection to her feet. Her small classroom is filled with old and broken desks, built many years ago by a local wood-worker, but she expends great energy in trying to maintain some sense of order and cleanliness in the classroom. Her fourth-grade children are also poor, undernourished, and poorly dressed, but they appreciate her concern, cooperate generally with her, and assist her by sweeping the concrete floor and cleaning the room, because there is no custodial help available. They are even willing to help her wash the floor in an attempt to maintain some physical order.

Much of her time is spent acting as a surrogate parent to what almost becomes a large family. One of the major services provided by the school is soup for the pupils, most of whom come to school because they can obtain something to eat. Some pupils even bring a small brother or sister who looks forward to the food. Maria allows them to be a part of her family, even though she recognizes that they must somehow be looked after during the day. Other pupils simply bring a bottle with them to carry food home to their smaller brothers and sisters.

Life at school is difficult for Maria. There is no security and the school is open to the streets so that burglars and vandals constantly assault the building looking for food and whatever else of value they can find. There is actually very little of value in the building. Expecting the children to bring their own pencils and notebooks, the school offers no materials to the students. Maria recognizes that some children are unable to supply even the basic materials, so she makes certain the pencils she has purchased and cut up into smaller pieces for the children are gathered and carried home with her each afternoon.

There is a chalkboard along one wall of the classroom, which is in poor repair, full of holes and without color, so what little chalk she is given is quickly used up. The school also has no library, only a shelf with between ten and twenty books, but they are of little value outside the school, so though occasionally damaged, they are rarely taken by intruders. By the way, Maria also spends as much of the day as she is able teaching her children. This is her greatest source of pleasure, although it is also her greatest source of sorrow. She knows that only a small number of her children will complete the full primary school.

Maria's case is certainly not out of the ordinary in the developing world. In fact, it is better than some areas. It is rare, for example, that food is provided for children in Africa, and in most places of the developing world the basic fabric of government schools is usually dilapidated and dirty. Equipment and especially consumables are frequently in short supply. Maria, at least, teaches in a school building that provides the basic conditions for learning. One of the authors of this essay observed children in Africa sitting on the floor of their classroom, while several hundred desks were stored in the playground of another school. There was no money to pay for the transportation costs.

Some years ago, the International Federation of Teachers conducted a survey of seven so-called "new nations," and found in all of them the lack of teaching materials, inadequate buildings, large classes, poor housing for teachers, and a host of other problems, including inadequate teachers, unjust dismissals, opposition of parents to schooling, poor supervision, etc. (International Federation of Teachers, 1963). If Maria's case has general validity, we must conclude that conditions probably have not improved much since that Federation of Teachers study.

Working conditions extend far beyond physical matters. The international organizations, such as UNESCO, OECD, and the ILO, have given considerable attention to certain factors that can be easily quantified, such as health and safety provisions, hours of work, and class size.

In terms of class size, the developing world continues to suffer from excessive pupil-teacher ratios. Whereas 97% of all developed countries were maintaining a pupil-teacher ratio of 30 or fewer students in 1984, only 55% of the developing countries could make the same claim. Another 27% were maintaining a ratio between 30-40 pupils, and 18% were maintaining ratios of more than 40 pupils. Nowhere in the developed world has this latter ratio existed for several decades (UNESCO, 1986a, II-24). It is encouraging to find that the pupil-teacher ratios are falling in many developing countries, but we have noted that financial constraints place severe limits on the kinds of changes possible. In fact, there is some movement in the opposite direction, as some policy makers and scholars argue that the lot of teachers will never be good if the number of teachers expands at the same rate as the number of pupils. The resources available are simply too limited.

One of the most visible projects to increase the pupil-teacher ratio has been a modified version of the old monitorial model. Initiated in the Philippines but expanded into several other countries, Project IMPACT has maintained a goal of expanding the number under a single teacher's charge of up to 100 pupils. Teachers would make use of extensive self-instructional materials, have access to teacher's aides, and rely on some voluntary community assistance to offset other disadvantages. At this point it is unclear whether such notions would be helpful either in offsetting fund limitations, retaining pupils in school, or increasing student achievement (Cummings, 1984; Theisen, 1987).

In terms of working hours, a number of factors come into play, including the number of hours each day devoted to teaching, the number of hours devoted to extra-instructional activities such as supervision of lunch breaks, preparation time, evaluating students, and staff meetings. We must also calculate the number of days each week the teacher works, the number of weeks each year the teacher instructs, and the number of weeks the teacher is obliged to be on the job when students are out of school. There is considerable variation in all of these factors in the developing world. For example, whereas Ghanaian secondary teachers are only expected to work 165 days a year, teachers in Thailand work 220 days a year (ILO, 1981a, p. 77).

While teachers in Sierra Leone and Singapore are reported to be expected to work but 20 hours a week, those in the Bahamas, Grenada, and Jamaica must work 25 hours, those in The Gambia, Ghana, Ivory Coast and Tunisia must work 30 hours, and those in Fiji, India, Papua New Guinea, the Philippines and Zambia must work 35 or more hours a week (ILO, 1981a, p. 75). Of course, these figures typically refer to the number of hours a teacher must be in school and do not reflect out of school hours devoted to their profession.

From other ILO reported information, it is unclear what the trends are in the developing world. It is also unclear whether teachers in those areas devote more or less time than is the case in the developed world. One thing is certain: teacher time is taxing in terms of emotional energy. Free periods are usually occupied by marking and preparation, breaks by administrative chores, and even lunchtimes by supervisory duties. For many, the pressures during school hours are unremitting. This is particularly so in primary schools, where the children cannot be relied upon to look after themselves to the same extent as older pupils.

In terms of other more subtle factors related to teaching, it has been widely observed that teachers exercise considerable autonomy in the classroom, more in respect of how they teach than what they teach, but are subject to stringent control otherwise. Management styles still tend to be autocratic in developing countries, in decentralized systems as much as centralized ones, although authoritarianism is mostly on the retreat, except for countries such as Iran (Smart, 1979). There is relatively little consultation and even less joint decision-making, and this applies to the relations between head teachers and their staffs as much as to the relations between head teachers and the administrative hierarchy.

The way that schooling is organized also tends to mean that teachers interact and collaborate with each other rather less than in many other professions. Some teachers, especially but not exclusively, of adolescent boys face a continuing problem of maintaining discipline, which is particularly wearing. Although students in the Third World countries are often better motivated than their Western counterparts, this is not always the case. There can be racial and religious tensions between teachers and students, for example, and several studies have shown that in groups that are highly discriminated against and disadvantaged, dropout, absenteeism, and poor performance in school are higher than average, which is generally attributed to student perceptions that school is unlikely to alter their life chances. Privacy is non-existent. Few teachers have or even share offices. Given the general impotence of teachers' unions, the priority of securing satisfactory salaries, and the general economic pressure on education budgets, there is little scope for optimism about dramatic improvements to these working conditions.

STATUS AND SELF-ESTEEM

The regard with which teachers are held by the community and their own self-regard do not appear to be widely studied. It generally appears that teachers are much less valued by the public than used to be the case, and their own self-esteem has followed suit, at least if surveys from the developed world have validity for the developing world (Edman, 1968, pp. 18-23). At a time when there were few literate people, even primary teachers held positions comparable to the priest. The teacher was actively involved in decisions of great importance and was consulted regularly concerning policy and community decisions. With the expansion of educated people, the teacher began to loose status and eventually came to be regarded as of little value (Bude, 1982, p. 110).

The rapid expansion of schooling itself helps explain some of the decline in status. The enormous expansion of enrollments and the enlargement of the teaching force means that teachers are neither so rare nor so much more educated than the rest of the community. There simply are so many teachers that the profession has lost its elite status. In Brazil, there were 913,000 primary and 204,000 secondary teachers in 1982, comprising .90% of the entire population and 2.3% of the economically active population. In Kenya there were 115,000 primary and 18,000 secondary teachers comprising .68% of the entire population and 10.5% of the economically active population. In Malaysia there were 83,760 primary and 60,502 secondary teachers comprising 1.0% of the population and 2.6% of the economically active population (*Encyclopedia Britannica*, 1985).

The situation for teachers has been exacerbated by attempts on the part of governments to control teachers and deprive them of what little professional status they have. Teacher groups in Latin America have become rather active in raising questions about the prevailing political ideology of the various countries where they have been expected to help reproduce the divisions and hierarchies of society, and governments tend to react against such activism

(Marquez, 1975). Because of the tremendous costs of education in countries with very limited resources, some policy makers come to advocate a "barefoot doctor" model, consisting of teachers having enough training to do the job, but not so much expertise as to be separated from the community and its people (Dove, 1986, p. 112). Even when officials are somewhat more enlightened and committed to quality education, the demand for teachers has, at times, been simply so great that they have turned to unqualified and underqualified people to staff the classrooms. Because of its status decline, teaching is rarely seen as an attractive option for young people entering the labor market. In 1972, for example, only 23.2% of primary school leavers in Nigeria were positively interested in teaching, while only 6.9% of the secondary school leavers in the survey showed an interest (Knamiller, 1981, p. 83). It is important to note that the status of the profession does not seem to be the cause of its lack of attraction. In the situation noted above, great changes were made in salary and working conditions after 1972, and interest in teaching rose substantially. In fact, by 1977 more than half of the general school leavers expressed an interest in teaching, while the percentage of secondary school leavers interested in teaching had risen to 22.4% (Knamiller, 1981). Of course, the secondary school leavers rarely considered primary school teaching. In a survey of ex-secondary grammar school students, Adeyinka found that only 2.0% wanted to become primary teachers, and only 0.5% actually became primary teachers. On the other hand, 11% indicated an interest in grammar school teaching and an astounding 31% eventually became secondary grammar school teachers.

Whereas more than three times (355%) as many secondary grammar school leavers in the survey mentioned above eventually chose grammar school teaching, as opposed to indicating an interest in it while in school, only 20% of those who indicated they wanted to be a doctor were actually able to enter the profession, and 25% of those who indicated they wanted to be a lawyer actually entered that profession (Adeyinka, 1973). In other words, grammar school teaching appears to be the profession of second choice among the elites of Nigeria.

Given the number of teachers and the relative impotence of teachers' unions, it is doubtful if they ever will achieve the professional status enjoyed by doctors and lawyers. Teachers do not control entry to their profession, they do not regulate the price charged for their services, they do not have wide options for mobility and promotion, they do not formulate their own disciplinary codes, and they do not enjoy high regard for entering the profession--all features of the high-status professions.

Teachers themselves have been responsible, in some respects, for the decline in their status. They have tended to fragment themselves through infighting between groups possessing various levels of qualifications and certificates, creating a condition where there is no solidarity or unified voice in professional matters. Confidence has been particularly eroded in countries where certain groups of teachers have become somewhat militant and have even engaged in teachers' strikes.

There are, of course, status differentials within teaching, lowering the self-esteem of those on the lower side of the division. There remains a marked difference in the status of the primary and the secondary school teacher in most countries of the developing world. Not only do teachers at the two levels come from differing social class backgrounds, but they also represent two distinct groups, with the secondary teachers almost always entertaining a higher status. In Latin America, for example, primary school teachers generally come from lower classes or lower middle classes, while secondary teachers generally come from the lower middle class or upper middle class (Oliveros, 1975a, p. 231). Because primary teaching holds a lower middle class status, teaching actually represents a way to gain "greater respectability, prestige and stability in society" for large numbers of teachers. Because secondary teaching represents an upper middle class status, many young people also seek to enter the profession because it means improving or maintaining their original status (Oliveros, 1975a).

There are also clear distinctions between various types of secondary teachers. In Africa, graduates with teaching certificates are distinguished from graduates, who are also distinguished from non-graduates. Those who have an academic background are more prestigious than those engaged in vocational and technical subjects (Blakemore & Cooksey, 1980, p. 133). Men invariably seem to do better than women in promotion terms and completely dominate the higher administration cadres. There are local differences too. For instance, expatriate Arab teachers in the Gulf enjoy a lower status than local counterparts, whereas the opposite is true of European expatriates in East Africa.

HOW TEACHERS REACT TO EDUCATIONAL INNOVATIONS

While most studies of educational innovation and reform are sociological in character (e.g., Beeby, 1966) and concentrate on structure and process rather than individual actors and their interactions, our interest in change is rather different and attempts to construct a theoretical model of the logic employed by teachers, and others, in deciding whether to adopt of reject an innovation, some proposed change in practice. This approach is quite common in anthropological and economic studies of peasant farmers, fishermen, entrepreneurs, investors, and other decision makers, but it is unusual to study teachers in this light (Hurst, 1983). Of course, context is extremely important in the innovation process, and there is empirical evidence that it plays a vital role, at least with regard to certain types of innovation (Morris, 1985). Nevertheless, teachers may be the main determinant of innovations having to do with factors such as curriculum or teaching style (McConnelogue, 1975; Doyle & Ponder, 1977), and they must play some role in all innovations affecting the school (Spaulding, 1975, p. 212). According to our model, the teacher appraises or evaluates a proposal in deciding whether to adopt some innovatory change of practice.

The process of making such an appraisal is quite complex and the way it is interpreted is usually guided by one or another theoretical perception. Marx observed, for example, that decision makers make choices in situations not of their own choosing, and these choices are largely determined by the material life surrounding them (Marx, 1959, p. 359). While people such as Karl Popper agree that our minds, our decisions, are in certain respects products of our environment, our minds certainly are not fully and solely determined by it. The world is differently perceived and "constructed" by the actors (Popper, 1966, p. 211). His theory also applies, in principle, to coercive situations. An actor can choose whether or not to comply with an order to adopt an innovation, and assesses the risks and rewards of noncompliance and compliance along with the risks and rewards of adoption and rejection. More subtly, the actor can choose to comply with an order without actually doing so, to comply temporarily until the threat of punishment is withdrawn, or to comply while covertly sabotaging the innovation.

There are, of course, differing models for teachers' decisions. Doyle and Ponder (1977) claim that teachers use three major criteria in deciding on an innovation: Is it instrumental in terms of classroom contingencies? Is it congruent with prevailing conditions? What are the costs involved in using the innovation? These are all worthy considerations and are not inconsistent with our model, which suggests that teachers choose to adopt an innovation using one or more of the following criteria:

Information: Information about the proposed innovation must be perceived by the teachers as adequate and accurate, and there should be feedback channels for the teachers to communicate their experiences to the managers of the innovative project.

Relevance and Desirability: The outcomes of the innovation must coincide with the values of the teachers in such a way that they are perceived to be beneficial. For example, teachers, who have been trained in an elitist academic form of education are unlikely to be attracted to democratized and vocationalized curricula without some persuasion.

Effectiveness and Reliability: Teachers, like most other people, will be averse to taking risks with newfangled ideas, especially if their existing practices are satisfactory. This is especially important in education, where failure has a significantly damaging effect on the children for whom the teacher is responsible.

Feasibility: Teachers will abandon innovations of necessity if they lack the resources and skills to put them into effect.

Efficiency: Innovations will succeed in the long term only if they offer more benefits for the same inputs, or the same benefits for fewer inputs. Teachers will not work harder to achieve the same results as before.

Trialability: Because of the risks involved in adopting new practices, we generally prefer some sort of trial or experiment on a limited scale to see what happens. Some innovations are easier to experiment with than others, and their implementation will be correspondingly more difficult.

Adaptability: Often we see that a new idea could fit our particular situation and needs if there were some modifications to it. Pre-packaged, centrally mass-produced innovations (e.g., some curriculum materials, radio broadcasts) are not susceptible to much adaptation, and this also restricts take-up by teachers.

Viewing teachers as decision makers according to our model provides some insights into the way their pay, status, self-esteem, and working conditions often affect efforts to improve education and make it more efficient. While certain scholars attribute the failure to adopt an innovation in terms of "a lack of motivation on the part of teachers" (Bude, 1982, p. 117), it is our position that teachers make rational decisions about the relative advantages of the innovation to them and their students.

We noted that many teachers are generally highly committed to teaching and are willing to make sacrifices up to a point for the sake of the more job satisfaction they derive. Paradoxically, this makes them more risk-averse than might otherwise be the case, since the victims of failure will be, not so much the teachers themselves, but the students for whom they are responsible.

Trying out new ideas and practices is much more time and energy consuming than practicing what is familiar and routine. Yet, we have seen that many teachers are very hard-pressed during school hours, and have very little unused time. Some are simply too busy to cope, especially where large classes are involved, with trying out new and possibly impractical ideas. Moreover, we noted that teachers do not get much opportunity for collaboration with each other, at least in conventionally organized schools. This means that there is little evidence in education of the so-called risky-shift phenomenon, the propensity of groups to expose themselves to riskier decisions than individuals. This is reinforced by the autocratic management styles which still persist in education in the developing world. All the evidence from other sectors suggests strongly that a more collaborative atmosphere and set of working practices in schools would lead to a lower aversion to risk.

The low pay and status of teachers tends to demoralize them, and to weaken their professional commitment. This, in turn, causes them to lose interest in working extra hard or extra hours in attempts to bring about qualitative improvement, and innovations aimed at reducing the cost of education are likely to be seen as adding insult to injury.

CHAPTER SEVEN

CLASSROOM TEACHING MODELS

Howard L. Jones
A. G. Bhalwankar

In geographical and political environments, which demand cost effective means for keeping or advancing the quality of life, education has been historically a valued resource. Even in the late twentieth century, with its heavy emphasis on technology, the key element in all educational endeavors remains the teacher. While the teaching act appears quite simple and mundane to students, parents, and many policy makers, its complexities are finally being identified and appreciated. Almost three decades ago, in the United States, Phillip Jackson (1968) counted over 1,000 interpersonal interactions between a teacher and his/her students on an average day. In a recent article (Clark & Peterson, 1986), teachers are reported to make an important decision on the average of once every two minutes. The teacher is responsible for planning and implementing instruction, often under less-than-ideal situations, to a broad range of learners, not all of whom wish to learn, in a range of subjects under the watchful eyes of often uncooperative parents, administrators and policy makers. For these actions teachers are paid very poorly in comparison to other service professionals. While considered necessary in all societies, the less-than-physical nature of the teaching act, and the fact that the immediate products of teaching are rarely seen, relegates teaching to the status of a tolerated necessity. There is one other reason for this less-than-positive situation: not all teachers are good or effective.

A key assumption for centuries has been that teaching is an art, and like artistic endeavors, the work of a gifted teacher is not amenable to scientific analysis, only to identification. Furthermore, the necessary knowledge, attitudes, and skills appear not to be uniformly distributed among teacher candidates. This recognition has led policy makers throughout the world to accept the IDENTIFICATION of teacher candidates as a necessary step in insuring adequate educational opportunities for youngsters. The prediction of success in teaching, the selection of candidates with the highest "artistic" probability of success in teaching, has demanded the development of selection procedures that were both valid and reliable. Dubbed with the term PRESAGE by Harold Mitzel in the early 1960s, these variables include the teacher's social class, age, sex, intelligence, personality traits, and the like. In fact, thousands of research and development studies have been completed that have examined the personal and social characteristics of teachers. Fortunately, or unfortunately, there have also been developed interview techniques and written instruments, that permit the separation of teacher candidates on the basis of intelligence, verbal fluency, dogmatism and, among a myriad of other characteristics, physical dexterity. But the effect of the identification of Presage variables in teacher selection has been considerably overrated; few such variables have been found that even modestly can predict the success of a teacher candidate.

What has been amplified as the result of recent teacher effects research is that teaching must be viewed as something more than a collection of teacher characteristics. Adding only slightly to Henderson's (1963) well-accepted mathematical notation, teaching can be conceived as a relationship:

IN A TEACHING ENVIRONMENT w, x TEACHES y TO z

The arena (w) in which the teacher (x) encounters the student (z) has recently come under careful scrutiny as having great possibility for influencing teaching quality. Throughout the world, billions of dollars have been spent to decrease the numbers of students in classes, to feed hungry students at schools, to initiate preschool programs, to purchase or print more textbooks or other written instructional packages, or to build libraries and learning resource centers that might assist the teacher in getting necessary ideas across to students. Parent education programs have been initiated with the hope that when the child reaches school age he/she will be better prepared to learn from the teacher. In Mitzel's terminology, these variables are CONTEXT variables.

However, the fact is that those efforts that have limited themselves to Presage and Context variables have not been as productive or effective as they might be. This view is identified in Dunkin and Biddle's (1974) model for the study of classroom teaching, outlined in the Preface of this book, which posits that Presage and Context variables are only usefully viewed when their interaction is examined in the classroom, alongside the PROCESSES of teaching. Similarly, Dunkin and Biddle, along with a growing number of scholars and practitioners, came to the conclusion that there existed inadequate criteria of teacher effectiveness-- PRODUCTS. This latter opinion has fueled a two decade search for valid and reliable measures of the impact of schooling on learners. The question, "How should the educational productivity of a teacher, a school, a province, a nation, a world, be measured?" is still without unequivocal answer.

Simply put, the problem is best seen in those numerous teachers (x), ranging in a wide array of Presage variables, who are able to generate significant student gains on a range of measures (y), within a wide range of contexts (w). Some teachers are simply able to generate greater student gains, regardless of the environment in which they find themselves. And, as a result, the focus of educational research for the past 20 years has shifted from Presage/Context to the Processes of teaching. In brief, the apparent complexity of the "art" of teaching has begun to be examined by the observations of "science." A world-wide search has focused on what happens in the classrooms of effective teachers, those teachers whose students constantly succeed, for hints about what Turney (1977) calls "the 'micro-criteria' of teacher effectiveness," well defined observable elements of the teaching act.

Several key elements pervade the research studies in the literature. First, a definition of teacher effectiveness has come to be accepted. Especially in the United States, teacher effectiveness has come to be defined mainly in terms of changes in student standardized test scores. The narrow range of standardized tests in reading, mathematics, and other subjects has been examined by researchers to pre-post treatment studies to identify student test "gains." This "empirical" change is seen as a measure of teacher PRODUCT and, in the past few years, has almost totally replaced previous indicators of teacher success, such as the teacher's use of "indirect" teaching behaviors--a criterion that had been generally acceptable for researchers since its invention by Flanders over 25 years ago (cf. Flanders, 1965). Instead of looking at the effect of some instructional treatment on the TEACHER'S behaviors, the criterion for teacher effectiveness has shifted to the LEARNER.

A second key element is that research findings have become more consistent as researcher's methods have become more sophisticated and at the same time simplified. Twenty years ago, required dissertations for young Ph.D. candidates were normally experimental. That is, two groups of teachers were trained to use different teaching strategies with learners, and teacher and/or students behaviors were observed. The reports of the studies usually ended with "no significant difference" or with reports of very weak correlations between teacher behaviors and student outcomes. This determination was not surprising, since most studies looked at only a small sample of teachers/students and, because of time and other limitations, focused on only a few variables. The results were almost always useless for policy makers, who were looking for some sort of "Salk vaccine" that would permit the curing of educational ills through the insistence that other teachers emulate research-proven and truly effective instructional or managerial behaviors.

This trend of "no significant differences" has been blunted in recent national and international studies. With increased governmental support more sophisticated experimental research and observational designs have been used to look at student learning and classroom interactions on a macro-scale. These steps, plus the availability of better controls, have permitted researchers to identify, with a high degree of reliability, a set of behaviors that are indeed exhibited by more effective teachers. There never will be a "Salk vaccine" for educational ills, simply because teaching is a very personal set of actions that intermingle humans in a complex set of activities. But there have been identified trends that are certainly promising for policy makers. Recent publications point out that effective teachers, regardless of subject matter and age of student clients, are more alike than different in their behaviors in the classroom. Our guess is that this similarity also is evident in most countries, developed or developing.

The rationale for such research in developed countries, of course, reflects more than intellectual curiosity. Regardless of the GNP of any nation, education is expensive. And, especially in developing countries, waste takes up a significant percentage of the monies that are invested. There is no question that by diminishing the educational output, however it is measured in a country, the rate of return of the educational investment is lowered (Huq, 1975, p. 15). Countries with wealth have long recognized this waste, and their apparent expensive education research efforts have a very pragmatic raison d'etre: taxpayers want a return on their investment. It is significant, however, that in studies of "profitability" of schooling in most countries, the criterion of success has not typically been classroom or school productivity. Instead, criteria like "number of students staying in school," "numbers of new schools," "numbers of books," have emerged from educational planning studies. In essence, in those reported studies of educational impact, the unit has been something different from the individual teaching act, the classroom or the school. Similarly, although large amounts of resources have been invested in improving school conditions, very little attention has been paid to the identification of effective teaching behaviors and, of course, the improvement of classroom teaching processes through in-service training programs.

All of the above is presented as a prelude to the description of teaching processes in the classrooms of developing countries. As will be seen, there is more prescription than description available about the scenarios within classrooms in developing countries. As C. E. Beeby noted in his *Assessment of Indonesian Education* (1979), "it is easier to assess the physical conditions of classrooms than to assess what goes on inside them." Yet, if policy makers are to be more cost-effective in their planning, such descriptions are crucial. In suggesting this, we are agreeing with Avalos and Haddad (1981), who in their review of teacher effectiveness studies from developing countries, concluded that:

> Macro studies of the effects of the educational system that follow the pattern of the input-output model probably are not adequate and cannot yield more information than what already exists. Insight into the teaching process and the interaction of its variables can probably best be gained by structured and non-structured observational techniques. On the basis of this information gathered in a variety of contexts it might be possible to suggest actions (in teaching and training) to be experimented with and evaluated.

In the section that follows, a brief review is found of studies that provide descriptions of what happens in classrooms. This is followed by a comparison of these data with research in teacher effects that has recently emerged in other countries. A third section focuses on those strategies that are available to teachers in all countries and some proposals are made of teaching models/

strategies that might be considered for inclusion into teacher education efforts within developing countries.

WHAT HAPPENS IN SCHOOLS IN DEVELOPING COUNTRIES?

The educational endeavors of any society appear to go through a set of developmental stages. Access to education for the majority of students occurs only after the stability of political and economic areas is assured. It is only after the access question is answered that the quality question can be seriously asked. Like Beeby (quoted in Lowe et al., 1971, p. 12), we argue that what can be done in a school setting depends first and foremost on the quality of teachers. Quality teachers emerge from quality training programs. But the problem for teacher education is that increased educational access often calls for massive increases in the number of teachers needed to educate the new students; and more teachers means more ineffective teachers, unless steps are made to insure quality before placing new teachers in the classroom (cf. Postlethwaite & Thomas, 1980), and to provide a support system for these new teachers with some form of in-service activities. It takes time to accomplish these steps, but until quality teachers are available, true cost-effectiveness in education is a moot point.

The focus of this section is ONLY on the quality question, and both Peterson and Clark (1986) and Huq (1975) agree with us that the answer to the question is easy only in theory. Definitions, as pointed out in previous sections, are difficult to come by. Huq (1975) correctly notes that the term "quality" is a semantically slippery one and has often been used to mean different things in different contexts. Yet it is argued in this chapter that "quality" must be defined as output, or in Dunkin and Biddle's terms, Product variables. At the same time, however, it is posited that a complete understanding of the processes of teaching is impossible without an understanding of the contexts in which teachers find themselves.

Certainly, Product variables vary from nation to nation. The recent emphasis on standardized tests in the United States points in one direction. The emphasis within other countries to identify special schools that historically have prepared youngsters with nationally recognized skills in leadership, technical or artistic skills, is another. In most developing countries, however, the criterion of quality is rather diffuse. Unfortunately, there exist very few studies that provide details about what actually takes place in instructional settings. The studies that have emerged from ethnographic and quantitative efforts within developing countries have primarily compared two different teaching methods, different curriculum slants, or have focused on questions such as whether it is possible for teachers to adapt teaching strategies or models that have emerged in other parts of the world. Even these are few in number. Dave reports only 109 studies in his yet unpublished review of past teacher effects studies in India from 1943-1982, and research efforts in most other countries lag well behind those in India. There exist virtually no ethnographic data about "Life in Classrooms" of developing countries. There are, however, some minimal data and more opinions:

> . . . there is little evidence in the school classroom that the children and the teachers (perhaps even in their capacity as Scout leaders) do such exciting practical work in the classrooms as they do outside (BP3K, 1975, p. 35).

> . . . (within Indonesia) there has been a marked deterioration in the quality of teaching in the secondary schools over the preceding years (Carpenter & Waskito, 1971).

Opinions like these focus on Context variables and do not describe what happens in the classrooms. Various approaches exist to collect that type of information. The psychometrician may use a questionnaire, because it is the simplest and least expensive approach in terms of person-power and money. Beeby (1979) took such an approach in his study of Indonesian education. Within 12 provinces, it was found that 75-95% of the teachers surveyed reported that they consistently prepared lesson plans, reviewed previous material with students, conducted examinations, and set and marked student assignments.

Beeby also did on-sight observations as survey teams followed up teachers who responded to the questionnaire and found the following:

- little evidence of planning
- only 36 of the 105 teachers observed had assigned homework in the previous month
- only 11 of these 36 collected the homework and marked it
- four months into the school year, 72 teachers had not examined the students
- of those who gave tests, only a third had returned the corrected papers to students

The survey teams also found the following conditions in primary and secondary schools.

PRIMARY SCHOOLS

The classroom emphasis was on a "thin store of facts," the teachers' explanations were usually restricted to a paraphrase of the textbook with an occasional reference to some relevant fact of village life, and a considerable part of the lesson was spent dictating notes or writing them on the blackboard and waiting for the students to copy them.

The 1968 national curriculum specified that teachers pay attention to the needs and abilities of individual children, but only in half the observed classes did the teachers work with individual children. Student learning to the observers appeared more passive than active.

SECONDARY SCHOOLS

In about 70% of the classes the majority of student notebooks observed reflected verbatim copying from the teacher's notes. The teacher usually talked and wrote on the board for half the lesson.

There was a very short time for questions and answers and what questions were asked were routine and recapitulatory.

Even in controversial topics rarely did a teacher's explanations present more than a single point of view. Only about two percent of the teachers clearly put forward a personal opinion about the lesson and in only three classes were students seen making extended verbal comments. Interestingly, however, was the survey team's finding that the teachers observed had a "tolerably good knowledge" of what they were teaching. In other words, the teaching processes were in question, not the content.

Beeby's findings are detailed above not to castigate the education efforts of one country or to describe the research design used but to present a scenario from which other data and opinions can be compared with other observational studies that have examined classroom processes in developing countries.

APEID (1975) noted a "persistence of rote learning in classrooms" and a failure to see any form of content integration in Southeast Asia schools. That is, subjects were seen as compartmentalized, not connected. Martaamidjaja (1981) found that teachers in West Java vocational schools seldom showed acceptance of feeling, gave praise or encouragement, and acceptance of student ideas. The teachers lectured most of the time; they also asked some questions and criticized students. In a large survey of secondary science teachers in the Philippines, APEID (1980a) reported that the majority used the textbook and chalkboard most frequently and that discussion groups and community resources were seldom employed. Arishi (1984) found that teachers in Saudi Arabia were generally direct and did not relate the content of their language lessons to students personal lives. He also found that student participation was limited and restricted. Malkawi (1984), in an ethnographic study in a Jordanian secondary school, found mostly direct teacher behaviors on the part of the teacher. Tanbanjogn's (1983) experimental study showed that students who used manipulative materials in Thai first grades demonstrated higher mathematics achievement although the teaching techniques implemented by their instructors were reported to be at odds with the usual strategies employed by most Thai teachers.

A TYPICAL TEACHING SCENARIO

Putting these observations together, we might provide the following scenario of a "typical" classroom in the developing world:

Teaching Scenario One: Mr. Sharad

Mr. Sharad is a secondary school teacher from Pune City, India. His favorite technique for teaching practical applications of mathematics--such as having students calculate the volume of solids--typically follows this format. On the first day he introduces the idea by writing the formula for finding the volume of a cuboid on the chalkboard. As he explains all parts of the formula, Mr. Sharad notes that this formula had been generated over 2000 years ago. The students are then expected to recite the formula a number of times. Students then watch as Mr. Sharad completes some example problems on the board. The students carefully write Mr. Sharad's calculations in their notebooks. Mr. Sharad is very careful to see that the students write his calculation steps correctly into their notes. In the following days, students are given problems to solve. And in succeeding days, Mr. Sharad follows the same steps in teaching the formulae for finding the volume of cylinders and triangular prisms. For some reason, however, Mr. Sharad does not attempt to relate the different formulae for finding volumes of cuboids, cylinders, and triangular prisms. The unit volume usually takes about 10 periods to complete.

The scenario reflects a series of teacher "strategies" (Taba, 1966b; Smith, et al., 1967; Smith & Maux, 1970; Hough & Duncan, 1970; Flanders, 1970) which represent a set of predetermined "moves" that the teacher predicts will facilitate student learning. The teacher in the scenario is obviously interested in having students master the practical computations of mathematics. He starts the lesson by writing the necessary formula on the board. This is followed by student recitation, performing practice exercises on the board for students, and finally having students practice themselves. Observers in the class see that Mr. Sharad does not use models of cuboids to show students but also note that the school in which he is teaching has virtually no teaching aids. There are also no textbooks in the classroom, so the teacher must present the necessary information to the students.

WHAT OTHER TEACHING SCENARIOS ARE POSSIBLE?

Given the number of teachers of mathematics in all countries, it might be expected that there are a large number of different strategies that might be used to teach the content that Mr. Sharad included in his lesson. However, teacher observation studies over the past 20 years show that, in fact, the differences are only superficial. Most, if not all, teaching activities that focus on imparting knowledge/skills to learners fit within three categories. (1) Expository: the teacher gives the principle under study, tells students what to do, monitors student performance as they practice the application of the principle. (2) Inductive: the teacher provides examples and nonexamples of that subject under study. The principles are either presented by the teacher or developed by the learners. The teacher then monitors student performance in applying the principles. (3) Inquiry: the teacher presents problems for students to solve. The solutions of the problems are the required knowledge. The teacher then monitors student performance in applying the principles.

Admittedly, even with this classification, there are variations of teaching moves that a teacher can use. But Henderson's classic study (1963) even shows that within these three categories there are similarities. After analyzing recorded tapes of verbal behaviors of mathematics teachers in the United States, Henderson noted that

there are only really four basic "moves." In teaching basic
principles, there must be:

1. STATEMENT OF PRINCIPLE (SP)
    A statement of principle under study may be made
    either by the students or the teacher.

2. CLARIFICATION OF THE PRINCIPLE (CP)
    Through the use of examples, demonstrations, evidence
    of proof, discussion of sub-principles

3. JUSTIFICATION OF THE PRINCIPLE (JP)
    This move identifies the veracity of that which is under
    study.   Cross-proofs, opinions of experts, student
    verification (such as takes place in the laboratory) are
    examples of JP.

4. APPLICATION OF THE PRINCIPLE (AP)
    In order to insure that the students are able to take the
    learned principle into other settings, there must be some
    form of practice.

We argue that these four moves are necessary to insure
meaningful learning for those outcomes that fit within what Gagne
(1985) and other learning theorists classify as concepts, rules, defined
concepts, cognitive strategies, and ideas. Instructional specialists
like Joyce and Weil (1986) argue that these outcomes are best taught
through what they call information processing teaching "models."
Table 1 reflects research-based teaching models that have stood the
test of time and classroom use in a number of countries. In the
remainder of this chapter we will show how several of these models
have relevance for classrooms in developing countries. We will also
show that the models reflect permutations of the order of SP, CP, JP,
and AP.

How does this reflect in Mr. Sharad's classroom? He starts
with SP, then follows with some minimal CP as he has students
recite the formula, and JP comes from his role as the expert in the
classroom. In situations where there are few aids and texts, there is

little more that he feels he can do. The AP at the end of the lesson is evident.

In fact, the sequence:

1.   SP (Statement of Principle)
2.   CP (Clarification of Principle)
3.   JP (Justification of Principle)
4.   AP (Application of Principle)

is one that most teachers experienced when they were students both in schools and teacher training institutions. Reuksuppasompon (1983) relates that it is definitely the most frequent technique found in Thai colleges. Our argument is that this is also the most frequently used series of instructional steps used in the majority of universities and colleges throughout the world.

There are few educators who would argue that Mr. Sharad's situation is ideal. With little or no materials or texts, his CP step is minimal. The JP step is also weak since there is no way for Mr. Sharad to have students see parallel verifications of the principle under study. What remains is an expository lesson that could, if care is not taken, reflect (1) student memorization of a principle whose value is not seen, or (2) student application of a principle to problems that have little perceived value. Mr. Sharad's lesson appears to be what Duck (1981) calls "amorphous." The problem with amorphous teaching, as shown in Mr. Sharad's classroom, is that no item in the teacher's curriculum is seen as being more important than any ʌther. What Bruner et al. (1977) call the natural structure of a discipline is, thus, not presented to the students, who, therefore, have difficulty seeing relationships among the components of the curriculum.

STRUCTURED TEACHING

Let us consider a second teaching scenario, illustrating what Duck (1981) calls "structured," which is the opposite of an "amorphous" lesson:

TABLE 1
Outline of the Major Research-Based Teaching
Models, Major Theorist, and Its Mission or Goal

INFORMATION PROCESSING MODEL

MODEL	THEORIST	MISSION OR GOAL
Inductive Thinking Model	Hilda Taba	Designed primarily for development of inductive mental processes and academic reasoning
Inquiry Training Model	Richard Suchman	or theory building, but these capacities are useful for personal and social goals as well.
Scientific Inquiry Research	Joseph J. Schwab	Designed to teach the system of a discipline, but also expected to have effects in other domains.
Concept Attainment	Jerome Bruner	Designed primarily to develop inductive reasoning, but also for concept development and analysis.
Cognitive Growth	Jean Piaget Irving Sigel Edmund Sullivan Lawrence Kohlberg	Designed to increase general intellectual development, especially logical reasoning but can be applied to social and moral development as well (Kohlberg, 1976).
Advance Organizer	David Ausubel	Designed to increase the efficiency of information-processing capacities to absorb and relate bodies of knowledge.

MODEL	THEORIST	MISSION OR GOAL
Memory	Harry Lorayne Jerry Lucas	Designed to increase capacity to memorize.

SOCIAL INTERACTION MODELS

MODEL	THEORIST	MISSION OR GOAL
Group Investigation	Herbert Thelen John Dewey	Development of skills for participation in democratic social process through combined emphasis on interpersonal (group) skills and academic inquiry skills. Aspects of personal development are important outgrowths of this model.
Social Inquiry	Byron Massialas Benjamin Cox	Social problem solving, primarily through academic inquiry and logical reasoning.
Laboratory Method	National Training Laboratory	Development of interpersonal and group skills and through this, personal awareness and flexibility.
Jurisprudential	Donald Oliver James P. Shaver	Designed primarily to teach the jurisprudential frame of reference as a way of thinking about and resolving social issues.

MODEL	THEORIST	MISSION OR GOAL
Role Playing	Fannie Shaftel George Shaftel	Designed to induce students to inquire into personal and social values, with their own behavior and values becoming the source of their inquiry.
Social Simulation	Sarene Boocock Harold Guetzkow	Designed to help students experience various social processes and realities and to examine their own reactions to them, also to acquire concepts and decision-making skills.

PERSONAL MODELS

MODEL	THEORIST	MISSION OR GOALS
Nondirective Teaching	Carl Rogers	Emphasizes building the capacity for personal development in terms of self-awareness, understanding, and autonomy.
Awareness Training	Fritz Perls William Schultz	Increases one's capacity for self-exploration and self-awareness. Develops interpersonal awareness and understanding as well as body or sensory awareness.
Synectics	William Gordon	Developments creativity and creative problem-solving.
Conceptual Systems	David Hunt	Increases personal complexity and flexibility.

MODEL	THEORIST	MISSION OR GOAL
Classroom Meeting	William Glasser	Develops self-understanding and responsibility to oneself and one's social group.

BEHAVIORAL MODELS

MODEL	THEORIST	MISSION OR GOAL
Contingency Management Self-Control	B. F. Skinner	Facts, concepts, skills Social behavior/skills
Relaxation Stress Reduction	Rimm & Masters Wolpe	Personal goals (relaxation of stress, anxiety), substitution of relaxation for anxiety in social situations.
Assertive Training	Wolpe, Lazarus & Salter	Direct, spontaneous expression of feelings in social situations.
Desensitization	Wolpe	
Direct Training	Gagne, Smith & Smith	Pattern of behavior, skills

Teaching Scenario Two: Mrs. Juariah

Mrs. Juariah is a secondary mathematics teacher in Rembang, Indonesia. She begins the study of volumes by introducing the concept of regular solids, showing the students different types of regular solids and describing their characteristics. She tells the students that the volumes of regular solids are equal to the product of the area of the base and height. After writing this rule on the board, along side of some careful two-dimensional drawings of the 3-D objects, she starts with the cuboid. With questioning, she is usually able to get students to identify the base and height of the cuboid, and at the same time she reviews ways to calculate the area of the base. Students are then given a number of practice areas, and when she is certain that the students can find the area, she asks them to calculate the volume of selected cuboids. The next day some hollow metallic cuboids are handed to the students, and they are told to find the areas of the bases and the volumes of each. The students then put their results on the chalkboard. Mrs. Juariah then fills each cuboid with water. Pouring the contents into a graduated cylinder, she identifies how much is in each and compares that number with the student calculations. On subsequent days, Mrs. Juariah gives volume problems of increasing complexity to be solved. Observers note a significant amount of interaction between the students and the teacher. When Mrs. Juariah is certain that the students can compute cuboid volumes she introduces cylinders and triangular prisms. Mrs. Juariah carefully relates the calculations of each type of object to the other types of objects. The entire unit takes about 10 class periods.

One thing is clear. Mrs. Juariah makes a conscious effort to connect the various parts of the mathematics lessons. The content is present, and it is hoped that it is received by the students, as having some form of connection with itself and with the world outside the school. However, even with the differences that are obvious,

Mrs. Juariah and Mr. Sharad reflect the same set and the same order of teaching moves. Both are using expository teaching strategies. Mrs. Juariah also starts with SP (Statement of Principle), jumps to CP (Clarification of Principle), uses JP (Justification of Principle) to verify the principle, and includes definite AP (Application of Principle). Her use of drawings, models, and materials, however, presents a CP that breaks the principle into small parts making it easy for students to see its interconnections and worth.

It is obvious that the availability of materials in her school makes it easier for Mrs. Juariah to insure meaningful learning. But it is more than the materials that focus on the efficacy of learning. In fact, Mrs. Juariah is using a kind of Advance Organizer teaching model (Table 1).

The Advance Organizer model (Ausubel, 1963; Joyce & Weil, 1986; Novak & Gowin, 1984) deals with three major concerns: (1) how knowledge is organized, (2) how the mind works in its processing of information, and (3) how teachers can enhance student learning. Ausubel is especially concerned with what he calls meaningful learning--learning that permits the learner to see interconnections. Mr. Sharad's amorphous presentations do not encourage students to make these intellectual leaps. Mrs. Juariah, however, recognizes the interconnections of her lessons focus on the interconnections. Ausubel also postulates that there is a strong relationship between how subject matter is organized and the way people organize knowledge in their minds. As a result, Mrs. Juariah first presents her teaching principle (CP), which Ausubel refers to as an "advance organizer." This is then followed with examples, activities and evidence (CP: JP), that are "subsumed" under the teaching principle. Application of the principle (AP) is also required in this model. Research in elementary and secondary schools within the United States (Novak & Gowin, 1984) and in India (Bhalwanker, 1984), as well as in higher education institutions in South Africa (Harley, 1982), indicates that the use of such teaching structures can, indeed, enhance learning, although Joyce and Weil (1986) point out that the Ausubelian teaching model is best reserved for learners who have developed to a point where they can think "about thinking" (Piaget's Formal Operation Stage). In Mrs. Juariah's case, this assumption is probably met since she is working with secondary mathematics students.

The past 15 years of research on teacher effectiveness has shown that more effective teachers, such as Mrs. Juariah, use instructional time differently than less effective teachers. Their students focus on "academic engaged time" (Rosenshine & Berliner, 1978) or "academic learning time," which is strongly related to student learning.

The question for teacher educators, of course, is whether Mr. Sharad can learn those skills necessary to implement the Advance Organizer model. The answer is yes. Recent research by Joyce and Showers (1983) on the "coaching of teaching" shows that teachers can definitely modify their teaching skills. And if Beeby's (1979) findings are correct, that most teachers have the minimum necessary subject matter, perhaps this form of in-service training is the best use of lean budgets within the educational directorates of developing and developed countries.

INDUCTIVE TEACHING

There are other ways that the volume of cuboids can be presented to students. Consider the following scenario:

Teaching Scenario Three: Mr. Sosa

Mr. Sosa is a mathematics teacher in suburban Caracas, Venezuela. His introduction to the volume of cuboids starts when he shows his students a number of cuboids that have the same area base but different heights. Mr. Sosa challenges his students to generate a rule that would permit students to calculate the volume of the different solids. He questions the students to focus on the differences and similarities of the cuboids. Then he distributes a number of plastic 1 cm. cubes to small groups of students. He reminds them that the volume of the small plastic cubes is 1 cubic cm. The students then build models of the larger cuboids by putting the smaller ones together and counting the number of 1 cm cubes that make up the larger cuboid. Mr. Sosa then demonstrates how water displacement methods can be used to determine the volume of solids. The students use this method to determine the volume of the cuboids. After doing this for a number of cuboids the students make a chart:

	Volume	Length	Width	Height	Water Volume
Cuboid a:	40 cc	2 cm	10 cm	10 cm	40 cc
Cuboid b:	60 cc	3 cm	2 cm	10 cm	60 cc

Then he tells the students to study their charts and find a relationship between the heights, widths, lengths, and volumes of the cuboids. The students usually come up with the rule, but if Mr. Sosa finds that students are having difficulties, he assists them in stating the rule. He also alerts them that this relationship between the area of the base and height is important in calculating the volumes of a number of geometric shapes. Practice exercises with other cuboids follow, and the following days are used to present the volume calculations of cylinders and triangular prisms in the same way. In the subsequent days, Mr. Sosa very carefully relates the formulae for finding the volumes of the three shapes so that students could identify patterns of volume calculations. The effort takes about 10 periods.

In essence, Mr. Sosa is using an inductive approach following the guidelines identified by Bruner, Goodnow, and Austin (1977) and popularized as the Concept Attainment teaching model by Joyce and Weil (1986). The original research by Bruner et al. notes that while there are differences in the ways that humans conceptualize, nonetheless, all means of conceptualizing call for students to identify the essential attributes of concepts in developing a principle that can be used in their application to real world situations. Mr. Sosa's use of examples permits his students to see the similarities of all of his cuboid models. In our terminology, this is CP (Clarification of Principle), since he is requiring that the students clarify what he is expecting. It should be noticed also that Mr. Sosa initiated his lesson by challenging the students to come up with a rule themselves, a form of anticipatory set that, like Ausubel's Advance Organizer, focuses student attention on what is expected in the learning activities. The JP (Justification of Principle) step here takes on a totally different form, however. The students are shown how the volume of calculations relate to some "external proof." Only then do the students state the rule and involve themselves in the application step.

Similar CP instructional steps could have followed Taba's (1966b) strategies or could have included some form of guided discovery through the use of manipulative materials, such as for the various mathematics projects that have emerged in the United States and the United Kingdom in the past 20 years, or through some form of funded laboratory exercises such as the PKG in-service program in Indonesia. The research studies that have focused on the relative effectiveness of inductive approaches are open to a number of interpretations. While some reviews have noted that those principles "discovered" or taught through some form of inductive activity are remembered longer and are more easily applied, there have also been a sizable number of studies that have shown that models like the Advance Organizer model are equally effective in the generation of meaningful learning in students (cf. Ausubel, 1963; Novak & Gowin, 1984).

The important issue for instruction, however, is that both Mr. Sosa and Mrs. Juariah include each of the four steps identified by Henderson. As a result, students of both instructors should acquire the principle under study and should be actively involved in the lesson. Both lessons fit within Duck's (1981) "structured" instructional format.   Whether a teacher in a school within a developing country has the materials necessary for the proper use of inductive teaching models is a key question.

PROBLEM-SOLVING TEACHING

Our last scenario reflects Mr. Sosa's efforts, but there are some interesting differences.   Let us turn to Ms. Meesin, who begins by presenting a problem to be solved.

Teaching Scenario Four: Mrs. Meesin

Mrs. Meesin teaches in urban Bangkok. Having grown up in the rural area, she believes that the best way for students to learn is to generate their own ideas about mathematical calculations. She believes that students will remember their own ideas better than those given to them. Her introduction to cuboids starts when she brings in a large metal cuboid and places it on her desk. She tells the students to see if they can find out how to calculate the volume of the cuboid by asking her questions. The students know the learning rules since this teaching strategy is one common with Mrs. Meesin. The questions that they ask must be answered by a yes or a no. Mrs. Meesin rewards the students' good questioning strategies with praise. She will not answer questions like "Am I right?" or "What is the answer?" No matter how long it takes, the students are on their own. They ask questions about the height, width, weight, or any other dimensions they wish. They can even ask the teacher "What would happen if. . . . ? If the students get stuck, Mrs. Meesin brings out another cuboid, and they continue their questions until a rule is generated. Once the students generate the rule, practice exercises are put on the chalkboard for the students to calculate volumes of other cuboids. Mrs. Meesin also might note that the rule is a special one in mathematics since it reflects a rule that was generated centuries ago.   In the following days, a similar procedure follows using cylinders and triangular prisms. During each of these exercises, Mrs. Meesin emphasizes the similarities of the various volume formulae. She also has the students focus on their own personal strategies that they used to generate the formulae. The entire process takes about 10 class periods.

Just as was the case with Mr. Sosa, the students are challenged by the teacher to generate a rule, which is not given at the beginning of the lesson, but there are some interesting differences. The CP (Clarification of Principle) step in this case involves the students in a series of questions, answerable only by a yes or no. When the students eventually do generate a rule (SP or Statement of Principle), they are required to apply the rule (AP) in other situations. The JP (Justification of Principle) step in this case is a simple statement of history. Ms. Messin's model is a form of Inquiry Training, a model developed first by J. R. Suchman (1958) in his efforts to investigate learner problem-solving strategies. The model, described well by Joyce and Weil (1986), calls for little equipment, involves students actively in the investigation of problems, and has a research basis that indicates that it is capable of enhancing student thinking and the generation of principles.

The similarities of the last two teaching models are evident. Each uses a strategy that generates an important principle as the result of the students' manipulation of their environments. Active learning is encouraged throughout. But there are sizable problems that are also evident. Materials could be a difficulty as could be the time needed for the students to generate the principle. In our hypothetical situations, we have noted that each scenario reflects a time period of 10 days, perhaps an optimistic time period in classes where students have great difficulty in conceptualizing or problem-solving. Furthermore, in the latter two scenarios there is a need for the teacher to have a significant background with the topic under study, since the open-endedness could easily permit students to explore areas or topics in which the teacher could be unsure.

SUMMARY STATEMENT

Like Joyce and Weil, we argue that an effective teacher is one who keeps in mind where he or she is attempting to take the students and is able to select from among a repertoire of teaching models those that will best enhance student learning. Yet, observational studies in the United States have shown that most teachers have a very narrow range of teaching skills, and many teachers are unable to modify their instruction with different objectives simply because they are not cognizant of other ways to teach.

Based on the work of Joyce and Showers (1983), we are convinced that the teaching behaviors of experienced instructors can be modified. Both within developed and developing countries, we feel that the teaching models identified in this paper appear to be logical choices for inclusion in the repertoire of teaching skills for mathematics and science teachers. They could, at least, provide the teacher with some alternative tactics. Other models could be added for other subject specializations. We noted that Joyce and Weil identify more than 20 research-proven models for a wide range of subjects and learners. We argue here that if the minimal data that exist on what happens in the classrooms of developing countries are correct, then the Advance Organizer, Concept Attainment, and Inquiry models could be excellent additions to teacher training elements within the countries. At the very least, it is recommended that the SP-CP-JP-AP sequence posited by Henderson be emphasized in all teaching efforts.

Henderson's ideas appear to some critical readers of teacher effects research to be overly simplistic. Yet, his ideas should alert all teachers and teacher educators to the need to structure lessons for learners in ways that can reduce an emphasis on rote learning. In our analyses of research-proven teaching models we have also found that the four steps are found with regularity.

There are obvious difficulties in implementing programs that will modify teaching behaviors in any society. With respect to inquiry models of teaching, a number of specific difficulties were noted.

There are others, not the least of which focuses on the effects of such teaching models on schools and societies. An example in point can be seen in the Cianjur project within Indonesia. This multi-year project has been aimed at increasing "student active learning" within primary schools. Within a relatively small number of schools, teacher's "indirect" instructional behaviors have, indeed, enhanced the number of student questions and demonstrated that students can be actively involved in learning. Of concern, however, is what happens when primary learners, after five years of indirect instruction, encounter teachers in advanced grades who have not been involved in similar types of instruction. What must be recognized is that any changes in teacher behavior affect not only the students in one classroom but could in many ways affect others as well. Planners of in-service activities must recognize the systemic nature of any change in teacher instructional training programs.

The broader question must be posed of the perceived role of the teacher within a society. Alternative teaching models to those identified by Beeby and a few others may enhance learning, but, at the same time, they could be in conflict with the traditional educational expectations of parents and national leaders. In selecting teaching models, teacher trainers of all countries must consider the social and pedagogical consequence of the model.

CHAPTER EIGHT

TEACHER EFFECTIVENESS:
MORE QUESTIONS ABOUT AN OLD THEME

Beatrice Avalos

When a superior man knows the causes which make
instruction successful, and those which make it of no
effect, he can become a teacher of others. Thus, in his
teaching, he leads and does not drag; he strengthens
and does not discourage; he opens the way but does not
conduct to the end without the learner's own efforts.
Leading and not   dragging produces harmony.
Strengthening and not discouraging makes attainment
easy. Opening the way and not conducting to the end
makes the learner thoughtful. He who produces such
harmony, easy attainment, and thoughtfulness may be
pronounced a skillful teacher (Confucius, Book
XVI-Hsio Ki).

INTRODUCTION

The topic which concerns this paper could not have been more
explicitly enunciated than the way in which Confucius did so in the
fourth century B.C. A successful teacher, in current terminology an
"effective teacher," would be the person able to discern from
alternatives what makes instruction successful and what does not;
and to that end, this person would hold views about what teaching
seeks to achieve.

We have grappled in our terms with the question of teaching effectiveness to the point that discussions and research on this theme have produced, in the developed world, no less than three thousand references (Powell & Berd, 1984), and close to six hundred in the developing world (Avalos & Haddad, 1981). Are we any closer to an agreement about what produces a good teacher? Can we say, for example, that teachers in the industrialized world are substantially different in their practices from those in the developing world, and that therefore different portraits could be drawn of effective teachers in these different contexts? Can we settle for a form of research that will address adequately the issues about effectiveness of teaching and of teacher effectiveness? These are the questions that we would like to discuss in this chapter.

TEACHER EFFECTIVENESS: DO WE MEAN THE SAME THING?

What are we looking for when we talk about teacher effectiveness? The issue can be posed from the perspective of the teacher (what he or she does and the way in which he or she does it), or from that of pupils (what they become after teaching); but it can also be discussed in terms of the interactive process (teaching as such), or in terms of the factors modifying whatever we can describe as quality teaching. It can be related to the efficiency of the school system, or more remotely, to changes in the social environment. In all these forms, the preoccupation with teachers and their effectiveness spans the century, both as far as theories of teaching and of actual research output are concerned. It does not seem necessary here to deal with the history of teacher effectiveness theory and research as this has already been done in a large number of works and reviews that deal with the topic (Biddle & Ellena, 1967; Gage, 1978; Medley, 1982, 1987; Good, 1983; Walberg, 1985; Cruickshank, 1986).

In seeking to produce a framework for the extensive review of teacher effectiveness research carried out in seven world regions (Avalos & Haddad, 1981), the reviewers settled on a number of aspects which in one way or another were seen generally as constitutive of the concept itself. Most important of these is what was termed the "outcomes" of teaching. Teaching has purposes and so do teachers; the educational system has purposes as well as parents and the society at large. Although these purposes may be included in a broad spectrum of immediate and long-range aims they all eventually converge on the pupil, on what he does here and now, and what he or she may be doing in the future.

Although people may not feel comfortable with defining these purposes solely in terms of school work (examinations or other officially agreed-upon forms), in practice this is taken to be a very definite and immediate indication of outcomes. But measured achievement as a criterion has its problems. There appears to be, on the one hand, practical agreement that scholastic success of the pupil is a measure of teacher effectiveness; on the other hand, the conditions that affect such success either have been too difficult to examine or have not generated agreements as to their importance. This situation makes the concept of teacher effectiveness, which is based on the criteria of measured outcomes, extremely vulnerable. It also partly explains so many attempts at teacher effectiveness research, which settle on other aspects of the process of teaching (teacher and pupil attitudes, skills and behaviors, or descriptions of interactive classroom processes). The goal of what has been called the "process-product" type of teacher effectiveness research, after an era of proliferation, is now being seriously called into question (Doyle, 1987). The perspective, however, of looking at how teaching contributes to outcomes is still a valid one. Teaching is undertaken for a pupil's benefit, and conceptualizations of teacher effectiveness need to be related to what that benefit is to be.

Pupils are human beings and as such require that their experiences with teachers not end in frustrated personal, emotive, and cognitive growth; they are also members of a society which rightly or not determines for them levels of qualifications and requires that they give evidence of abilities needed to be active in social development and change. As human beings, pupils have a right to experiences which will enable their preparation to fulfil such requirements; although at times and in some social contexts the preparation for social life may contradict in practice the needs of cognitive growth and emotional stability. That is, to follow the prevailing social rules may well be alienating.

We all know that something we perceive as "better teachers" and "better schools" produces pupils who more easily find their way in the bigger society; though we also know that generally those pupils in such schools also come from more privileged and comfortable social and economic conditions. In practice, then, we do have a concept of teacher and school effectiveness, which is largely related to what Confucius had to say abut the ease of learning and its assumed relationship to success, as well as to the capacity of being inventive and creative of new social avenues of development, if not blatantly critical of existing ones.

When we delineate as criteria for teacher effectiveness, the attainment of successful teaching outcomes, we cannot leave aside the other factors which affect the process of teaching: background of teachers (their experience, personality, training and qualifications), the context of teaching (school system, school management, teaching conditions), the process of teaching with its interactive forms, and the contribution from pupils and their background characteristics. All of these elements coalesce in the discussions about teacher effectiveness increasing the complexity of its definition and of the procedures for its study.   The history of teacher effectiveness research reflects these problems.

Despite such difficulties in conceptualizing and doing research on teacher effectiveness, the issue itself cannot be sidetracked as it also underlies the understanding of the teacher training process. Gage (1964) reminds us of the obvious when he says:

> the problem of discovering and developing more effective
> ways of equipping teachers with pedagogical knowledge

and skill is the same, in principle, as that of discovering more effective ways of teaching (p. 93).

A review of those elements in the theories which underlie the concept of teacher effectiveness points to a least four research concerns:

1.   Teacher skills and behaviors (competencies) which appear to influence outcomes of the teaching process. In this respect, a whole array of literature deals with teacher classroom behaviors, such as types of lecturing and questioning, the effect of praise or other forms of feedback, and managerial behaviors such as communication or rules and procedures and the consistent enforcement of these (Brophy, 1979; Brophy & Good, 1985).

2.   Teacher patterns of decision-making as they affect the long-term preparation of a school year, the more immediate lesson preparation, or the interactive decisions at the daily classroom level; all of these seen both at the instructional and managerial level (Burns, 1984).

3.   Teachers' modes of thinking and how they interpret the situations experienced in teaching. Such thinking patterns may respond to held theories of teaching or to theories about the effect of pupil background factors; they also may be influenced by views about what can be expected from some pupils as opposed to others (Stebbins, 1975; Clark & Yinger, 1979; Yinger, 1980; Shavelson & Stern, 1981; Woods, 1983).

4.   The relationship between teaching purposes and the way in which pupils mediate such purposes as well as the nature of teacher-pupil tasks (Doyle, 1977, 1983b, 1987).

These four approaches have inspired much of the current research in the developed world and to a certain extent also that of the developing world (mainly the first approach, centered on teacher skills and competencies). In addition, one notices a return, in the literature, to the notion that the actual knowledge base (command of what is being taught, together with sound "pedagogical" knowledge), constitutes a factor of crucial importance when it comes to defining an "effective" teacher.

The above theoretical approaches, however, underlie different and often antagonistic forms of research, and their results cannot be easily pooled together to describe effective teaching (though isolated teacher behaviors can and have been found to relate to achievement). Despite this, there continues to be interest in understanding teaching as a complex web of all the factors which are isolated in different theories, thus explaining the search for more comprehensive programs of teacher effectiveness research and more comprehensive efforts to understand the process of training teachers. Good examples of this direction are studies like those of Oracle (Galton, Simon, & Croll, 1980a, 1980b) and Scots (Powell, 1985) in the United Kingdom, which, though keeping within the process-product research paradigm, utilized concepts and approaches reflecting the intention to understand the complexity of patterns of activity in the primary classroom. The growing number of classroom studies within an ethnographic perspective, which also consider the influence of factors external to the teaching process, also illustrate the point.

TEACHERS IN INDUSTRIALIZED AND LESS DEVELOPED COUNTRIES: HOW DIFFERENT ARE THEY?

Part of the discussion that concerns research on teaching and that attempts to make recommendations for classroom practices and teacher training refers to whether or not it is acceptable to use research findings and experience from one context to apply to another, or whether cross-national studies on a topic make any sense at all. At the root of these concerns is the historical fact of educational colonization, which has not been eliminated with independence in much of the world south of the Equator. This was expressed in systems of education modelled on those of the ex-colonial powers or later on those in industrialized countries, without, for a variety of reasons, being equal to them in the quality of their services and products. As a result, school scenes involving teachers, pupils, classrooms, seats, chalk, and talk are found everywhere but with differences in material conditions ranging from less to better equipped, with teachers from less to better trained and with children from poorer to better backgrounds and with lesser to more promising opportunities for insertion in the world.

These similarities make the contention that the study and improvement of educational conditions in the Third World require perspectives and strategies which are "native" as opposed to imported to be true only to a limited extent. If we could liberate ourselves from the continuing domination of First World perspectives and strategies and eradicate the effect of history plus decide that the coming together of the contemporary world (through communication media and technology) is reversible, then we might sustain a radical context-bound approach to the problems of education. Then we could say that research approaches and pedagogical strategies and techniques are not adaptable or usable from context to context.

The most compelling evidence that this is not the case is brought home by the current position of China *vis-a-vis* the industrialized world. While respecting and believing in its culture and traditions as well as maintaining loyalty to its political philosophy, the Chinese people pragmatically accept that their welfare and development depend on their capacity to adapt Confucian aims to a socialist society capable of high technological development. This requires links with the technologically advanced societies and transformation of their educational services accordingly. The problem is then not one of simply repressing cultural invasion or domination but of determining also in each society what are its needs; what prevailing (autochthonous or imported) forms of cultural life exist, and what is required to further the social and individual development of its people. What is at stake in the poorer and lesser developed countries, as well as in the new developing nations, is the ability to describe their educational needs and to provide services accordingly. These needs, compared to developed societies, are obviously different in societies where literacy levels are low, where large segments of the population live in isolated rural areas or where professional and technical know-how remains meagre. They may come closer to segments of industrialized societies (the "inner city" areas of London or Belfast) in countries where modern urban centers grow along with the permanence of the traditional rural zones. But the prevailing mode of imparting education in almost every Third World context continues to be "classroom" (with or without buildings) teaching in two-level systems of primary and secondary education with a growing but insufficient tertiary sector. Teachers hold in these contexts as in all others a crucially powerful role *vis-a-vis* the development of children entrusted to their teaching actions. The possibility, therefore, of these teacher actions having a beneficial rather than negative effect underlies the concern for the study of teacher effectiveness. Equally, the sameness of the structure of teaching from context to context underlies the possibility of cross-cultural studies of teacher effectiveness as well as the possibility of a two-way transfer of knowledge about teaching from one setting to another.

But also, the differences in cultural and economic environments underlie the need for accurate descriptions and understanding of the conditions of variation. In particular, what is needed are descriptions of the way in which the teaching tasks and their difficulties are perceived by teachers, how these may effect teaching and learning, what strategies operate effectively, and which do not and why, granted the cultural variations. In many Third World countries innovation in the classroom responds to systems of teaching introduced from elsewhere, e.g., mastery learning in Korea or the Integrated Social Studies primary curriculum in Nigeria. How these have been interpreted locally is being and should be the object of further studies (e.g., Orungbemi, 1987).

In exploring what we know about teaching in teacher effective contexts, two recent studies provide information on how teachers perceive their practice as well as on characteristics of the practices themselves as observed by outsiders: the one was a typical process-product study of teacher effectiveness; the other was an ethnographic account of teaching processes leading to pupil failure. What these studies reveal is very much dependent on their initial questions and the research framework from which they operated; what emerges are pictures of classroom teaching with similar sets of events occurring but with substantial variations among them in quality and quantity interpreted, in turn, according to the theoretical and research framework under which they were produced. Consideration of these results together with other factors should help us to formulate in the third part of this paper what programs of research on teaching and training could be envisaged for the future.

THE IEA CLASSROOM ENVIRONMENT STUDY

A cross-national study was carried out between 1981 and 1984 under the auspices of the International Association for the Evaluation of Educational Achievement (IEA) in some twelve countries, three of these being developing nations: Republic of Korea, Nigeria, and Thailand. The purpose of the study was to assess by means of an observational/correlational design the characteristics and conditions under which effective teachers stimulate both pupil learning and favorable attitudes toward subject-matter knowledge. Results, it was posited, would serve as input for teacher training experiments. The research design was originally modelled along the lines of the descriptive-correlational-experimental studies, which had been carried out in the United States (Gage, 1978). It was subsequently modified in the light of both practical and theoretical considerations (Ryan & Anderson, 1987).

As background to the study and as a way of establishing whether the sample of teachers to be observed would be similar to a wider population of teachers, a survey of teacher perceptions about their practices and contexts was carried out in each country. The results of this survey provide some basis to assess how teachers behave in these countries.

Teaching Context and Teacher Background

With regard to teaching context and teacher background in the IEA study, various differences emerged between the developed and the less developed countries surveyed. In Thailand, Nigeria, and Korea there were bigger schools, larger classes, more lower socioeconomic pupils and more schools located in rural areas (with the exception of Korea). At the certification level, however, no startling differences were noted. Teaching resources appeared practically reduced to textbooks in the developing countries; and teachers, in the developing countries of the study, had less overall autonomy in the making of instructional and assessment decisions with regard to their classes, though with two exceptions on either side. Korean teachers reported similar autonomy to teachers in most developed countries,while the Netherlands teachers reported very little autonomy on instructional and assessment decisions.

Teaching Practices

Teaching practices, described in terms of the structure and content of lessons, the interactive processes observed, the use of correctives and provision for individual needs, and the assessment procedures used, were measured on a "frequency of use" or "agreement/disagreement" scale. In general, in all countries, teachers' responses to the various questions relating to teaching practices seemed to revolve around the middle point with few noticeable differences between developed and less developed countries. In other words, teachers perceived themselves similarly everywhere and the common pattern that could be discerned had the following traits:

- Teachers spent a "fair amount" to a "lot" of time on presentation of content as compared with review activities.
- Most teaching appeared to be done in whole group situations (to the whole class).

- *Interactions* consisted mostly of conventional forms of questioning and eliciting specific recall from pupils.
- *Assessment* was mostly for the conventional summative purposes of marking work rather than as a means of aiding learning and diagnosing difficulties.

Teachers in Thailand

The core of the IEA project was an observational study conducted in each participant country, searching for links between teacher practices and pupil attitudes and learning. The report from Thailand (Nitsaisook, 1985) serves to illustrate what was observed regarding teacher practices in 79 fifth grade mathematics classrooms containing 2,332 pupils.

The teachers were mostly female (71 percent) and had nearly 13 years of experience. Their mean workload was about 13 hours per week, but some of them were teaching 20 or more hours per week. The size of their schools ranged from 100 to 5,000; and the average size of their classes was of 33 pupils (the range being between 17 and 57). As far as training was concerned, 62 of the 79 teachers indicated that they were trained for primary, secondary or both levels. But 42 percent of those 62 indicated no special training in mathematics. About 70 percent of the pupils could be classified as coming from low socioeconomic environments in terms of father's occupation.

Fifty-six percent of the teachers perceived the average level of their pupils to be poor, and 35 percent thought that "nearly all" their pupils were in need of remedial attention. On the average, the teaching activities were those found in Table 1 with the percentage of time allocated to each activity also being shown (Nitsaisook, 1985).

Frontal teaching in the form of lecturing, demonstrating and explaining dominated the scene, and this was followed by seat work. Though various forms of "interacting" with pupils occupied some 76

TABLE 1
Distribution of Percentage of Time Devoted to Different Types of Teaching-Learning Activities in Thailand

Lecture/Explain/Demonstrate	54.39
Review	10.30
Discourse/Discussion	1.24
Oral Practice/Drill	2.52
Seatwork - Tests	.52
Seatwork - Reading	.08
Seatwork - Written	29.52
Seatwork - Manipulation	.13
Composite Management	1.02
Other Activities	.26

percent of the class time, this was mainly broken down in the following manner:

- high on   "teacher to group"
               "group to teacher"
- lower on   "teacher to student"
- low on   "student to teacher"

The second item, "group to teacher," might have signaled something significant, but it really only meant that pupils were giving responses in chorus to teacher-initiated recall questions (recitation). On the whole, there was accord between what was observed in these classes and what the teachers in the general survey said about their practices; they generally addressed the whole group and interactions were largely based on recall questioning with little feedback.

Despite the initial intentions of the study to relate teaching practices to outcomes, including context and background factors, the nature of the research approach and the design used did not allow important significant relationships to be established in the Thai or in any of the other studies (Mandeville, 1984).

Of interest, however, was the description of teaching that the researchers involved in the Thai study were able to put together.

> . . . as shown in the findings of the study, 60 percent of the Grade 5 mathematics teachers in the survey sample and 50 percent in the observation sample had never taken any courses or attended any intensive training in the teaching of mathematics. The results clearly illustrate the teaching weaknesses in some classes. The first weakness is that the teachers present the concepts of the lessons unclearly. The teachers' explanations are unnecessarily lengthy and not in logical orders. Besides, the teachers frequently ask students questions which are not yet taught. Thus, when the students do not give correct answers, the teachers waste time on emotionally and unsatisfyingly redirecting or prompting the students. The second weakness concerns the inadequacy of time utilization for teaching concepts. Some teachers spend too much time on explaining easy concepts and too little time on more complex ones. Such practices reflect the fact that those teachers themselves perceive the nature of the lesson concepts according to the length of text prescription-- more pages, more difficult, and more time. . . .

> . . . the findings show that 38 percent of the lessons consist of 83 percent of lecturing/explaining activities. These lessons include not only the presentation of new material but also the reexplaining of the material previously taught. This reexplaining always occurs when the teachers find the students either cannot give correct answers or do not solve the problems in the assigned exercises correctly. This finding seems to reflect the conviction of some of the

teachers that only explanations can help students to learn the lessons. One may wonder whether the teachers understand the concepts of reteaching and reexplaining.

Furthermore, even though a great number of questions are asked, most of them are either recall or simple direct questions mostly initiated by teachers. The main purpose of asking questions seems to be the maintenance of the students' attention to the teachers' explanations and of the students' engagement in teaching activities rather than to check the students' understanding of the lesson concepts.

In addition to the infrequent specific checking of understanding, most teachers do only general comprehension checks, e.g., the teachers ask students whether they understand or have any difficulties with the lessons. The teachers rarely provide an opportunity to the class to transfer their understanding into performance or types of practice which indicate how well the students comprehend the concepts right after the lesson presentation, so that the teachers can provide either feedback and correctives or reteach promptly before the students practice independently their incorrect concepts (Nitsaisook, p. 65).

The above description of teaching will be used at the end of this chapter to compare with what we know of other contexts.

Teaching in Latin America

An ethnographic study carried out in four countries of Latin America (Bolivia, Chile, Colombia, and Venezuela) provided rich descriptions of teaching practices and allowed inferences to be made regarding their effect on high rates of repetition and failure in the first years of the primary school (Avalos, 1986).

The description of teaching which resulted was similar to the one found in Thailand as well as in other contexts (Nunn, 1987). Teachers occupy a central role in the conduct of teaching. Most classroom activities are directed to the whole class, with the teacher appearing as a "benevolent dictator." The teacher solicits, requests, or orders responses from pupils who in turn must render such services. The children's personal world of experiences is seldom used as a learning input. Some children are selected to have a special position in the class, without it being clear what justifies such selection. The provision of feedback to pupils' responses is often arbitrarily decided by teachers who might choose to "ignore" a response or treat a child's error as a personal insult. Children often respond to these manifestations of authority with acceptance, indicating that "that's how things are supposed to be." Hence, they interpret failure to learn mostly as a result of their own real or assumed irresponsibility rather than having anything to do with the form of teaching to which they are subjected.

An excessive emphasis on order and cleanliness determines the conduct of lessons. Copying from the blackboard or books takes an important part of lesson time, though checking for correctness or understanding is seldom practiced. Equally, the teaching of norms and rules of conduct overshadows other teaching activities, and even while these are taking place often there are interruptions to remind the students that they should be paying attention or looking at their books or sitting up straight.

The effect of poor expectations about children's ability and, especially, of labelling practices was noted. At least in one of the countries the habit of pejorative nicknaming and the communication of poor hopes for achievement affected substantially the situation of many children, who began a school year in equal standing to other children, who were differently treated.

Though there is some structure in most lessons (introduction, recitation activities, presentation of new content, seat work, and perhaps a conclusion with a homework assignment), within that structure all sorts of variations occur. There can be a sudden and arbitrary change of topic, or recall-type questioning leading not to assessment of knowledge but to "guessing." The teaching of language skills is ritualistic, involving the syllabic method, using meaningless sentences and reading without checks for comprehension. Teachers interpret the reasons for poor learning in terms of what might be called "determinist" theories. Teachers claim children cannot learn if they come from poor backgrounds as they will be affected by malnutrition and insufficient parental support. These interpretations are also found in other research studies of teaching in Latin America (Tedesco, 1983; Nunn, 1987).

Teachers, in most Latin American countries, constitute the professional group with the lowest salaries and prestige; their workload usually includes teaching in more than one school in order that they may subsist (sometimes 40 to 60 hours per week). In some situations, the bureaucratic requirements of the system are irritating and mean large amounts of time spent in the filling of forms sent by ministries and other local authorities.

The teaching conditions in schools vary. There are no excessively crowded classes by comparison with other poor countries, but school buildings, size of classrooms, and teaching resources can be meagre.

Lack of stimulation from educational authorities, poor teaching resources, and sheer fatigue help explain what was observed; but not everything could be attributed to these conditions. The possibility of finding, as did the authors of the study, the teachers who are "different," that is, teachers who introduce changes into the common teaching style, who believe pupils are not irreversibly damaged by their background, who avoid as much as possible the "labelling" pitfall, suggests a renewed confidence in the possibilities of training or in-service experiences.

WHERE TO MOVE?

An overview of the studies presented in the preceding sections allows some generalizations to be made. First, the IEA survey does not indicate that teachers in developed countries perceive themselves very differently from teachers in the developing countries. Moreover, if one sets aside the differences produced by better buildings, more material, and teaching resources, most teachers still see themselves preferring to teach whole groups and using very limited interactive styles (recall questions, recitation), limiting provision of correctives, and mostly evaluating in a summative way. The Thai observational study corroborated the teachers' own perceptions and noted the almost exclusive concentration on lecturing and group questioning centering on requests for factual recall.

What this indicates is that differences between countries may exist in the quality but not in the structure and style of the preferred methods. The Scottish study referred to earlier (Powell, 1985) also found teachers (not necessarily the majority) in Scotland who exhibited "weakness in "teaching skills," poor feedback, dullness, excessive allocation of time to work so repetitive as to serve little function other than that of keeping pupils occupied, and failure to identify and respond to individual differences found both where group methods were employed and where they were not" (p. 162).

Second, both the IEA study and the Latin American ethnographies, as well as other relevant research, suggest that within styles and patterns of teaching there are variations which affect different sorts of pupil outcomes, including learning. They need to be brought out into the open for teachers to see and reflect upon.

Third, the different research approaches of the studies referred to yield different perspectives of what goes on in teaching; but in the end they are not incompatible, and seen together they offer descriptions where a variety of components of the teaching process can be observed. Structured observation allows concentration on particular teaching skills and behaviors, on time allocation to various parts of a lesson, on the observation of particular types of interactions, and so on. Narrative observation provides insight into the quality of events and interactive processes. Structured and unstructured interviews as well as survey practices help to complete the awareness of contextual factors and indications of teachers' thinking and patterns of decision-making. What is difficult, however, is to pool together the information provided by these means to produce correlations between observed events and behaviors, and pupil outcomes, while also attempting to consider contextual factors and interpretative processes of actors.

Fourth, if the above is to be taken as reasonable, then there must be a recognition that research on teaching, though in need of a theoretical basis,cannot look for that theory purely in one of the social science disciplines, or in one of the four research approaches outlined in the first part of this chapter. As far as developing countries are concerned, preoccupation with actual learning and the satisfaction of a child's basic right to knowledge and skills which are required from any member of society, must override all other considerations; hence, understanding of how teaching takes place and what can be done to improve it must also override the slavish adherence to one or another of the existing academic paradigms (often of more interest to the sociologist, psychologist, or anthropologist than to the actual pedagogue).

In their critique of the Process-Product tradition of research on teaching, Garrison and Macmillan (1983) suggest that perhaps something new should emerge that is not a defense of the tradition (with its bias on correlational procedures). They suggest a new tradition "should provide a coherent way of showing why the earlier one got the results that it did. If such a 'paradigm' can grow from present research on teaching, there is much hope for the future" (p. 274). Equally, Sharpes (1983, p. 10) suggests that "studying teacher education concerns in the developing world demands something of an overall set of strategies from the combined social sciences, and a probable balance in methodology from each.

Conventional academic boundaries are not always appropriate, and the quest for a new methodological framework will continue to conform to the active consciousness of researchers."

Finally, the analysis of the studies included here, and the literature on Teacher Effectiveness, as well as the above quotation, inevitably remit us to the area of training. The review of Teacher Effectiveness in the Third World (Avalos & Haddad, 1981) concluded that training was related to the way teachers conducted their teaching and to pupil outcomes. However, training alone, as the teachers in the studies considered in this chapter attest, is not sufficient insurance against poor teaching. It remains an open question for which we have few answers: "how is this training (initial or in-service) actually carried out?" Without doubt, an important step ahead is to increase the number of descriptive studies that tell us what prospective teachers learn in teacher training institutions, that follow graduates through the first years of practice, and that experiment with modes of in-service which cover both teacher attitude change and improvement of teaching skills in particular subjects as well as of their pedagogical style. There is no lack of ideas, suggestions, practices that tell us how to improve training (Goodings, Byram, & McPartland, 1982; Bude & Greenland, 1983) and these are increased with other articles in this volume (Shaeffer, Vera). But the research that penetrates the mysterious world of training institutions, including the curriculum knowledge provided (Denham, 1985) and pursues awareness of how young teachers cope with their practice in all sorts of contexts, must be undertaken with urgency.

CHAPTER NINE

TO THE DEFENSE OF TRADITIONAL TEACHING IN LESSER-DEVELOPED COUNTRIES

Gerard Guthrie

The schools of lesser-developed countries are littered with the remnants of attempts to change the quality of teaching. Well-meant but inappropriate reforms of syllabuses, teacher training, teaching styles, inspection systems, and examinations have been marked by considerable failure. Some successes, usually under well-funded but difficult to replicate pilot conditions, merely serve to highlight the more numerous exceptions. All too often the failures have been blamed not on the innovators, who lacked understanding of the theoretical and practical barriers to change, but on the teachers who did understand.

Underlying much innovation have been Western philosophies of education that denigrate the formalistic teaching which traditionally prevails in so many countries, both "developed" and "lesser-developed." Implicit, therefore, in many innovations has been an equation of change in the quality of teaching with change in teaching styles. Rather than concentrating on student learning as the criterion variable against which quality of teaching should be assessed, many innovations have taken teaching styles themselves as an end product. Several of the assumptions made about the relationship between teaching style and learning are open to the charge that they are insufficiently validated or that they are valid only in some cultural context.

In this chapter we consider some of the theoretical and methodological objections to equating teaching style with quality of teaching, as well as the practical difficulties, which would make implementation difficult even if the more abstract objections did not exist. In doing this, we shall refer to recent empirical research from a number of lesser-developed countries which provides evidence to support the preceding statements. Conversely, we also consider some of the positive advantages of formalistic teaching and discuss findings on some relatively cost-effective successes at improving teaching quality in a manner which is not inconsistent with the dominant formalistic teaching. We thus attempt to play "devil's advocate" to the conventional theme of change and innovation in teaching but in a manner which is constructive rather than destructive. One outcome, we hope, will be increased appreciation that the opposition of many teachers to inappropriate change is rational and well judged.

EDUCATIONAL DEVELOPMENT AND TEACHING STYLES

To illustrate the theoretical and methodological problems inherent in many attempts to reform teaching, we will address the issues as raised by C. E. Beeby's "stages of educational development," formulated some 20 years ago (Beeby, 1966). Our comments outline aspects of a detailed critique of the stages (Guthrie, 1980a, 1980b; and Beeby 1980a, 1980b in response to the critique). Beeby's stages are relevant to the concerns of this book as they were widely influential on attempts to change curriculum and teaching styles in the late 1960s and early 1970s (Barrington, 1980; Guthrie, 1980a, pp. 416-18), when many attempts were made to improve the quality of teaching by changing teaching styles. The empirical evidence now available on some of these innovations should caution our attempts to find alternative models to traditional teaching practices. While many of the innovations were made quite independently of Beeby's analysis, his stages serve to illustrate many of the issues raised by reforms based on other theoretical grounds, particularly in the circularity inherent in their formulation. Beeby has also had considerable involvement in education in Indonesia, as witnessed by his book on the education system in this country (Beeby, 1979).

Beeby argued that there were four stages of primary schooling in developing countries: the Dame School, Formalism, Transition, and Meaning. Movement through the stages, he considered, is normally evolutionary, the key being teachers' ability to promote change. This ability is itself a function of teachers' confidence, itself partly a function of their levels of general and professional education. Five major factors affect teacher conservatism and inability to promote change: lack of clear system goals restricts teachers' thinking, lack of understanding and acceptance impedes reforms, conservative systems restrict the tendency of teachers to innovate, isolation of teachers in classrooms slows diffusion rates of reforms, and a wide range of teacher abilities creates uneven diffusion rates.

Here are the seeds of many systems-based approaches to modernizing the curriculum and improving the quality of teaching: upgrade teacher education, in both professional and academic terms; provide new syllabuses and teaching materials; give in-service training, especially to "sell" reforms; introduce new teaching techniques. A common expectation has been that teachers' ability to promote change will be improved, as indicated by changes in their teaching style towards liberal, student-centered methods. Where this has not occurred a frequent interpretation has been that failure is due to the inability of the teacher to take advantage of the extra inputs.

Unfortunately, the results of innovations taking the view that the curriculum should be modernized have been very uneven. Some of the fundamental reasons have been indicated in the analysis of the theoretical and methodological properties of the stages (Guthrie, 1980a, pp. 418-22, 427-29). Four main theoretical arguments exist:

1. the logic of the stages is circular;
2. the criterion of judgment is culture-bound;
3. the association of an ability to enquire with enquiry teaching techniques is not a necessary one; and

4.   attempts to have students learn higher-level cognitive skills may be inappropriate to their level of intellectual development.

Where attempts to improve the quality of teaching are based on similar grounds to Beeby's stages, there is a considerable risk that the logic is circular and therefore invalid. The fundamental criterion of educational progress in the stages model, for example, is an *a priori* bias that changes in teaching style represent progress. Subsequently, progress is assessed in relation to the achievement of these changes and a self-fulfilling prophesy ensues. The empirical referents, which change propositions provide, tend to be assumed as likely outcomes rather than being tested under controlled situations to see whether they will indeed occur.   The sort of independent reasons for change which should be posed as research questions are, for example: Will the new style upgrade student achievement? Will it increase student creativity?

In the case of Beeby's stages, and of much curriculum theory, the bases of judgment that change is desirable are the educational norms of a liberal Western academic subculture. These norms often favor student-centered learning, enquiry methods, integrated curricula, school-based innovation, and the like. Although the attempts to change syllabuses are usually put in cognitive terms, the hidden agenda is often affective moral and philosophical values about desirable psycho-sociological traits for individuals and for society. The most explicit expression of such views is in the physical and social sciences where scientific enquiry is designed to question revealed truths--but commonly anti-authoritarian values exist as well.

Formalistic teaching provides a ready butt for those who want to effect change based on these grounds, but their values are questionable in the international and cross-cultural context of the lesser-developed nations. While culture-bound innovators are quite likely to be the expatriates, employed in many countries to upgrade the quality of teaching through curriculum development and teacher education, national staff, particularly those with overseas study to their credit, are also vulnerable to the questionable transfer of fashionable educational theories.

Educationists in societies which place great value on respect for elders, on respect for wisdom and knowledge, and on respect for religion, need to be consciously aware of the potential for conflict over curriculum innovations based on different values. These societies are not the proper place for naive experimentation with the effects of different Western value systems. Two recent analyses of the literature on curriculum transfer both found cautionary tales to tell (Crossley, 1984a; Guthrie, 1986), while a recent study of attempts by expatriate and African elites to reform secondary education in both mathematics and literature in Kenya indicates that viewpoints out of keeping with mainstream values may not be the sole prerogative of expatiates or be confined to the science areas of the curriculum (Lillis, 1985).

The common association in educational theory of liberal, student-centered classroom methods with positive attitudes to enquiry among students and with appropriate intellectual skills is also questionable, even within Western culture. At their most rigorous expression in scientific research, problem-solving skills demand a high degree of personal and intellectual discipline, which has for decades been taught quite formally in Western colleges and universities. While, as educational researchers, we can readily find sound reasons for students to learn scientific thinking, schools may be the wrong part of the educational system to do so. This is particularly the case once the Piagetian level of formal operations is required for problem-solving, for high school students are predominantly at the concrete operational level, as was found by Lewis and Ransley (1977) in a survey of Piagetian research in the South Pacific. Formal operations are more likely to be a proper function for university education, yet many high school science and social science syllabuses attempt them and attempt to get teachers to change teaching styles in order to accommodate them. The functional effect of this type of curriculum in schools is to maximize the potential for failure by asking teachers to use styles which are not necessary, and which they are unlikely to successfully use, to teach what their pupils will not learn.

There are also methodological objections to the stages concept in that an inappropriate and poorly defined measurement scale is used, leading to the assumption that teaching styles are discrete entities rather than typical or modal behaviors representing complex continuous variables. This view has tended to direct the attention of evaluators to assess teaching styles rather than the changes to which they are supposed to lead. The criticism which Flander's Interaction Analysis has received in developing countries (Avalos & Haddad, 1981, p. 49-51) can be partly understood in this light, for this technique is designed to collect classroom interaction data on the assumption that a high level of student interaction is an indicator of teaching quality.

To be fair to Dr. Beeby, a man for whom we have great respect, the critique on which this brief summary is based (Guthrie, 1980a) is founded on strict criteria, and he did not subscribe to all the views alluded to above. Although Beeby did regard long-term progress as being represented by modern teaching methods, he did not share the inference that progress was to be made by attempting to accelerate teachers through the stages. Rather, he viewed the difficulty of change in lesser-developed countries as a reason to attempt to slow down change and to use more traditional teaching methods (Beeby, 1980a, p. 439).

PRACTICAL BARRIERS TO CLASSROOM CHANGE

Even if the case put in the previous section is not valid, and the theoretical case for increasing educational change rates is sustained, there are many practical barriers to change. As Morris (1985, p. 15) has recently concluded, curricular changes should be influenced by the realities of the classroom and the constraints within which teachers and pupils operate. Innovations should be selected with regard to their probability of success as well as their desirability. The implication is that many changes desirable on more abstract grounds may not succeed for practical reasons, and therefore they should not be attempted. Four main practical problems exist:

1. teachers may have insufficient time to innovate;
2. classroom facilities may not be appropriate for some teaching styles;
3. examinations may emphasize learning inconsistent with the innovations; and
4. education ministries may be unable to provide appropriate organizational support, particularly during extension phases.

The pressures on time, which confront many teachers in their day-to-day work, prohibit the sort of long-term input which many innovations require. The normal work of preparation, teaching, marking, school administration, playground supervision, and extracurricular activities simply leaves little time to spare for many teachers. Family persons with obligations to spouse, children, and relatives, as well as to community groups to which they belong, simply may not have hours in the day to undertake major curriculum innovations. This is particularly so for teachers in communities with few modern facilities, where the sheer mechanics of daily life occupy greater time than for the more comfortably located innovator at headquarters. Low rates of pay may not provide the motivation to put any spare time into extra school work. Under pilot conditions, it is possible to obtain considerable commitments of time from those singled out for special attention through, for example, in-service. But extension phases requiring the same high levels of commitment, and without relief from normal duties, can tax the most willing and overtax those who are not so willing or those for whom fewer resources in the extension phase mean less in-service support. Watson's (1983) description of programs in Cameroon, Iran, and Thailand, using primary school teachers as social change agents, one of which is reasonably optimistic, nonetheless indicates a number of these constraints which are as applicable to the curriculum internal to schools as to a curriculum involving community education.

Attempts to upgrade teacher quality by requiring changes in teaching style may find the situation in the classroom overwhelms the desired behaviors. Where teachers have to cope with large classes, in particular, changes in teaching style, which require small group work, experiential enquiry, or experimental activities, may not be practicable because of lack of space, inadequate classroom furniture, absence of equipment, and lack of classroom insulation, making even moderate noise levels a disturbance in other classrooms.

Where syllabus reforms promote open-ended activities or heuristic teaching styles to develop enquiry skills and attitudinal change but examinations emphasize recall of lower-level cognitive knowledge, teachers face a dilemma. They will often tend to be led by their own and their students' expectations of exam-oriented teaching, as Lewin (1984) has shown for Sri Lanka and Malaysia, and Morris (1985) has shown for Hong Kong. This is particularly understandable where schooling is dominantly seen as an investment in the possibility of future employment rather than as consumption of something valued as good in itself. The lesson from the literature on the effects of examinations on classroom practice appears to be that it is a necessary but not sufficient condition of attempts to change classroom practice. These attempts should be consistent with teachers' and students' perceptions of the requirements of any public examination system (Crossley & Guthrie, 1987). The effects of formalistic teacher training and inspections systems reinforce the role of examinations.

Finally, insufficient support from ministries of education may inhibit the desired change. This may be simply a problem of shortage of funds, but it may be embedded much more deeply in the formal bureaucracies which surround so much formal teaching. With an inadequate travel budget, headquarters support for school-based in-service may not be possible. If funds severely limit continued provision of support materials or equipment, problems will occur. If there is insufficient administrative capacity or there are administrators not sympathetic to change, the innovation is vulnerable. Field's (1981) detailed analysis of the failure of generalist teaching in Papua New Guinea shows a particularly clear example of an inappropriate and incompetently managed attempt to promote an integrated curricula at lower secondary level without even a pilot project. Although pilot projects are increasingly used to generate and promote educational innovations, Crossley (1984b) has a number of cautionary messages about their potential to create unrealistic expectations, the difficulties of extension phases, and the resource implications. Above the implementation level of ministries, political commitment to educational change needs to be supported by appropriate economic and managerial policies, as Saunders and Vulliamy's (1983) analysis of attempts to promote practical curricula in Papua New Guinea and Tanzania demonstrates.

What the preceding indicates is that in analyzing any failure to shift from formalistic to meaning style teaching, to use Beeby's terminology, we should not necessarily look to conservative teacher resistance as a rationale. Crossley (1984a) and Morris (1985) emphasize that the conceptual approach provided by the barriers to change implies that failure of teachers to innovate may be rational. This approach suggests that teachers' perceptions of the realities of the educational system and the context in which it functions govern their professional behaviors to a marked extent. The mental constructs used by teachers to classify this reality are influenced by the educational environment in which they operate, providing stability in educational systems marked by change. The perceptual and contextual factors, which the systems view tends to overlook, can therefore have a major influence on attempts to change the quality of teaching, as Beeby (1979) himself has emphasized in his assessment of the Indonesian education system.

POSITIVE ADVANTAGES OF FORMALISM

The preceding may be misconstrued as supporting formalistic teaching by default, by virtue of a series of negative verdicts on the alternatives. This is not our intent. Formalism may also be considered as having positive value in itself. To some extent, the case for this is, of course, a mirror image of the preceding.

Formalistic teaching involves organized processing of fixed syllabuses and textbooks, with the main emphasis on memorizing of basic facts and principles. Teachers dominate roles, with students generally passive, although limited overt teacher-student and student-student interaction may be permitted under conditions strictly controlled by the teacher. Students are often set individual work, but other types of activity, such as group work, are infrequent. While many modern educationists do not approve of formalism, it is desirable and effective in many educational and cultural contexts. It is compatible with societies which value respect for authority and which regard ritual as meaningful in itself. It is consistent with formalistic teacher training, inspections, and examination systems, providing a base on which to build in the many situations where teachers and students feel comfortable with it. With lower cognitive levels, in particular, formalistic teaching is effective at promoting learning. Its functionality in schools and classrooms with poor facilities is a positive asset, although good facilities will make it more effective. In these contexts, the question to ask is not, how can we improve the quality of teaching by promoting alternatives to formalism, but, how can we improve the quality of formalism?

The main barrier to an acceptance of formalism as having desirable properties is, it seems to us, its connotation to Westerners of a domineering authoritarianism. More typical is a benevolent paternalism, as found in a classroom observation study in Papua New Guinea. The study found teachers did nearly all the structure, soliciting, and reacting; pupils did almost none of these but did all the responding. While critical of such an approach, Dunkin (1977, p. 10) found it appropriate to comment that "the teachers were warm and supportive in their dealings with the children and the atmosphere in all classes was one of enthusiasm and interest." If this is typical of other countries, then the affective consequence of formalistic teaching may indeed be rather more positive than is commonly assumed.

IMPROVING THE QUALITY OF FORMALISTIC TEACHING

One of the characteristics of educational innovations is their high cost and, given some of the evidence referred to in this paper, their apparent lack of cost-effectiveness. What does the research literature indicate to us about cost-effective alternatives to current practice, which are nonetheless compatible with the predominant formalism in the classrooms of the lesser-developed countries? We shall refer to four possibilities:

1. modification of examination systems;
2. provision of textbooks;
3. provision of supplementary language readers; and
4. use of distance education for in-service programs.

The most complex of the available options is to utilize the power of the examination system to change teachers' and pupils' expectations. If curricular innovations are unlikely to succeed because they are incompatible with the requirements of the examination system, one solution within the power of educational authorities is to change the system. The dominant function of examinations is selection for higher levels of education and for employment. This practice is usually norm-referenced as the assessment system merely has to differentiate students according to their relative performance. One alternative is criterion- or domain-referenced testing, which concentrates on assessing students' ability to achieve defined educational objectives, although the same information can also be used to rank students on their performance and can therefore meet the selection function as well (Quansah, 1985). Indeed, under criticism from proponents of criterion-referenced testing, norm-referenced examinations are now much more likely to be tied to explicit learning objectives than formerly. The value of doing this is that the objectives themselves can be made to promote the desired types of learning. This is simple in principle, but the practice is time consuming, highly technical, requires computer facilities to do even on a moderate scale, and is therefore expensive of time, skills, and money. It also requires the will and finance to systematically rewrite syllabuses in performance terms and to continuously provide appropriate materials. Clearly, we are looking at the sort of curriculum change which could easily take 10 to 15 years to work its way through a school system, and which is not to be undertaken lightly.

More limited and cost-effective, especially in large-scale systems, is the provision of textbooks. Since the mid-1970s, a considerable literature has built up since a range of research generally revealed positive associations between textbook provision and student achievement (Heyneman, Farrell, & Sepulveda-Stuardo, 1978). In light of this, the World Bank has been notable for funding a considerable number of textbook projects. While school texts will tend to be more effective if carefully written in relation to integrated performance objectives, it is possible to do so without rewriting the original syllabuses or renovating examination systems. Once written, large scale production rapidly reduces unit costs, although the design and logistical problems can be considerable (Altbach, 1983). Formalistic teachers normally find textbooks compatible with their teaching style and can use them to set practice tasks, class reading, and homework. The bottom line is that a student with a teacher ill trained in a particular subject can at least continue to learn independently from a textbook.

One innovation to do with book supply has been tested with high success in Fiji (Elley & Mangubhai, 1981a, 1981b). The "Book Flood" made available to students in grades four to six large quantities of books for daily reading. The interesting thing about this experiment was that classes taught by teachers who had undergone in-service training in a shared book method did not perform significantly better than those where teachers were not provided with assistance other than instruction to have 20 to 30 minutes of silent reading a day. Both groups had much higher proportions of students passing the grade six examination than a control group, with the benefit of the program accruing to all examined subjects. Here is a simple method for improving student achievement involving low costs, little support, and easy for even the most lackluster teacher to implement.

Finally, the potential of distance education for teacher in-service can be considered. In a simple experimental study, Biniakunu (1982) found improved student performance in Zaire was associated with a correspondence in-service course for teachers untrained in teaching the language. No other assistance was given teachers. As a cost-effective alternative to other types of in-service, this approach bears investigation, although it should be noted that the economics of distance learning are such that it is better reserved for courses with large-scale enrollments (Guthrie, 1985, pp. 87-90).

CONCLUSION

Formalistic teaching is not an aberration distorting the goals of education systems. It is frequently part of, and highly compatible with, a symbiotic whole. It is not problematic, it is symptomatic. Given the inability of educational systems to cope with revolutionary change, the future for improving the quality of teaching in many lesser-developed countries lies in operating within the constraints of formalistic systems and in working at improving the quality of formalism.

In citing four examples of cost-effective innovations compatible with formalistic teaching, we are not recommending their uncritical adoption. Borrowing innovations from other lesser-developed countries can be as questionable as from developed countries. Educational effectiveness is so dependent on context that sweeping solutions are unusual. Indeed, a survey of research by Avalos and Haddad (1981, pp. 22-24) found that in some countries liberal alternatives to formalism can be effective, particularly with higher cognitive skills. However, the types of innovation summarized above do merit investigation and, perhaps, experimentation. Importantly, they indicate that there are alternatives to improving the quality of teaching which do not involve complex curriculum development projects and which need not threaten the competence of classroom teachers. The tendency is to look for complex solutions to complex problems, but on occasion simple solutions may suffice.

SECTION THREE

INTERVENTION MECHANISMS FROM THE DEVELOPED WORLD

CHAPTER TEN

EDUCATIONAL RENEWAL AND STAFF DEVELOPMENT

Per Dalin

In this chapter, we will outline our present best understanding of educational renewal, particularly as it relates to teachers and efforts to improve the quality of teaching. Educational renewal is defined here as any systematic attempt to improve educational practice in relation to desired objectives as seen by the appropriate decision-making body. Any systematic attempt to improve a school or classroom is a time consuming, complex, and difficult process. It is not an event but a process involving the thinking, attitudes and behavior of many people, not just the students and the teachers, but other people both in a school, and institutions beyond the school (Hoyle, 1973; Carnoy & Levin, 1976; Dalin, 1978; Hurst, 1983; Lillis, 1983).

Although most of the literature available to us comes from the developed world, some valuable literature is beginning to emerge from the developing world. The Asian Programme of Educational Innovation for Development (APEID) has produced some important works (e.g., APEID, 1981a, 1981b, 1985), as well as the Paris office of UNESCO in its Experiments and Innovations in Education series (e.g., Huberman, 1973; Churchill, 1976; Ariyadasa, 1976b; UNESCO, 1978c). A growing number of doctoral dissertations focusing on the process of change are beginning to emerge (e.g., Ahmad, 1986).

The developing world is beginning to face problems that have existed for some time in the developed world (Crossley, 1980a, 1980b). Whereas in recent decades countries in the developing world have defined their problems as simple access to school and the supply of schools and teachers, they are now beginning to face the problem of quality improvements in their schools. As they do this, they have been adopting similar models and making similar assumptions about schools as organizations that industrialized countries have adopted and made, even though these are now being challenged and replaced by new models and assumptions (Huberman, 1976; Oliveros, 1975a; Salamone & Salamone, 1982; Wells & Chang, 1986). One intention of this chapter is to suggest new directions that may be taken in the developing world in terms of the process of educational renewal.

THE CONVENTIONAL CHANGE MODEL

Most of the change process literature is based on a linear model, on the assumption that intentional change can be understood as a Planning-Development-Implementation-Institutionalization-Dissemination process. That is, innovations are assumed to follow a sequence of phases, including a basic and applied research phase, followed by a development phase with field testing and evaluation, followed by a demonstration and dissemination phase. A basic assumption of this model is also that the teacher at a school plays a relatively passive role in the process. The teacher is regarded as a "target of change," a person who is in need of new materials and techniques.

This model has usually been maintained in most government and donor agency projects involving the change process. The "products" of development projects are typically "put on" schools to help them improve (Watson, 1983). Even though the managers of these projects have long recognized the shortcomings of such a model, the conditions under which they operate necessitate that they continue to use that model, because of the following:

1. The model fits well with the idea of someone planning, someone developing, someone else implementing, and so on. It fits with the picture of a *rational bureaucratic organization*. In this

tradition, therefore, research questions related to *roles,* to the use of different *interventions*, and the use of *resources* are central to a change process.

2.   The model fits well with the assumption that organizations are *goal-seeking*, and, therefore, that the renewal effort is something of value to schools. From this perspective "innovations" are unquestionably good things. After all, a major change effort, well planned and with large amounts of development funds, must surely be beneficial for schools The *value* of the innovation is seldom questioned.   In this tradition, researchers would ask questions related to the *degree of adaptation* (change in the original concept), *conditions* in the system that would favor adoption, and interventions that would "tune" the system to accept the innovation would be central to a change process research study.

3.   The model also fits well with the assumption of consensus. Innovations with a "hierarchical base," being decided at a high level of the organization or being supported by "heavy" research and development work, tend to iron out local criticism. After all, it has been tested in a number of settings and found superior to present practice. It supports a consensus view of the world. Therefore, research questions related to value and ideological differences, such as the extent to which new practices would benefit some students, teachers and schools more than others, are seldom asked.   Questions are rather *pragmatic*, like what kind of professional support is most effective? It fits with a *technocratic perspective* of educational change (House, 1981).

4.   The model fits with the picture of the teacher as a *consumer*. He/she is at the end of the change-chain. Somehow a number of people and institutions have worked to develop something that will benefit the teacher and his/her students. There is just one little problem: the teacher needs to appreciate this, get the necessary skills, and "implement" the innovation. With a sufficient number of teachers demonstrating the new practice, somehow, it will be institutionalized.

5.   The model also fits the concern of researchers, who typically focus on the fit between traditional and new practice, on the *concerns* of teachers (Hall, 1979), on the teachers' mastery of new practice (Huberman & Miles, 1984) and on the conditions that would favor *implementation* (Fullan, 1982).

We have observed several schools that have attempted to innovate according to the traditional change model, by adopting externally developed "innovations." In a great number of cases we have found that although some of these projects may have improved practice in some way, they have had several unintended side-effects. Some schools have used so much extra time and energy that they have no more left for other development needs. More seriously, the real problems of the school are often put aside, and may even worsen over time, so that the staff becomes less willing to use extra energy to cope with them. Some school problems are clearly *caused* by the same external forces and conditions. That, however, does not mean that they can be *resolved* by the same remedies, because the unique mix of people, processes, and resources in each school defines how external conditions are dealt with. We may find excellent strategies to assist schools to adapt and implement externally defined and developed "innovations." The school may well gain in some aspects, but it may be left with its real problems unresolved.

In recent years, a growing number of change process researchers have come to recognize the problems related to the traditional change model and have challenged it. Scholars such as Matthew Miles (1980; Huberman & Miles, 1984), Richard Schmuck (Schmuck, Runkel, & Arends, 1977), and Michael Fullan (1982) are beginning to formulate a different type of paradigm, which takes a broader cultural perspective on educational change. In the remainder of this chapter we shall provide some insights into this paradigm.

THE SOURCE OF PLANNED CHANGE

In our work at IMTEC, based in Oslo, Norway, we have engaged in over 200 studies of educational change, where the school as an organization has been the focus. We have been interested in how the school as an organization is able to renew its practice. Sometimes the change process has been facilitated due to external assistance, pressure, or resources. Sometimes it is a locally initiated and supported change process, and in other cases it is a school-internal process, initiated by the school head, one or more teachers, or even the students. In most cases school change reflects a "Mutual Adaptation and Development Process" involving the interaction of internal, creative interests and external pressures for change (Dalin, 1973, 1978). The capacity of the school to engage in internal reform activities and the capacity of the school to respond to external pressures for reform are outlined in Figure 1.

Four extremes are described as follows:

(Low, Low): This is a type of school that favors traditional practice. It is usually "loosely coupled," teachers are classroom-based and fairly isolated from their colleagues, few changes are initiated internally and the school does not respond easily to pressures from the environment.

(Low, High): This is a school that responds easily to pressures from the environment (including the Superintendent's office). The staff responds to demands for change, participate in in-service activities and try to adopt "innovations." It is only by chance, however, that these new practices help the school to resolve any of its basic problems. "The school" has not worked sufficiently as an organization to understand itself, to appreciate its strengths and identify its weaknesses. The simple adaptation of new practices may be "a good thing"--but the school adopted innovations are rarely connected with the school itself.

FIGURE 1
Mutual Adaptation and Development Process

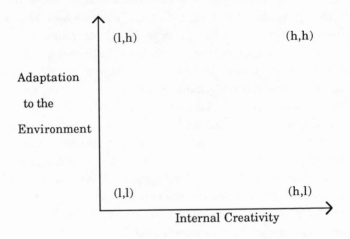

(High, Low): This is a school that is constantly working to improve its internal processes. It goes through regular internal organizational analysis, has developed a cooperative climate, develops a number of internally driven innovations and becomes known as an "innovative school." Teachers usually work together in "projects," and the school functions as an organizational unit. It becomes, however, increasingly less and less interested in demands from the environment. It begins to "protect" itself from "the market," and continues to pay little attention to the environment. It becomes isolated and runs the risk of becoming irrelevant in terms of satisfying community needs.

(High, High): This is a type of school that has the capacity to deal with its own internal needs for change and to adapt positively to environmental pressures. It will not adopt innovations from the outside but rather try to "fit" an innovation into its own needs, through a process that is openly discussed and understood. It will use external assistance when needed; however, it will usually try to manage its own development processes.

Our investigations of school change has demonstrated that only "High, High" schools, as a rule, engage in genuine educational renewal. We usually refer to these as creative schools (Huberman, 1973). For any change process to take root in a school, it needs to meet both external needs, based on real needs of the community/society, and internal needs of students and staff.

THE "REAL NEEDS" MODEL OF CHANGE

We at IMTEC have found that four factors, as illustrated in Figure 2, are essential conditions for effective educational renewal to take place. The interaction of these four factors constitutes a general model of educational renewal, which we call a "Real Needs" model:

Real Needs: The term "Real Needs" is problematic. Who's needs? Who's understanding of "needs?" Short-term or long-term needs? Are the needs in conflict with each other? Are they the same *across* schools? We understand *real needs*

FIGURE 2
The "Real Needs" - Model of Education Change

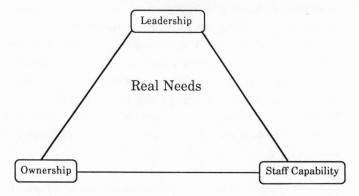

as those expressed by the collective students, parents, teachers and leaders at the school level. In order to determine real needs, a "needs assessment" must be conducted at the school level.

Leadership: Many researchers have observed the need for leadership in educational change. It is somewhat unclear what role the headmaster and the superintendent play and should play in the change process; however, there is little doubt that there is a leadership function to be played. We have found that effective "change management" is dependent on a number of situational variables, e.g., the characteristics of the innovation (e.g., complexity, need for resources, etc.), the decision makers of the school, whether it is a traditional loosely coupled school, a school with a project tradition, or a "problem-solving school" (Dalin, 1986), and the characteristics of the leader. In general the effective leaders fit their style to the culture of the school ("situational leadership") to stimulate creativity, and acceptance and mastery of new practices. They provide "shelter conditions" for experiments (new practices need time to succeed), a "forum" to exchange experiences, and sufficiently close and relevant follow-up.

Ownership: Even if a project meets real needs of individual students, groups of students or teachers, it may well be rejected. Teaching is a value-based profession. Teachers do *believe* in what they do. It may not always be clear why certain practices are valued; however, teachers must be convinced that new practices support their basic perspectives on teaching and learning and the upbringing of children. They must, therefore be actively involved in the process of deciding what to do, somewhat akin to the early design of the Peruvian model for innovation in the 1970s (Churchill, 1976).

We do not find that it is necessary for teachers to *invent* a project to own it. Teachers may welcome a project from other staff members or external agencies. The crucial element is that teachers are *participating as professionals*, not as passive consumers. They need to air their concerns, discuss the basic assumptions of the project, be convinced that it "works," and *contribute* with their experiences. This certainly will result in an *adapted* project, sometimes even a different project from the originally conceived idea, but the chances that the project fits real needs and will be "carried" by the teachers are much higher.

Staff Capability: Most educational change efforts imply changes in attitudes and behavior of staff. We know from a number of studies that changes in teaching behavior is a complex and time-consuming process. It may take as much as 10-15 times of practice of a new skill until it can be used effectively and creatively (Joyce & Showers, 1980). Huberman and Miles (1984) found that it may take 6-18 months of practice under supervision and support before "mastery."

LIMITING ORGANIZATIONAL FACTORS

Even when the factors listed above are all in place, there remain certain *necessary organizational conditions* for educational renewal to take place.

Diversity of Goals: Educational objectives are many, diverse, and often in conflict with each other. Any effort to improve practice would usually strengthen some part of the objectives, neglect or even reduce the importance of others. Discussions over values and the mission of the school may, therefore, often block an innovative project.

Unclear Technology: Although we do increasingly know more about how learning takes place and the effects of various instructional strategies, our knowledge base is still weak. It is phenomenological in nature, i.e., it is contingent upon a number of situational variables, and in the school setting, as we know it, it becomes more of an art than a science. Teachers know that they have to rely on their own experience, that the educational theory they once learned has helped them only marginally, and they are therefore quite hesitant to move into "another experiment."

Documentation of Outcomes: Partly as a consequence of goal diversity, but also due to the nature of the objectives it is very hard actually to *document* that certain outcomes have been achieved. In certain rather narrow areas of educational achievement we do have somewhat reliable measures, in others we are far from being able to document results. In some cases we do not know how to do it, in other cases outcomes can only be appreciated several years after schooling has taken place. This often leads to one-sided measurements (and thereby goal shifting). More important in this respect, it does not provide the necessary *incentives* actually to reach the objectives. When no one can ever document what I do--why do it? And, moreover, why bother trying to do something different from what I do today?

Professional Autonomy: The teaching job is a lonely job. In only very few schools do teachers work together. The normal pattern is still one teacher to one class. The individual teacher has considerable professional autonomy. Since objectives often are unclear, the technology uncertain and results difficult to document, the dangers are that teachers *do not share* their experiences in a systematic way. It becomes more comfortable, with all the uncertainties and contingencies that a teacher has to deal with, to keep it to one's self. Isolation becomes the norm.

A number of *second order* characteristics follow from the above. Several organizational researchers have, for example, observed that teachers seldom are supervised, that students are fairly tightly controlled and have little influence, that parents have minimal influence, and that instruction is traditional and standardized.

THE PHASES OF PLANNED CHANGE

In our studies of change in different schools, we have found that schools engage in fairly predictable phases of a cyclic nature. We have identified three major *cycles of development,* the first phase of which is outlined in Figure 3.

Contractual Phase

The needs for change within the school are matched with perceived pressures for change from the environment, and preliminary "negotiations" take place. Usually only a few teachers and leaders are involved in these first efforts. From Figure 3-1, we see that both environmnental and internal conditions lead to a recognition of the need to change in the school.

Mobilization Phase

Necessary resources, assistance and cooperation are established. At this stage the partners begin to develop a common ideology and norms--essential to the climate for development. Still, only one or a few teachers and leaders are involved.

First "Trial and Error" Phase

New practices are tried, "project learning" takes place, and the first rough experiences are gained. At this stage the developmental activities may come to an end. It depends, according to our data, among other things, on 1) the perceived value of the new practices, 2) the degree of support received, 3) the degree of internal leadership support, 4) the degree of organizational consensus, and 5) the position of the innovators in the organization. In Traditional schools (see above) where "loose coupling" is the norm, it is usually one or two teachers who volunteer to try a new practice. It may start and end in their classrooms. They may also, however, gradually recruit

FIGURE 3-1

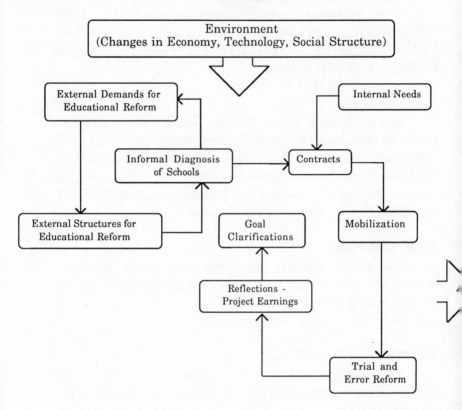

new teachers if the conditions are right, and leaders understand and play their roles (see Dalin, 1986). In schools that come through the first "trial and error" phase, a reflection phase is begun.

Reflection Phase

Many schools have difficulties moving from an "individual" trial-and-error phase to a more cooperative phase, probably due to the degree of "loose coupling " that characterizes so much of education.

Those educators who are able to move beyond individual endeavors, usually devote great time and energy to a reflection of their previous experience. In the process they begin to engage other teachers in what they are doing, leading to the second phase of the cycle as outlined in Figure 3-2. Their initial activity is to assess critically what has been going on. This reflection is seldom based on formal "evaluations." The practicing teachers reflect on the value of the innovation and the process of managing it. Based on the early experiences the *real needs* of the teachers and students become more apparent, which leads to further adaptations of the innovation, which leads into the next cycle, having the general outline found in Figure 3-3.

FIGURE 3-2

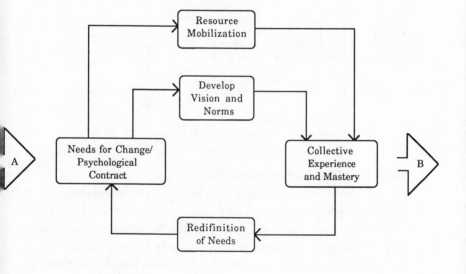

FIGURE 3-3

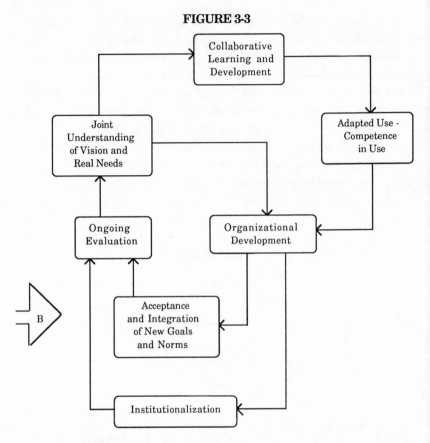

Experienced Based Development Phase

Values, norms, and needs are more clearly established, where several people in the school may "negotiate" conditions for further work, and where "contracts" with those in the external environment (usually the superintendent) are more clearly defined. As the school moves into the second cycle, more teachers have joined, and although external assistance may be available, the most experienced teachers take a lead and support newcomers. The development of values, ideologies and norms continue (and changes take place partly due to new members). The school may move into the next phase.

Mature and Cooperative Phase

Several factors, other than the "loose coupling" characteristic of schools seem to have importance to move into a cooperative phase, including:

1.   The greater the advantage of the innovation as seen by the practicing teacher, the more the chances for a cooperative activity.

2.   The more relevant support, technically and professionally, to assist in the mastery of new practice, the more likely the school will master a more cooperative phase.

3.   The degree to which the early innovators and the school leaders invite constructive criticism and participation of newcomers the more the innovation will be shared.   The "mature and cooperative" phase may lead, over time, to the next phase.

New Common Practice Phase

Most teachers in the school are involved in the fine-tuning of new practices and it becomes the norm, which, if the practice is sufficiently different from old practice, may lead into the next phase.

Organizational Development Phase

In this phase procedures, organizational structures, and resource allocations are altered to better fit new practices. This may lead to the "generalization of new goals," and possibly to new needs for change.

What this paradigm illustrates is that the process of educational change is a complex, time-consuming, cyclic, and fragile process. It usually takes years. It goes through several "cycles" with increasingly more teachers involved. The *nature of the school* and school-related cultural factors determine the direction of the change process.   In addition, in all cases the motor to development is the contradictions found between existing external and internal needs.

STAFF DEVELOPMENT AND EDUCATIONAL RENEWAL

Because our focus in this book is on teachers, we shall give some detail to the issue of staff development, as it operates in the context of educational renewal. By staff development, we mean "school-focused in-service education," an attempt to provide an entire staff with the necessary knowledge and skills to run an effective school.

In studies of educational renewal from OECD countries (Bolam, 1981) as well as from the developing world (Verspoor, 1987; Peiris, 1983), staff development is coming to be seen as one of the key strategies to improve educational practice. Since Lortie's classical study, *The Schoolteacher* (Lortie, 1975), an increased interest in the actual work situation of teachers has resulted in a number of school improvement studies focusing on *implementation issues* (Fullan, 1982). We are beginning to know more about the *concerns* of teachers facing the challenges of behavior change (Loucks & Hall, 1979; Huberman & Miles, 1984). We have a better understanding of how different individuals can gain from staff development (Joyce, Hersh, & McKibbin, 1983). We know more about how to make staff development more effective (Joyce & Showers, 1980), and we are beginning to move toward a comprehensive theory of educational renewal (Dalin, 1986).

The picture we have been drawing of the change process is a complex one, and it takes different forms in different kinds of schools. The natural consequence is that *staff development* will also take different forms. Let us first try to answer the question, why should a teacher want to participate in staff development?

A Challenging Job

A routine job that does not challenge the jobholder does not stimulate the need for staff development. It is when the job is a *real challenge* that a need for more knowledge and skills becomes apparent. Most teachers are confronted with new and challenging problems in their job, not the least by the changes in the *social capital* of children coming to school (Coleman, 1987), in the diverse demands made on the school, in that the subject areas themselves are continuously expanding. There is no doubt that most teachers feel a need for further education.

Joint Problems to Resolve

Although the individual teacher may find his or her job a challenge, and may feel a need for further education, this need may best be understood and interpreted as an individual training need. In spite of this, we find that many of the new challenges schools are facing can be best resolved jointly by the entire staff or groups of teachers. We also find, however, that due to the loosely coupled school organization, in many schools an understanding of the problems as common problems is not developed.

A New Mandate to Fulfill

Schools sometimes get new challenges as organizations. An example is to "mainstream" handicapped students who earlier have been in special institutions. This represents a new challenge for the school as an organization to resolve. There is no need to have a joint understanding of a problem, but there is a need to appreciate a new organizational challenge.

We see these three above issues as typical illustrations of the need for staff development. How schools are going to meet these needs depends largely on those making the decisions in the school and the available resources for staff development. It would, for example, be premature to introduce a full-scale staff development program as a support for an innovative project when only one or a few teachers are trying out a new practice, and others may not even know about it. More appropriate would possibly be a close collegial or consultant relationship with the concerned teachers. This may develop into a staff-development program, as the school moves from a first trial-and-error phase into a more mature cooperative phase.

RESOURCES FOR STAFF DEVELOPMENT

Before we discuss staff development in schools, it may be of interest to see what other organizations do to meet the challenges of staff development. As organizations meet new challenges and understand the need for staff development, they usually go through three phases of development:

Individual Phase

Needs for new competence are "discovered" by individuals and work units throughout the organization. Needs are met without any systematic organizational plan, basically by the individual identifying training opportunities and finding the resources to attend.

Project Related Training

As an organization gets involved in major development projects needs for staff development become clearer and are identified as common needs. The organization usually organizes staff development by purchasing external courses. Usually such courses are of a general nature, not directly connected with the needs of the organization--and they are usually expensive. This is the time for consulting firms, colleges and universities to offer their standard programs.

Integrated Staff Development

As organizations mature, they begin to learn the costs and benefits of external courses and begin to discover their own internal resources, a new and mature phase of staff development takes place. Staff development is seen as an integrated part of organizational development, and tailor-made to the needs for development. As much as possible staff development takes place *on-the-job,* the essential learning takes place close to the individual and the group, and external assistance is seen as a necessary *supplement* to internal activities.

Figure 4 illustrates the strategies that can be applied for staff development. It starts with a *challenging job.* It provides for *collegial cooperation and feedback,* it provides for supervision and *performance appraisal,* and it gives opportunities for individual reading and studies.

Most organizations also use *job rotation* as a means to exploit the resources in the organization for staff development. The resources in the *work group* should first be explored. Then the resources of other work groups can potentially be of use, or an individual with project-experience can be used as a resource person in a new work group.

When these learning opportunities are fully exploited, then tailor-made development-relevant courses and consultancies are utilized. These are courses with a rather narrow skill-oriented focus that draws on the experiences of other individuals and organizations. At this stage there might still be a need to utilize *standard* courses from the educational system (e.g., colleges or universities).

So far, schools have been rather immature in their staff development efforts. Most schools are in the "individual phase" mainly using the *external* standardized courses--the least effective strategies for staff development and probably the most expensive approach. As we have seen from other organizations, effective staff development is a question of *organizing* internal and external resources. To move schools towards more effective staff development, we would suggest the following strategies:

Collegial Cooperation

Even in the most traditional schools there would be opportunities for collegial cooperation. This may be the first opportunity to appreciate the resources that are available in the school already.

FIGURE 4
Staff Development Resources

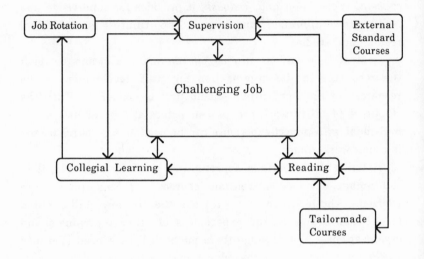

Supervision

Many schools are not used to any form of supervision. In the most traditional school cultures the least threatening form of supervision is a *collegial* form. In other cases it is the job of master teachers or the headmaster. Regular supervision will help to identify strengths and weaknesses and to give staff appropriate work challenges.

Performance Appraisals

Few schools go to the next step, namely to institutionalize a form of performance appraisals. Through regular appraisals (e.g., once a year) it is possible, not only for the supervisor to discuss the need for staff development, but also for the teacher to discuss ways in which the school can help in his/her development.

School-Based Review

We have seen that needs assessment is a weak part of the change process. Teachers are also often isolated and a sufficient *shared* understanding of strength and weaknesses does not exist. It is difficult then to develop a strategy for staff development. For 12 years IMTEC has used the "Institutional Development Program" (IDP) as the main vehicle to school-based reviews (Dalin & Rust, 1984). It provides a broad data-base as a resource for a school-based development process, and necessary assistance in defining needs and to develop a school-based program.

Improving Staff Development

Joyce and Showers, as well as other staff development experts, have identified critical elements in successful staff development activities (Joyce & Showers, 1980). Effective courses, in their view, need relevant theory, demonstration of new practices, opportunity to use new skills and get feedback, and coaching over time in the classroom. Much attention should be given to the actual process of staff development.

Organized Job Rotation

The teaching profession gives very few possibilities for meaningful job-rotation. It has only career-ladder possibilities, which severely limit the opportunities for professionally concerned teachers (Derr, 1986). We see opportunities to better utilize local pedagogical centers, active use of colleges and universities (external staff opportunities) to provide opportunities for "job rotation."

SUMMARY

Schools need to discover their own needs and resources, to organize the school in such a way that internal resources are fully utilized, to cooperate more effectively with external research, development and training agencies, and to integrate all staff development activities in a strategic plan for development.

For all of this to take place we believe that both schools, local school authorities and "support" institutions need to work more closely together. There is a need for *partnership*. There is a need to *train educational leaders* in the process of educational change, to train external and internal school based development consultants, to develop materials and procedures for the processes suggested above and to free resources for a different kind of professional development than what we have experienced to date.

Educational renewal implies organizing the school and the local school system in such a way that internal resources can be fully utilized. The approach to *staff development* taken in this paper is a low-cost approach. The total skill level of the organization needs to be strengthened, not only the skills of the individual teacher, and that is why staff development is a key strategy to ensure educational change capabilities. From this perspective staff development and educational renewal are *mutually* dependent. It is unlikely that school and classroom improvement will occur without staff development. It is also unlikely that genuine staff development will occur without educational renewal as the driving force.

CHAPTER ELEVEN

DEVELOPMENT AGENCY SUPPORT FOR THE IMPROVEMENT OF TEACHING IN ASIA

H. Dean Nielson
Pauline C. P. Chan

QUANTITATIVE EXPANSION VS QUALITATIVE IMPROVEMENT

In Asia, as in other parts of the developing world, the expansion of educational capacity has been dramatic over the past two decades. In part a reflection of rapidly growing economies and in part a demonstration of the cultural and political value placed on education, the countries in the region have given high priority to increasing the participation of its youth in education at all levels. For example, in the past few years universal primary education has been attained or approached in several countries (notably those in East and Southeast Asia plus Sri Lanka) and has been made the object of campaigns in the others. Countries with oil reserves experienced particularly rapid expansion in the late 1970s. For example, Indonesia during this period provided one million new primary school places per year. Others, experiencing rapid industrialization, like China, Thailand, and Malaysia, have developed plans to universalize lower secondary education in the foreseeable future.

In South Asia, investment in education has lagged behind that in the rest of Asia. For example, in Pakistan the proportion of national budget spent on education has never risen above 5% in recent years, whereas in Malaysia it has been over 20%. In addition, participation rates have been lower, especially for girls (in

Bangladesh, Pakistan, and Nepal 50% or fewer of the girls in the appropriate age group attend primary school). Nevertheless, even in this sub-region commitment to quantitative expansion has been growing--in Pakistan the proportion of GNP devoted to education increased by 25% between 1982 and 1986--and enrollment rates have been moving constantly upward.

There is a sense, however, that this expansion has been purchased at the price of educational quality. The new rural schools which have been built have often been staffed with inexperienced and "unqualified" teachers, youth barely out of the grades they will teach, whose only training has been a "crash course." The new generation of trained teachers, although growing to fill the gaps, is disappointing in many ways since teacher salaries are becoming less and less competitive. Despite this, teacher salaries still typically represent 80-90% of the recurrent costs of education, leaving precious little for books, teaching aids, equipment, building maintenance, supervision and curricular reform, all needed in order to produce effective student learning (Heyneman, 1984).

COMMITMENT TO IMPROVING THE QUALITY OF TEACHING

Since the mid-1970s policy-makers in the region have seemed to become more aware of the trade-offs they have made and have begun to place a higher priority on improving educational quality. In most cases, such efforts have begun with teacher training and upgrading. This choice seems to have been built on conventional wisdom rather than exhaustive study of alternatives. As simply stated in a recent UNESCO regional office document, ". . . pupil performance is a result of what teachers do . . . it follows that if teachers can be trained to do better, then the achievement level of pupils should rise" (UNESCO, 1986c, p. 3).

While this statement might appear simplistic and overly optimistic in light of research findings in Western industrialized countries (Coleman et al., 1966), the literature on determinants of educational achievement in developing countries does seem to support the general direction of this argument. For example, Heyneman and Loxley (1983) present evidence which seems to show that factors internal to the school, such as teacher quality and physical facilities, explain a much higher percent of the variance in achievement scores in poor countries (India, 88%; Egypt, 68%) than they do in relatively rich countries (United States, 35%; Sweden, 27%).

Such findings underscore the desirability of improving teacher quality but provide little insight into how this can be done. As mentioned above, constraints on teacher salaries make it difficult to attract highly capable and motivated new recruits. Conventional training programs, both pre- and in-service, are being expanded but with difficulty because of development fund shortages. Even as they expand, however, their effectiveness is being called into question. A review of research on teacher training in developing countries by Schiefelbein and Simmons (1981) has revealed findings echoed elsewhere in the literature (Lanier, 1986; Sykes, 1985), namely, that conventional teacher training and upgrading programs have little or no impact on student learning, that they are generally irrelevant to teacher needs and conditions, and that they are longer and more costly than necessary. The relevance of these findings to Asia, although not empirically established, is reflected in the conclusion from a recent UNESCO regional meeting of teacher educators that "traditional teacher training methods were not sufficient to cope with problems of underachievement" (UNESCO, 1986c, p. 5).

In response to this challenge, nontraditional teacher training programs are being developed in many parts of Asia. Two kinds of programs are becoming increasingly popular: teacher education through distance education and "field-based" teacher training. Such systems allow teachers to be upgraded "on site" using either self-instruction or small group learning processes. Although these new approaches seem to show promise, their development and dissemination are impeded by financial and bureaucratic constraints.

In sum, the developing countries of Asia have expanded their education systems rapidly over the past two decades but, it seems, often at the expense of quality.   Concerned about this imbalance, policy-makers have recently been placing more emphasis on improving school quality.   This has meant, among other things, taking steps to improve teacher effectiveness, either through expanding conventional teacher training programs or by experimenting with innovative programs which are field-based or self-instructional.   Their attempts to attract more capable and motivated trainees into the teaching profession have been frustrated by their inability to maintain competitive salaries.   As it is, teacher salaries consume 80-90% of recurrent costs in education.   Few funds are left for increasing teacher salaries, expanding training facilities, promoting research and development, and disseminating promising innovations.

DEVELOPMENT AGENCY SUPPORT: POTENTIAL AND PROSPECTS

Given inadequate domestic funds for improving the quality of teaching, the developing countries in Asia have turned to development agencies for financial and technical assistance.   They have sought help in building new teacher training facilities, in developing teacher training curricula, in the training of trainers, in research and experimentation and in the establishment of teacher support systems (in-service training and supervision).   Time pressure, the urgent need to put qualified teachers before a growing number of students, has spawned a variety of reforms and innovations, providing ample opportunities for creative assistance from the donor agency community.

But how receptive have development agencies been to this role? Has their support to educational development reflected the growing concern for educational quality and improved teaching in the developing countries?   What have been the trends in their support in this area over the past two decades?

Some observers (Weiler, 1979; Husen, 1979) have documented a growing sense of disenchantment with education and its role in development within donor countries starting in the mid-1970s. That and the conservative political and recessionary economic forces in the late '70s and early '80s might have led to reductions in levels of development agency support to education in recent years, just when concern for educational quality has been at its peak. Weiler (1983) demonstrated that donor OECD support for education development during this period reached a "steady state" in which domestic and donor agency spending on education barely kept pace with inflation. Has this been the case with development agency support in Asia, a region of relative optimism and respect for education and learning? What about the special case of support to programs for teaching quality improvement?

The purpose of this chapter is to examine some of these questions, using secondary data from development agency reports. Its particular objectives are to: 1) determine the magnitude of development agency support for improving the quality of teaching in Asia; 2) determine the distribution of such support according to development level (national income) and sub-region; 3) assess changes in that support over a recent 15-year time period; and 4) examine variations in the type of support provided.

APPROACH TO THE STUDY

Since we found no prior attempts to do this kind of analysis in the literature and since development agencies rarely consolidate information on topics, our initial approach was to consult individual development agency reports. Annual reports from 1970 to the present were examined in order to capture a wide enough time frame to reveal funding trends. Our interest was to identify projects which appeared to be mainly concerned with improving the quality of teaching. In cases where reports in the public domain did not provide us enough information to determine this, we sent away to the development agency for detailed project descriptions. In order to qualify as a "quality of teaching" (QUOTE) project, a project had to deal primarily with teacher training or upgrading, teacher supervision or support, improvement of teaching-learning systems at the school level, or the development of teacher training curricula. We further restricted the field to projects in primary and secondary (academic and technical) education. We did not include projects in nonformal education, adult education, higher education (except that for training teachers), curriculum development (except that for teacher training), physical facilities development (i.e., school building construction, materials development, textbook production), educational planning and management and teacher training in specialized subjects such as population or health education. Multifaceted projects covering teacher training as part of an integrated system (like some primary education projects) presented a special dilemma, since generally the documents we received did not provide separate cost estimates for the teacher training components. We decided to count the entire project as a QUOTE project if it seemed basically geared to improving teaching quality, even if some of the funding was for building construction, textbook development, and so forth. This has inevitably inflated our estimates of donor agency financial support for the improvement of teaching; on the other hand, we left out teacher training and upgrading efforts which were part of projects which were primarily for purposes other than teacher training, such as curriculum or textbook development. Since teacher upgrading efforts in such projects may have been substantial, this exclusion was seen as off-setting (with an undetermined degree of equivalency) the above overestimates.

An attempt was made to look at financial support, grant and loan, of the major "Western block" bilateral, multilateral, and private organizations (foundations and NGO's). It turned out that data on many European organizations were unavailable and the NGO's active in Asia did not cover formal education. In the end we included projects from the following development agencies:

- Aga Khan Foundation (AKF)

- Asian Development Bank (ADB)
- Australian Development Assistance Bureau (ADAB)
- British Council
- Canadian International Development Agency (CIDA)
- Ford Foundation
- International Bank for Reconstruction and Development (World Bank) (IBRD)
- International Development Research Centre (Canada) (IDRC)
- Swedish International Development Agency (SIDA)
- United States Agency for International Development (USAID)
- UNESCO
- UNICEF[1]
- United Nations Development Program (UNDP)

The recipient nations in Asia which we considered were the five major nations of South Asia (Bangladesh, India, Nepal, Pakistan and Sri Lanka), the five original members of ASEAN (Indonesia, Malaysia, Philippines, Singapore, and Thailand) and Papua New Guinea. Because of the recent emergence of China as a recipient nation, we also decided to include her but did not include the other nations and colonies of East Asia, namely North and South Korea, Taiwan, and Hong Kong. This list of twelve nations is thus not exhaustive of Asian nations, but it does cover most of the major development agency recipients. Also, since our search was based primarily on annual reports and project selection made on the basis of brief project descriptions, we expect that some important initiatives have, regrettably, been overlooked. Nevertheless, we feel that the list of over 100 projects which we compiled does present a fairly accurate general picture of development agency support in the above 12 countries over the past 15 years.

---

[1] Since UNICEF's independent contributions to teacher quality improvement were not available in summary form, we only included its contributions in concert with other organizations.

MAGNITUDE OF DEVELOPMENT AGENCY SUPPORT

Table 1 provides an indication of the level of development agency support for QUOTE projects during 1972-1986. A total of 106 such projects was identified, sponsored by the 13 agencies in 12 countries. The overall funding level was nearly a billion US dollars ($925,867,000), with 94% ($870,855,000) in the form of loans and 6% ($55,012,000) in the form of grants. Although these funding levels seem impressive, it should be pointed out that they only represent a small fraction of national educational expenditures. For example, the national budget for Indonesia for 1986-87 was US $126,728,000[2] or almost 2 1/2 times the total amount given in grants over the 15-year period.

In Table 1 the various countries are sorted into groups according to GNP/P per capita. The two relatively high income countries mounted 17 QUOTE projects over the period whereas the middle- and lower-income countries mounted 30 and 59, respectively. Large differences appear across groups when type of funding is compared. Higher and middle income countries acquired 80% of the loan support given whereas the lower income countries acquired fully 95% of the grant funds! Among those countries the two poorest, Bangladesh and Nepal (both having a GNP/C of around $150), acquired two to three times more than any other country or about 61% of all QUOTE grant funds. Among the recipients of loan funds, two countries, Indonesia and Malaysia, acquired the most--over 50% of all loan funds issued. Two other countries, China and India, the most populous in the region, acquired no loan funds at all.

TRENDS OVER TIME

Tables 2 and 3 present a view of the trends over time. In Table 2 the countries are sorted into groups according to development level (GNP/Capita), namely higher, medium, and lower. In Table 3

---

2   INDONESIA Education and Human Resources Sector Review, Economic and
Financial Analysis, Jakarta: Ministry of Education and Culture and US
Agency for International Development, April 1986.

TABLE 1

Number of Development Agency Supported QUOTE Projects and Funding Level (in 000's of USD) during 1972-86 by Country

	Country	Projects	Level of Funding Grant	Level of Funding Loan	Devt.Agencies Involved [1]
A.	GNP/C>US$2000				
	Singapore [2]	5	124	19,000	ADB,BC,IDRC
	Malaysia [3]	12	691	254,500	ADB,BC,IDRC,FF,WB
	SUBTOTAL	17	815	273,500	
B.	US$5000>NP/C <US$2000				
	Thailand	9	856	--	BC,IDRC,FF, UNESCO/UN
	Papua New Guinea	3	--	71,300	W B
	Philippines	6	801	100,000	WB,IDRC
	Indonesia [2]	12	460	240,000	WB,IDRC,ADB,CIDA
	SUBTOTAL	30	2,117	411,300	
C.	GNP/C<US$500				
	Pakistan	17	4,857	83,500	WB,ADB,AID,AKF, IDRC,UNESCO/UN
	Sri Lanka	8	4,036	16,250	UNESCO/UN&FIT, FIT,ADB,SIDA
	China	9	7,672	--	ADAB,CIDA,IDRC, UNESCO/UN
	India	6	2,224	--	FF,AKF,IDRC, UNESCO/UN
	Nepal	15	15,954	8,305	ADB/UN,AID,IDRC, UNESCO/UN
	Bangladesh	4	17,337	78,000	WB/UNICEF/SIDA/ UN,UNESCO/UN,AID
	SUBTOTAL	59	52,080	186,055	
D.	OVERALL TOTAL	106	55,012	870,855	

1 Development Agencies are as follows: ADAB=Australian Devt Asst Bureau; ADB=Asian Development Bank; AID=US Agency for Intl Devt; AKF=Aga Khan Foundation; BC=British Council; CIDA=Canadian Intl Devt Agency; FF=Ford Foundation; IDRC=Intl Devt Research Centre; SIDA=Swedish Intl Devt Agency; UNESCO; UNICEF; UN=UNDP; WB=World Bank

2 Funding level for one project not available.

3 Funding level for two projects not available.

TABLE 2

Number of QUOTE Projects by Development Level and Time Period
(Nos. in Brackets Are Average Projects Per Country)

Dev't Level*	1972-1976	1977-1981	1982-1986	OVERALL
Higher	4	9	4	17
n=2	[2]	[4.5]	[2]	[8.5]
Medium	6	17	7	30
n=4	[1.5]	[4.2]	[1.8]	[7.5]
Lower	6	18	35	59
n=6	[1]	[3]	[5.8]	[9.8]
TOTAL	16	44	46	106
N=12	[1.3]	[3.7]	[3.8]	[8.8]

*   Based on GNP/Capita. Higher=GN P/C>US$2000;
    Medium=US$500>GNP/C<US$2000; Lower=GNP/C<US$500.

TABLE 3

Number of QUOTE Projects by Geographic Region and Time Period
(Nos. in Brackets Are Average Projects Per Country)

Region	1972-1976	1977-1981	1982-1986	OVERALL
SE Asia	10	26	11	47
n=6	[1.7]	[4.3]	[1.8]	[7.8]
South Asia	6	16	28	50
n=5	[1.2]	[3.2]	[5.6]	[10.0]
China	--	2	7	9
TOTAL	16	44	46	106
N=12	[1.3]	[3.7]	[3.8]	[8.8]

they are sorted according to sub-region, Southeast Asia, South Asia, and China. The time periods are five-year blocks, 1972-1976, 1977-1981, and 1982-1986.

Earlier we mentioned that the middle 1970s were the years in which disenchantment with education as a key to development began. We also mentioned that in the late 1970s developing country educators began to focus on problems of educational quality. Our data show very modest levels of support during the first five years, 1972-1976. Without data from the preceding periods, it is hard to determine whether this is a reflection of agency disenchantment. What is remarkable is the dramatic increase in support during the subsequent five-year period, 1977-1981. During that period, the number of projects begun was almost three times greater than that during the previous period. Again, without data on the entire education sector, it is hard to tell whether or not this represents an overall increase in donor agency support to education or whether it represents a relative increase in the proportion devoted to QUOTE projects. In any case, it does represent a dramatic increase in support to this sub-sector, a level which is sustained in the most recent time period.

Although the overall number of new projects in the most recent period (1982-1986) was nearly the same as that in the second, the level of support across the various development levels changed radically from the second period to the third. For example, during 1977-81 the lower income countries negotiated almost the same number of new projects as the middle income countries did. During 1982-1986, however, lower income countries acquired five times more new projects than the middle income countries did! The average number of new projects negotiated by the poorer countries in that period was around three times that by in the upper- or middle-income countries. Over the entire 15-year period it appears that support to higher- and middle-income countries peaked in the second period, whereas support to the lower-income countries experienced accelerated growth.

Table 3 presents basically the same kind of analysis, except the groupings are by sub-region. Since the higher- and middle-income countries are basically in Southeast Asia, it is not surprising to find that support to them peaked in the second period. The poorer countries are those in South Asia and China. The table shows that much of the dramatic change among those countries from the second to the third period came as a result of developments in China. Whereas that country negotiated no new QUOTE projects in 1972-76, in 1982-86 it negotiated seven. All of this seems to signal a shift in development agency policies and global strategies, a point which will be covered briefly in the next section and in more depth in the last.

THE POLITICAL GEOGRAPHY OF DEVELOPMENT AGENCY SUPPORT

Table 4 shows the countries in which the various development agencies have supported QUOTE projects over the past 15 years. The countries on the table are arranged according to their relative geographical location from West (left) to East (right). The development agencies are arranged according the number of projects they supported, from high to low.

The International Development Research Centre of Canada appears to have supported the greatest number of QUOTE projects in Asia (28). Although its support appeared in all parts of the region, the bulk of it (over 70%) has been in the four ASEAN nations, Thailand, Indonesia, Philippines, and Malaysia. Since it was basically in support of research, its amounts were relatively modest (generally from $50-150,000). UNESCO (using funds from UNDP or "funds in trust" from developed countries) provided the second highest level of project support (22 projects). In contrast to IDRC its support was concentrated in the relatively poor nations of South Asia, especially Pakistan, Sri Lanka, and Nepal. Also in contrast to IDRC is the fact that its projects were generally large infrastructural development projects with funds averaging around $1,000,000 each.

TABLE 4

Number of QUOTE Projects by Development Agency and Country

Dev't Agency	PAK	IND	SRI	NEP	BAN	THA	MAL	SIN	INDO	PAP	PHI	CHI	TOT
IDRC	1	1	-	1	-	6	4	2	5	-	-	3	28
UNESCO/ UNDP	6	1	5*	4*	2	1	-	-	-	-	-	3	22
WORLD BK	2	-	-	-	1**	-	5	-	4	3	1	-	15
USAID	1	-	-	7	1	-	-	-	-	-	-	-	9
AFK	6	3	-	-	-	-	-	-	-	-	-	-	9
BR COUN	-	-	-	-	-	1	1	2	-	-	-	-	4
FORD FN	-	1	-	-	-	1	1	-	-	-	-	-	3
ADAB	-	-	-	-	-	-	-	-	-	-	-	2	2
CIDA	-	-	-	-	-	-	-	-	1	-	-	1	2
SIDA	-	-	1	-	1**	-	-	-	-	-	-	-	2
TOTAL	17	6	8	15	4	9	12	5	12	3	6	9	106

* Includes one project financed through "funds in trust."
** Since this is a jointly funded project, it is only counted once.

This, in fact, explains why such a high proportion of QUOTE grant funding has gone to the poor countries of South Asia.

The World Bank was next in the order of project support (15 projects). Like IDRC its support was concentrated in Southeast Asia. But like UNESCO/UNDP its funding levels were high, in fact, in the tens of millions of dollars. Of course these are all loans which the countries will have to pay back, but about half of them (those to the South Asian countries and some to Indonesia and Papua New Guinea) were "concessional loans" through the Bank's subsidiary, the International Development Association (IDA). Next on the list is the Asian Development Bank. This bank has specialized in loans related to technical vocational education and has been active across the region. Its loans have generally been smaller than those of the World Bank, but its terms are always concessional.

Further down are the bilateral and private sector agencies. Nine projects were identified for AID, all but two of them in Nepal, where there has been a large effort to provide radio assisted teacher upgrading (among other efforts). With the same number of projects is the Aga Khan Foundation, which is active only in the two countries, Pakistan and India, which have substantial numbers of Ismaili Moslems. After that are the British Council, the Ford Foundation, the Canadian International Development Agency, the Australian Development Assistance Bureau, and The Swedish International Development Agency. The first four of these five have been mainly active in Southeast Asia and China, whereas the last one, SIDA, has concentrated on South Asia.

Looking at the horizontal axis, it appears that Pakistan negotiated the highest number of projects (17) involving the greatest number of development agencies (6). Nepal negotiated the second highest number of projects (15), almost half of which were with USAID. Indonesia and Malaysia negotiated 12 projects each, mostly with the World Bank and IDRC. Thailand acquired nine projects, mostly from IDRC, and China the same number, the donors being IDRC, UNESCO/UNDP and ADAB. Those acquiring six projects or fewer were the Philippines, India, Singapore, Bangladesh, and Papua New Guinea: those to the Philippines were mostly from IDRC; to India from Aga Khan; to Singapore from IDRC and the British Council; to Bangladesh from UNESCO and the World Bank (and their associates); and to Papua New Guinea from the World Bank only.

From this brief look it is clear that agencies tend to have their special clients and, conversely, that countries tend to deal with only certain of the agencies. Such relationships have tended to hold over time, although recently there have been some changes, as the poorer countries begin to receive a larger proportion of the QUOTE support.

OBJECTIVES OF AGENCY SUPPORT

Project descriptions allowed us to examine the objectives of the various programs of support. Five different types of objectives appeared most frequently, namely: 1) technical assistance/specialist advice; 2) personnel training/teacher upgrading; 3) materials development; 4) Research studies/policy development; and 5) provision of facilities and equipment. Table 5 shows the types of support provided to each country by the various projects. Since one project may include more than one of the types of objectives, there are often more types listed for a country than there were projects. Types of support have been broken down by level of education (primary and secondary) as well as by country, and countries have been grouped by income level.

Table 5 shows that overall about the same number of project components went into the improvement of secondary education as into primary. In the higher- and lower-income countries there were somewhat more components in secondary education and in the middle-income countries more in primary education. At the individual country level the countries which put twice as many or more components into primary education projects were Thailand, the Philippines, India, and Bangladesh. Conversely, the countries

TABLE 5

Types of Agency Support by Country for Primary and Secondary Education

Type of Support Country	Primary						Secondary					
	TA	PT	MD	RS	PF	Total	TA	PT	MD	RS	PF	Total
Higher-Income												
Singapore	1	1	2	-	1	5	1	1	-	-	2	4
Malaysia	2	-	3	2	-	7	4	4	-	1	2	11
Sub-Total	3	1	5	2	1	12	4	4	-	1	4	15
%	25	8	42	17	8	100	33	33	-	7	27	100
Middle-Income												
Thailand	1	1	3	5	-	10	1	1	1	2	-	5
Papua New Guinea	-	1	-	-	2	3	-	1	-	-	2	3
Philippines	-	1	2	3	1	7	-	-	-	-	-	-
Indonesia	1	4	3	3	1	12	3	4	1	1	2	11
Sub-total	2	7	8	11	4	32	4	6	2	3	4	19
%	6	22	25	34	13	100	21	32	10	16	21	100
Lower-Income												
Pakistan	2	8	4	2	5	21	3	8	3	3	4	21
Sri Lanka	1	3	3	-	-	7	3	6	3	-	-	12
China	4	3	2	-	-	9	7	7	1	2	1	18
India	-	3	2	2	3	10	1	-	1	-	1	3
Nepal	-	5	3	3	1	12	4	3	2	1	1	11
Bangladesh	3	2	-	-	2	7	2	1	-	-	1	4
Sub-total	10	24	14	7	11	66	20	25	10	6	8	69
%	15	36	21	11	17	100	29	36	14	9	12	100
TOTAL	15	32	27	20	16	110	29	36	12	10	16	103
%	14	29	24	18	15	100	28	35	12	10	15	100

which devoted twice as many or more components to secondary education were Sri Lanka and China.

At the primary level the higher-income countries tended to channel their support towards materials development and, to a lesser extent, technical assistance. Middle-income countries tended to find support for research/policy development, and, to a lesser extent, materials development and personnel training. In the lower-income countries personnel training was the most prevalent kind of support, with materials development the second. Aggregating across all countries, the types of support which were the most common at the primary school level were personnel training, materials development, and research/policy development.

At the secondary level patterns were hard to discern in the higher- and middle-income groups but in the lower-income group the most frequent component was generally personnel training, followed by technical assistance. At this level across all countries personnel training accounted for about 35% of project components and technical assistance 28%.

These patterns probably reveal both what recipient countries have been seeking and what the agencies have been "offering." On the supply side, IDRC has been offering support for research over the past 15 years but has given priority to research on primary education. On the demand side, the countries which have had huge teacher shortages and relatively little domestic training expertise have tended to opt for support for personnel training support, whereas those which have been relatively well-staffed have concentrated more on research, policy development, and technical assistance. Although these are the general features of the "marketplace" the actual process of project identification and negotiation is subtle and complex, involving the reconciliation of numerous agendas on and across both sides. An examination of this process is expected to be part of the next phase of this research.

DISCUSSION

"STEADY STATE" AND INTRA-REGIONAL DISTRIBUTION OF SUPPORT

At first glance the results of this study appear to be consistent with Weiler's (1983) findings concerning the "steady state" of donor country support to education in recent years. Taking the region as a whole (or at least the countries in this study), the number of new projects in support of teaching quality in the most recent five-year period was virtually the same as that in the previous five-year period, even though the region has been growing steadily and optimism concerning the role of education in development has carried into the 1980s. However, the results for the region as a whole mask the striking changes which have been taking place in the distribution of support across sub-regions. Whereas support to projects in Southeast Asia peaked during the five-year period 1977-1981, support to projects in South Asia and China has grown exponentially over the entire 15-year period. Moreover, whereas in the period 1977-1981 there were 30% fewer new projects in the latter group of countries than in the former, in the period 1982-1986 there were 300% more.

ECONOMIC AND POLITICAL EXPLANATIONS FOR DISTRIBUTIONAL CHANGES

Explanations for this phenomenon are numerous (however, since direct questioning of agency decision-makers was not possible they are all somewhat speculative). First, it is highly likely that the vast disparities in national wealth between the sub-regions had something to do with investment decisions. In 1985 the median GNP per capita in Southeast Asia was around US $770, while in South Asia and China it was approximately $280. Many of the Southeast Asian countries (Singapore, Malaysia, and Thailand) have become or are now becoming newly industrialized, whereas some in South Asia (Bangladesh and Nepal) are still among the poorest of agrarian countries. By the late 1970s many of the Western donor nations (for example, the United States under President Jimmy Carter) had begun to develop a doctrine of priority support for the poorest of the rural poor. And although conservative governments in North America and Europe seem to have taken some of the force out of this movement, its basic principles have recently been reaffirmed by agencies like Canada's IDRC.

Global politics are also likely to have influenced investment decisions. The upsurge in QUOTE project support to Southeast Asia in the mid-1970s was almost certainly related to the emergence of communist governments in Indochina. Support to education and development projects in neighboring ASEAN[3] countries can be seen in the context of the West's interest in guarding against the further spread of Marxist ideology and insurgency movements. The ASEAN Secretariat itself became the conduit for some of this support as did the Southeast Asian Ministries of Education Organization (SEAMEO) set up during the Vietnam War.

By the early 1980s ASEAN nations seemed secure, and "hot spots" began to appear in other parts of Asia. Islamic nationalism was brewing in the Moslem countries of South Asia, and one of them, Pakistan, had become a "front-line" state in a new East-West struggle in Afghanistan. In addition, ethnic conflict threatened to tear Sri Lanka in two. It is reasonable to assume that the West's concern for blocking Soviet expansion in Southwest Asia and for preserving the integrity of friendly nations like Sri Lanka entered into the decision to increase social sector aid in those and neighboring countries.

At about the same time China was becoming a hot spot of a different sort. China's new obsession with modernization and its simultaneous opening to the West made it an ideal place for new donor agency activities in the 1980s. Support to social sectors started slowly, taking a back seat to the physical and industrial sectors, but

---

3   ASEAN stands for the Association of Southeast Asian Nations. It originally consisted of Indonesia, Malaysia, Philippines, Singapore, and Thailand. In 1986 Brunei was added.

gradually they have grown to the point that now the demand is greater than the agencies can meet. For example, IDRC now has to put a ceiling on support to China, since that one nation is capable of absorbing virtually all of the funds available for Asia.

One interesting feature of changes related to politics is the time lag which can be observed. The height of support in Southeast Asia came in 1977-1981, four years after the end of the Vietnam War. Now that Soviet troops have been pulled out of Afghanistan the bulk of USAID support to education is about to come on line. The most aid support ever to social programs in China is in the "pipeline," but no one knows if the country will still be open to the West by the time that funding is available. This is all because of the long gestation time for project development (typically two to four years).

CONTINUITY IN DEVELOPMENT SUPPORT

The above explanations are not meant to imply that all development support is carried by the winds of economic and political change. Certain donor agencies are "chartered" to work with certain kinds of countries (i.e., Aga Khan Foundation with those having Ismaili Moslems; ADAB with countries in the Pacific Basin; SIDA with those having left-leaning governments). In certain cases programs of aid build up a certain momentum, one project generating successive stages (i.e., IDRC support for the low-cost learning systems in the Philippines, Indonesia, and Malaysia; USAID support for radio teacher training in Nepal; World Bank support for teacher training colleges in Indonesia). This is justified within the agencies as a way of maintaining continuity of support and of building lasting institutional capacity, although it may sometimes keep agencies involved with countries longer than justified given new political and economic realities.

Continuity in support may also be justified on the basis of the recipient's capacity to meet certain conditions. For example, earlier it was noted that most of the loan funds were provided to the relatively wealthy countries. This pattern seems to have held up in the most recent period, as illustrated by the fact that during 1982 to 1986 four of six new World Bank loans for QUOTE projects in Asia went to Southeast Asian countries. It may be that loan funds are more available to countries which are sufficiently healthy economically and stable politically that debt repayment will not be too great a burden. Similarly, research funds (notably those from IDRC) have gone primarily to relatively wealthy countries. This would appear to be a reflection of the absorptive capacity of the various sub-regions for research funding. The fact that four of the six most recent IDRC QUOTE projects in Asia went to countries outside of Southeast Asia does not contradict this observation, since three of those projects went to China where the absorptive capacity for research is higher than would be expected given its GNP per capita.

PROSPECTS FOR THE FUTURE

It seems likely that the current trend of growing support to the relatively poor countries in the region will continue. All of these countries still have not come near providing the number of trained teachers they need to provide an adequate education for the numbers of students currently enrolled. Beyond that most of the South Asian countries are now making special efforts to increase enrollment rates among disadvantaged groups (especially girls), an effort requiring the training of new waves of minority group and female teachers. In addition, some countries like China are now expanding the concept of universal education to include the lower secondary grades, a move which will require the provision of millions of skilled new teachers in a hurry.

Political and economic conditions also favor the continuation of current trends. Major support efforts appear to be in the pipeline for Pakistan which is still considered a hot spot.[4] Sri Lanka will require

---

[4] As the Afgan War winds down, it is not certain how long external support will last, given Pakistan's relatively low domestic support for education and its unstable internal politics. It may be that donors in the future will want to see more internal commitment to education as a condition for continued support.

assistance in developing the decentralized systems it has committed itself to in order to maintain national integrity. Nepal and Bangladesh are still desperately low on local resources and infrastructure. India, while it has vast local resources and a solid infrastructure, has huge pockets of marginal groups which cannot be reached using local resources alone. Finally, China continues to be open, to be growing at a dizzying pace, and to be able to absorb all the resources the development agencies can provide.

In addition, there may be a certain resurgence in support to QUOTE-type projects in Southeast Asia; this for two reasons: first, because communist insurgency is increasing in the Philippines and Western governments are inclined to give support to the relatively popular and democratic Aquino government, and second, because Southeast Asian countries (e.g., Thailand and Indonesia) are now, like China, in the process of universalizing lower secondary education, a prospect which will require teaching resources beyond the countries' own capacity to provide. (Because of these countries' relative wealth, one may expect to see loan funds being allocated to this cause.)

Our final points are ones which stretch beyond the scope of this chapter. We have focussed on development agency support to the improvement of teaching in Asia. We have seen how the magnitude of support increased dramatically in the late 1970s in both the relatively wealthy and the relatively poor countries, falling off dramatically in the early 1980s in the former and continuing to grow in the latter. We have interpreted this in part as an indication that funds are flowing to where they are needed the most. If this is the case within a region, might it also be the case across regions? In order to address this question, one would have to examine the amount of QUOTE support that has been flowing into the poorest regions in the world (e.g., those in Africa) in recent years. Our observations here lead us to believe that support in these regions may also be on the increase, just as it is in South Asia.

Finally, this study has not made any attempt to evaluate the impact of any of the projects reviewed or enumerated. Acquiring financial support is one thing; using it effectively and with impact is quite another. A worthwhile extension of this study would be to ascertain which of the projects identified have been particularly successful (and unsuccessful) and why. Does success depend solely on conditions and managerial skill in the receiving country or do donor-recipient relationships have something to do with it as well? Such questions are open for future investigation.

CHAPTER TWELVE

COMMUNICATION TECHNOLOGY PROMISES IMPROVED TEACHING

Val D. Rust
Ladislaus Semali

Despite progress made during the past decades, the quality of teaching in the developing world remains suspect. Two major innovative directions seem evident as developing nations have attempted to improve the productivity of their educational delivery systems. On the one hand, efforts have been taken to change the quality of conventional teaching, including changes in teacher training, instructional methodology, textbooks, and teacher supervision (see Chapter 14).

On the other hand, efforts have been undertaken to redefine the conventional delivery system altogether. Traditionally, instruction has involved direct face-to-face contact, where a teacher meets on a regularly scheduled basis with a group of learners to deliver instructions or communicate information about new practices. That instructional model has been called into question. Advocates of a new mode of instruction predict a transformation or structural change in the entire delivery system, described by some as a "breakthrough in educational development" (Swahn, 1987), that will alter the very structure of educational systems (Bork, 1987).

These proponents hold to a vision, at times, shocking and unreasonable to most conventional educators. They claim the present crisis calls for outrageous proposals, it demands a plunge into new mental and technological territory. The new proposals, they claim, must be unreasonable, because reasonable solutions define our options in such a way that the developing world will remain programmed to failure.

It shall be our task in this chapter to address some of these new endeavors.   Within this perspective, the break-throughs envisioned inevitably turn on technology.   Until recently, technological innovations have usually been seen as supplementary to the more conventional learning environment.   That is, the position of the teacher has been readily acknowledged, and the new technologies have been viewed as supplementing and assisting the teacher.   Instructional technology has been intended to improve teaching by improving the quality of classroom instruction and raising the productivity of the individual teacher.

Within this mode, a variety of educational materials and media has been introduced into the conventional classroom environment, including demonstration objects such as flip charts, pictures, photographs, booklets, and fliers, as well as electronic systems such as films, video, slides, transparencies, and audio cassettes.   Many of these have been labeled audio-visual aids to the face-to-face human interaction.   However, these have rarely been considered adequately innovative to bring about a breakthrough in instruction.   The technology has had the purpose of supplementing and enriching classroom teaching but has not been meant to transform it in any fundamental way.   The teacher and classroom have remained the dominant elements in the instructional process, and the media has only supplemented the teacher's work.

However, it has become increasingly difficult to justify this mode of education.   Some experts claim that the old labor intensive process of instruction must be replaced.   The educational process is terribly inefficient, and the bottle neck seems clearly, at least to some, to have been the lack of well-trained and qualified teachers.   In spite of heroic efforts on the part of the developing world, the economic situation and the state of the art of teaching have prohibited any possibility of recruiting and training these teachers to the point that they would be adequately qualified. Another mode of education seems necessary if the educational needs of the developing world are to be satisfied.

In recent years, as technology has advanced, a new vision of education has begun to emerge. The notion of a teacher in a classroom with a small number of students is being altered or replaced by a new educational format. In that format, the high-quality teacher ceases to be restricted to the isolated classroom and becomes a teacher to the nation, with a salary and status commensurate with the responsibility. Other less-qualified teachers are relieved of the burden of satisfying all the educational needs of their pupils, and they can rely on information inputs from a variety of communications sources. Individual students are no longer dependent on what is taught to the group in the isolated classroom, but they are able to gain access to whatever information, in visual or auditory form, they require, independent of the local teacher's personal knowledge. And the system has the possibility of being so structured that it is easily and regularly updated so that the latest and best information is always available.

Just how all this is to be accomplished has depended on the particular technological instruments and media that has come on the scene. Probably the first really innovative instructional format was the old correspondence school, which recently has become a part of a more diversified "distance learning" operation. Diversification has come about through radio broadcasts, telephone hookups, various types of television, programmed instruction, and more recently, computerized instruction.

In the process, two major shifts have occurred. In the first shift, the media has moved from a supplementary learning aid to become a primary source of information, referred to as direct instruction. That is, comprehensive courses of study have become available on the video screen, tapes, and written learning modules. Ostensibly, these possess the potential of actually replicating or improving classroom instruction. In the second shift, especially with the new media, we find not only information packages of various sorts becoming available, but interactive technologies being developed that allow for learner driven learning, either between people or media programs.

Consequently, for the first time in our history, we are able, on a mass basis, to operationalize a concept of individualized instruction. Most forms of individualized instruction stress diagnosis of a person's individual learning requirements and abilities and the assignment of the student to a program of studies which will best satisfy those needs. A number of steps are usually identified in this process. Harold Mitzel, for example, outlines five major dimensions. First, the learner is allowed to proceed on a learning continuum at a self-determined pace that is comfortable to him. Second, the learner can work on a given learning sequence at times convenient or appropriate to him. Third, the learning begins on a learning continuum at a point which is appropriate to his past achievement rather than at one which the teacher finds appropriate for the majority of a class of students. Fourth, the learner should be allowed to detour from the learning sequence in order to undertake remedial efforts for skills or knowledge necessary to continue in the learning sequence. Fifth, the learner has a wealth of instructional media from which to choose, which will assist him in learning the same intellectual content as every other learner (1970, pp. 434-439).

We must take care, however, not to interpret individualized instruction in such a manner that it takes away the possibility of social learning and interaction between students. In fact, the newer interactive technologies have the potential of actually facilitating interaction between students as they work in small groups with interactive computer programs and video disks (Bork, 1986).

In the developing world it is unrealistic even to think about individualized instruction to the extent that Mitzel sees it, although there remain some who feel we are on the brink of a major breakthrough that will benefit the developing world. However, most of the new delivery systems remain within the framework of the first shift mentioned above, having very limited aims and restricted purposes. In the next sections we shall discuss five approaches currently being used as alternative delivery systems to instruction in the developing world and examine their major aims, characteristics, target group or population, and context within which they operate.

INSTRUCTIONAL BROADCASTING

Instructional broadcasting today consists of two kinds of delivery systems: radio broadcasting and television broadcasting, including satellite broadcasting.

RADIO BROADCASTING
Aims

The objective of using radio as an instructional medium has been based on the assumption that it has high potential to reach a large number of learners in an effective manner, not only as a supplement to the regular classroom instruction but also as direct instruction. McAnany (1973) describes some 30 countries using educational radio under five conditions, ranging from unorganized mass audiences to radio rural forums or radio clubs. Bearing these case studies in mind, the aims of using radio as an instructional medium could be placed with three major categories: (1) to reach distant populations, where radio is used as a mass medium, (2) to broadcast to schools where radio is used as a direct instructional medium, and (3) to provide contact to adult students engaged in correspondence and distance learning with the radio being used to supplement reading materials.

In the case of radio being used as a mass medium, many projects in developing countries have been documented to show the effectiveness of radio. Mass audiences are sought in the same ways that commercial broadcasts build their audiences--through humor, drama, or through other popular programs.

One successful application of radio for educational purposes in recent years has been its use in conjunction with low-cost learning systems in Indonesia, Liberia, the Philippines, and Thailand. These programs were designed for maximum student involvement, peer tutoring, and the use of simple print and audio media, all organized in a systematic way in order to ensure that learning takes place effectively (Nichols, 1982).

Begun as a campaign to improve classroom teaching, direct broadcasting to schools has been used by schools in developing countries since the 1950s. Direct instruction covers a range of intensities of use, such as providing several lessons a week in the same subject. The best known example is the case of Nicaragua, where students received 30 minutes of radio instruction in mathematics daily. The radio has also been used, as it were, to extend school instruction to regions otherwise unreached, as in the case of rural Mexico (McAnany, 1978, p. 36).

As a component of a distance learning system, radio has become a useful medium to enhance and support professional development, as in the Kenya Teachers' Training project (Kinyanjui, 1977) or the Radio Educational Teacher Training (RETT) project in Nepal. The aims of the USAID sponsored program in Nepal were conceived as a research and development project to develop and test a training program for untrained teachers through the medium of radio, but reinforced by written self-instructional materials and periodic workshops.

The Characteristics

In general, the characteristics of radio instruction consist of broadcasting programs of instruction from a central station. However, the characteristics of radio for instruction vary somewhat with the objective and the target audience in mind. For instance, in the case of direct instruction, some of the features include: (i) a specific announcer, (ii) specific instructions, (iii) specific subject matter, (iv) specific target learners, (v) questions and/or assignments, (vi) review of a previous lesson, and (vii) comments on written submissions of students. Routinely, students are expected to follow prepared notes, textbooks, or any other printed materials during a broadcast, page by page, as the instructor leads them on the air.

However, in the case of reaching distant populations or masses, the characteristics change. Some of the Latin American Radiophonic schools in Colombia and Honduras offer useful insights. As a matter of practice, radio broadcasts deliver practical information on agriculture, home development, health and so forth, with the motive of helping the rural families change their living practices. The method used could be described as persuasive communication, combining mass education with interpersonal contacts (Musto, 1971). From the evaluation studies done by Beltran (1976) and Musto (1971) on the ACPO *(Accion Cultural Popular)* program in Colombia and by White (1977) on ACPH *(Accion Cultural Popular Hondurena)* in Honduras, some typical features emerge. Basically, radio provides instructional input supplemented by written materials, with a focus on a rural group of villagers who listen in an organized way to selected programs. In the radio forum technique, radio is used to stimulate social and economic development through active participation by the members. Other approaches similar to this include the radio listening group campaigns as experienced in Tanzania (Hall & Kidd, 1973). It should be noted that these programs were directed primarily to out-of-school audiences, whose learning needs lie beyond the scope of formal school and relate to everyday living needs.

Although it is acknowledged that the use of radio in formal education is for enrichment and for direct instruction, no systematic evidence exists on the effectiveness of lessons (Sudame & others, 1985). However, in many developing countries, radio has been used to broadcast to schools with varying success.

The Target Group

The possible radio target audiences are (a) elementary pupils, (b) secondary pupils, (c) adult education learners involved in literacy classes, radio campaigns, radio forums, radio listener groups, and (d) adults undertaking tertiary or university instruction by radio.

In order to meet the listening needs of these diverse groups, broadcasting stations, both private and government, cater to particular group needs. Even in the case of countries with only one radio station, program services cater to different needs. In Kenya and Tanzania, for example, school-age broadcasts are aired in the mid-mornings and adult programs in mid-afternoons and early evenings. This feature helps learners identify closely with a particular program or time period offered by the station.

Sometimes an insufficient number of trained teachers has led to the use of the radio specifically for teachers. For instance, the lack of mathematics teachers in Mexico, El Salvador, and Nicaragua, contributed to the establishment of instructional radio programs in the subject. Radio lessons provide comprehensive instructional units especially in the remote areas of these countries (McAnany, 1973; Searle, 1975). The Radio Educational Teacher Training Project (RETT) in Nepal, mentioned above, was expected to create a cost-effective mechanism and methodology for assisting untrained teachers to meet certification standards (Graham & Paige, 1980, p. 175; Okwudishu & Klasek, 1986). Expected to provide training for about 6,000 untrained teachers in the country, the program covered five one-hour programs each week. Each program covered a subject area with three segments, two providing formal instructions based on the curriculum and one discussing general interest elements.

The Context

Radio broadcasts operate within the context of socioeconomic and political factors. Radio is only a tool, and, like schooling, its function in society depends on the political power distribution in the country. The budget allocated for educational programs reflects the ideological commitment as well as the willingness to support such programs. Success and failure are often indicators of such commitment.

Radio instruction may be sponsored both by private and public enterprise, in capitalist or socialist, poor or wealthy countries.   In Latin America, for example, many adult education programs have been sponsored by the church and other private organizations.   In Africa, one finds a style of managing broadcasting stations similar to that found in many European countries, perhaps a result of the colonial legacy.   In that context, governments have a monopoly control of the stations and most educational programs are directed and managed or supervised by the Ministry of Education in cooperation with the Ministry of Information.   In Asia, the situation is very similar to Africa in that school broadcasts are controlled by government.

TELEVISION AND SATELLITE BROADCASTING
Aims

To this point, the basic aim of instructional television has been mainly to supplement textbooks, to change the pace of lessons, and to bring new resources into the classroom.   Research distinguishes two uses of television in the classroom, direct and supplementary use. Direct teaching relies on a studio-based instructor conducting the lesson for students watching the picture tube.   Supplementary use of television in the classroom refers to film clips, slides, video, narration of research information, or interviews organized into a single unit or theme on a given subject.

Bearing in mind the long held contention that instructional media threatens to replace the teacher, it would seem that the supplementary use of television is less threatening to the classroom teacher.   The one quality of instructional television that merits its use in the classroom is its extraordinary capacity to combine vision and sound simultaneously to classrooms over large areas.

Unfortunately, research studies have typically compared instructional television with conventional instruction in an effort either to promote instructional television or to defend conventional instruction.   However, almost nowhere in the world is television being used in the classrooms without being built into a learning context managed by the classroom teacher, and most successful uses seem to depend on the studio teacher and the classroom teacher working as a team toward the same learning goals.

The Characteristics

Owing to prohibitive costs, the diffusion of television has been very slow, especially in the less-developed countries. Originally, programs were broadcast by narrow beams by regional transmitters that covered a certain broadcasting area or part of a nation. The regional transmitters then rebroadcast the signal from locations custom designed to optimize reception in the schools within the reception area. Usually, each local area would have a small microwave or receiving antenna connected to a receiver tuned to the frequency of the regional transmitter. The output of the receiver would be amplified and integrated into a distribution system and viewed on standard television sets. In this way a particular school was able to benefit from the various programs designed to supplement textbooks and other learning materials. With the advancement of satellites, this method has been changing and in some places is already outmoded.

In the last decade, satellites have come to be used in many developing countries for telecommunication purposes. First generation satellites were designed to be used in connection with general television, but they have begun to be used for educational purposes. A good example of this shift would be Indonesia's SISDIKSAT: The Indonesian Distance Education Satellite System. Today, improvements in transmitting over satellites now make it possible to broadcast directly from satellite to home via reception on a roof-mounted dish about one meter in diameter. These so-called Direct Broadcast Satellites (DBS) make television reception possible in the most remote areas.

A frequently cited example of use of satellites for instructional purposes is the well-known SITE project in India. This project began operations in 1975/76 and has been described as the largest satellite communications project of all time (Mody, 1978; Karnick, 1981). SITE (Satellite Instructional Television Experiment) was designed to test the effectiveness of direct one-way Instructional Television (ITV) as an educational medium for the rural population.

Cable television is another technology waiting to be taped for educational purposes. It first began as a system to provide television to communities unable to receive a broadcast signal.   As communication satellite use increased and sending costs and receiving dishes became more competitive, the opportunity for widespread distribution of specialized programming (sports, movies, religion, news) became possible. However, educational services have not, as of yet, utilized network cable TV on a truly national scale in the developing world, even though institutions in industrialized nations have taken advantage of the medium.

The Target Group

The use of television in the classroom is mainly directed to school age children. Out-of-school use is principally directed to the adult learner in large audiences. The adult learner, as a target group, is described by Dr. Bernard Luskin as being older, employed-- at least part-time--or home bound, with dependent children (quoted in Kraig, 1980). These adult learners are generally non-campus focused and their need for convenience and flexibility in learning is far greater than that of campus-bound learners. They are the targets for self-posed instruction (through video courses and broadcast television). It is now possible to earn a degree from the university via TV. The best-known case is the Open University of Great Britain, which has served as a model for many developing countries. That model mandates well-prepared television and radio programs and integrated self-study booklets with tutor/learner correspondence and occasional week-end group meetings on a campus. Thus, the mass media-television and radio enable community colleges and universities to serve people literally in their living rooms, enabling working men and women to fit college into their busy schedules.

The Context

The context of television as an instructional medium is less defined than radio. Television has been used both for distance education and direct instruction. In both instances, it has been used in the context of the school or college. Because of the rising costs of hardware and software, countries of the developing world face an increasing handicap in terms of applying this medium to education. With the exception of the Ivory Coast, where television has been used for the masses, in the case of *Tele Pour Tous*, the medium has proven too expensive to be diffused widely like radio. Among the reasons cited are costs and the fact that television and most of the new technologies must be imported. For example, in an attempt to prepare youngsters for primary school, "Sesame Street" was produced and shown in the United States and has subsequently been translated into several languages and distributed in several developing countries. However, no systematic attempts have been made to evaluate this experience.

With the exception of Latin America, where instructional television is owned or sponsored by universities, it is usually owned by the governments. The same could be said about satellites, whose technology is equally prohibitive to most developing countries. Satellite communication systems are invariably established for political, economic, or technological reasons. Consequently, the educational aims of these networks have often been subservient to political or technological motives (White, 1984).

CORRESPONDENCE EDUCATION
Aims

Early experiences of correspondence education consisted of a form of "teaching letter." In many countries, as schools were set up, it soon became evident that many prospective candidates could not attend class owing to distance or inconvenient working hours. It was determined that contact with the teacher might be maintained through correspondence. The objective of correspondence education was usually to help candidates prepare for qualifying examinations at secondary or other pre-collegiate institutions. The educational system was so structured that passing examinations represented a ticket to a job. Certainly, this was the case in Tanzania and Kenya and in other former British colonies where the British Tutorial College was engaged in preparing students for the School Certificate examinations from the London and Cambridge Universities. It was not until recently, when these examinations were discontinued, after these countries achieved independence, that the service of correspondence education was taken over by internal adult education institutes.

Such courses were criticized from the very beginning for their lack of personal contact and interaction. Although they were by no means inexpensive to many students of the Third World, they did represent a "cheap alternative" to formal education (Halliwell, 1987).

Because the qualifying examinations rarely changed, any improvements in correspondence education consisted of higher-quality printed materials, notes, exercises, and evaluation procedures, including marks and comments on written home work. Finally, in the 1930s, more fundamental improvements began to find their way into correspondence courses. Radio was added to what was becoming referred to as "distance education." The use of radio was only a beginning of a whole series of electronic media, such as video equipment, television, computers, and satellites.

Although correspondence education has undergone many changes over the years, its basic aims have remained the same: to provide an opportunity to youth and adults to pursue courses which they could not otherwise take in the formal school, eventually complete a course of studies, pass a qualifying examination, and obtain the ticket to enter a certain job market. The establishment of the Rapids College in England catering to those interested in business and commerce courses, especially in the Third World, was within this objective. Today, we can identify various kinds of correspondence education: (1) elementary adult correspondence education, (2) professional education in accounting, journalism, and vocational training, and (3) open university education, which has been adapted with different names, such as the Extramural University in Africa, the University without Walls in the United States, and the Book University in Indonesia.

The underlying assumption of this operation is that students will be motivated enough to pursue the course to the end and that adequate learning is possible through this mode of instruction.

The Characteristics

Typically, we can identify three kinds of correspondence education prevailing in the world today: (1) pure correspondence education, entirely limited to written two-way communication between student and the correspondence school; (2) a combination of correspondence and counseling or tutoring, with a small amount of oral communication, and (3) a combination of correspondence and tutoring with a considerable amount of oral communication. As a matter of practice, most participants opt for combined forms. A multimedia approach is presumed to consist of several media, including a combination of some or all of the following: (1) radio programs which are broadcast on a regular schedule; (2) regularly scheduled television programs; (3) a semi-programmed handbook written by experts; (4) meetings of learning groups; (5) newspaper presentation of themes; and (6) telephone or teleprinter connections used in radio and television contact programs.

It should be noted, however, that correspondence education utilizes printed materials a great deal, including textbooks for independent study, letters, and in some cases study guides to the textbooks. The texts are meant systematically to disseminate selected information and act as guides to all phases of study. Besides, the process of two-way correspondence is indispensable to monitor the learning process by means of assignments. Thus, written exercises are sent to the teacher to be corrected, the assignments are returned to the student by mail with appropriate corrections. Various forms of periodic oral communication are also used. Individual and group face-to-face consultations of students and teachers, selected lectures, short seminars, and courses are sometimes given. However, digest lectures are occasionally used to facilitate the study of difficult materials or to compensate for the lack of certain written material. More recently, audio-cassettes have also been used. But written texts are still the basic teaching material, and all other forms of contact remain secondary.

Some distance learning programs provide types of learning equivalent to that provided by formal schools and colleges to audiences beyond their practical reach. One example is radio combined with a correspondence program in Kenya, which has provided many school teachers and other interested learners, mainly in rural areas, with an opportunity to pursue various secondary school subjects. By far, the best-known and most influential example, however, is the Open University in the United Kingdom, which was mentioned above. Through a combination of well-prepared television and radio programs and integrated self-study books, supplemented by learner, tutor, correspondence and occasional week-end group meetings on a campus, adequate university education is being provided to thousands of mature learners studying on their own at home and at the same time working full time. As a radical educational innovation, the open university has created a whole new teaching and learning system. Its results have been so successful that the model has been adopted in various forms in numerous other countries such as Japan, Thailand, Pakistan, China, the Netherlands, and West Germany. Some 30 open universities and open colleges of different varieties are scattered across both the developed and the developing world.

The Target Groups

The target groups benefiting from correspondence education are mainly adults. The majority of distance learning programs are directed, to a large extent, to out-of-school audiences, whose learning needs lie beyond the scope of the schools. Specifically, we could list here (1) high school and secondary school level adults seeking an equivalent form of schooling as is found for youth in more conventional schools; (2) youth and adults seeking education to increase knowledge and skills of management positions; (3) adults retraining themselves as part of continuing education and for better job opportunities; (4) parents seeking information about self-improvement; (5) individuals or groups of people seeking professional knowledge for their private business; and (6) individuals seeking professional licenses, including real estate, public accounting, journalism, etc.

The Context

The environment in which correspondence education takes place is that of a mixture of formal and nonformal institutions. Because correspondence education is adult oriented, it typically is more learner driven than other alternatives. That is, correspondence courses exist in large measure if they satisfy a demand within a free-market framework. In this context, the quality of correspondence education is measured against the more conventional institutions of education, especially in the developing countries. The cultural issue related to the impersonality of written communications, whether it be with those living in the same culture or in distant environments, continues to plague this sort of education. Other context issues include the kind of content being offered, the types of assignments given over quite different social situations, and the way in which students are evaluated. Of crucial importance is also the broader technological situation, which determines the efficiency of the mail and telephone systems.

PROGRAMMED INSTRUCTION
Aims

Programmed instruction aims to use a highly structured curricular program in an effort to equalize the instructional treatment and classroom interactions experienced by students across different classrooms and schools. It can be developed at a relatively low cost and is seen as a means of compensating for poorly prepared teachers. The approach offers a means for content to be more logically sequenced and presented in a more task-oriented manner than is typically found in a conventional classroom. The method also is intended to place more responsibility for learning on the pupil than does more conventional teacher-directed instruction.

Programmed instruction is also intended by many of its advocates to better equalize the educational experience received by the pupils, who claim that teachers discriminate, either consciously or subconsciously, in their instruction between boys and girls, different cultural groups, or pupils of different maturity or age levels. It has the potential of minimizing disparities in student achievement across subgroups.

The Characteristics

Programmed instruction received its major impetus from the work done by B. F. Skinner and is based on the theory that learning is best accomplished by small, incremental steps with immediate reinforcement of positive response. The original programs were in written form. The student is presented with a bit of information to learn and is then presented with a "frame" that requires the student to demonstrate that the student has mastered the information. If the student gives an appropriate response, the student moves on to the next frame and repeats the process. Over time this linear process was enhanced with a branching program, which would allow the student to detour from the learning continuum in order to undertake remedial efforts for skills or knowledge necessary to continue in the learning sequence.

Programmed instruction has often been used in connection with other technologies. In South Korea, for example, a scheme was devised to combine programmed instruction with the use of tethered balloons, which would facilitate television broadcasts to schools throughout the country (Spaulding, 1987, p. 8). In recent years, with the introduction of the computer, programmed instruction has become much more sophisticated; however, in the developing world, this technology has not been widely enough introduced to really have had an impact on programmed instruction in schools.

The Target Group

Programmed instruction is appropriate for any age level or ability group.   A number of instructional programs have been developed for the primary grades in the developing world as well as for various subjects in the upper grades.   A recent educational project in Liberia provides a good case in point.   A USAID funded project was developed and employed a combination of programmed teaching for grades 1-3 and programmed instruction materials for grades 4-6.   Both were designed to instruct primary school students in five areas (reading, English, mathematics, science, and social studies) (Chapman, 1986).   This mode has rarely found its way into other teaching environments.

The Context

Programmed instruction has been heralded mainly by a specific school of psychological thinking: behaviorism.   From this vantage point, its political orientation comes from developed world specialists, who have carried their ideology into the developing world, promising to produce teacher-proof instructional modules.   Even though the idea of programmed instruction has been available for a quarter of a century, it has remained highly experimental and project based.

COMPUTERS IN EDUCATION

Aims

Of all the alternatives available, computers are the only electronic devices that promise to fulfill all of the dreams of the visionaries thinking to transform the educational process via the new technologies. However, the level of development of computers for educational purposes in the developing world is so experimental and recent that little can be said about its actual potential for achieving these aims.

Two major aims appear to have emerged in using the computer. First, educational planners and consultants have promoted the introduction of the computer as an administrative device to facilitate data processing and information management. Honduras and Guatemala, for example, have been very active in the past decade in developing such systems at the ministerial level (Cuadra, 1987). Second, projects have been initiated that explore the possibility of introducing computer-assisted and computer-managed instruction. For example, projects in Belize, Granada, and Lesotho, sponsored by the US Agency for International Development, are intended to determine what computerized applications are feasible, manageable, culturally acceptable, effective, and affordable in the developing world (Block et al., 1987). The present quest is to enhance the productivity of teachers as well as to motivate students and raise their achievement levels. However, at this point in time, almost no programs yet exist, which are beyond the experimental stage.

Research seems to be taking three main directions: (1) assessment of the present state of computer literacy in developing countries; (2) development of quality programs suited to the entire range of users; and (3) inquiry into the impact of computers on human relationships, e.g., student-teacher, teacher-student, parent-school relationships. All this research activity shows one thing: computers in education promise much, but their application to the classroom and to instruction in general remain experimental.

The Characteristics

In general, computerized instruction has now moved to the level of microcomputers. The programs are made available either by disks or through telephone channels linked with a central station. The effort put into computer-assisted instruction extends from simple familiarization and exposure to computers to real learning projects, where the computer can be used as the primary source of information or instruction and as a learning vehicle of instruction. At this stage, the computer might be looked on as an alternative to books, with the added advantage that the computer is used interactively.

In the experiments sponsored by USAID, mentioned above, computers were used to teach mathematics, spelling, and reading, with the computer playing the role of a learning aid. It is envisioned that through such experiments, in the future, computer facilities would be expanded so that they would be placed in environments ranging from remedial work to vocational education for school leavers.

The Target Group

So far, computer-assisted instruction has been directed mainly to school children. For instructional purposes, the use of computers has also been limited to school-age children, but is slowly expanding to adult learners. Seminars and conferences have been held to introduce teachers to computers and to expose them to the variety of uses that could be applied to instruction. School administrators and board members have also been exposed to the potential of utilizing the microcomputer as a tool for fast storage, retrieval, and analysis of administrative and policy related information for improving schools.

The Context

As indicated above, the use of computers in developing countries is still experimental, and it depends on donor agencies to supply the hardware and software, although these experiments have been conducted with the understanding that the host country can benefit and make suggestions about modifications required to make computers more appropriate and effective for instruction in developing countries. Computer instruction remains highly dependent on political, economic, and technological conditions in the various areas of the world.

DISCUSSION

There is no question that the new technology has great potential as a delivery system in education. Mass education is very expensive and it has enormous limitations. However, the new systems have not only possibilities but potential liabilities that must be confronted within the framework of the issues we have raised.

We find that educators have actively used the new media as supplementary learning aids for the regular classroom. They have also, in more limited ways, begun to use the media as a substitute for classroom learning environments, although these typically take place in conjunction with school-type environments. We have found that most of the delivery systems have been able to compensate for deficiencies in a conventional educational program in areas where sufficient personnel are not available or the young are so dispersed that they are unable to be gathered together into a typical school setting.

We find that some of these delivery systems are, in many respects, able to replicate the school task, at least in terms of pupil performance. In fact, as experimental programs, they have often been able to demonstrate that they are superior to the conventional school. For example, the USAID funded programmed instruction project in Liberia demonstrated that students engaged in programmed instruction had a significantly higher level of achievement than students in the more conventional modes, though the difference was small (Chapman, 1986).

However valuable the new technology may be, so far it has not been able to demonstrate that it is able to transcend the old form of education in any fundamental manner. It may be somewhat more cost effective in certain situations. It may reach young learners isolated from schools. It may overcome some limitations in terms of teacher preparation and quality.

In addition, these systems have been able to transcend certain limitations almost inherent in the conventional classroom. One of the limitations often noted is that teachers are often either unwilling or unable to provide an equally valuable experience to all students in a classroom. They often discriminate on the basis of age, gender, ethnic background, or some other factor. Machine-driven instruction could better avoid the prejudices and predilections of the live teacher, and there is some evidence that equality of instructional opportunity may actually be enhanced through the new technology (see, for example, Chapman,1986).

However, the new delivery systems that are presently in place are not revolutionary. They have not been able to break through the learning barriers nor have they been able to insure far greater learning efficiency or substantially higher student outcomes, even when those outcomes are higher in a statistical sense. There is some anticipation that microcomputers may overcome all the technical limitations of the other modes of instruction, breaking through the barriers that now exist. Microcomputers especially open the way for extensive multidimensional interactive learning to take place. It certainly is the only electronic instrument that is, in theory, adequately able to satisfy the criteria set down by Mitzel for individualized instruction. However, even microcomputers have had such limited use in the developing world that no judgment can be made about their ability, operationally, to satisfy the criteria.

A number of the new delivery systems have been used successfully with younger people, but the major inroads that have been made have to do with adults. In fact, some of the systems are only appropriate for adults or at the very least young people who are rather mature. Essentially all activities falling under the category of distance learning and correspondence programs are strictly for the more mature learners. Within this context, one major demonstrated value of the new technology, in terms of the conventional classroom may be in its capacity to assist teachers themselves, not so much in their teaching role, but in upgrading themselves and maintaining a greater sense of morale and purpose. Teachers are able to overcome their sense of isolation, especially in isolated rural areas, and to remain in touch with their professional colleagues. They are also able to keep abreast of the latest developments in different fields of study. A substantial number of adult learners are mature enough to cope with the inconveniences of machine learning and are able to transcend poor communication links, inadequate equipment, power breakdowns, etc., in their quest to improve themselves as teachers.

Our conclusions reflect a tempered optimism. The potential of the electronic delivery systems are theoretically great, but their practical ability to provide education more efficiently and effectively than conventional schooling has yet to be demonstrated. The technic ideology of the developed world mandates that we use the new technologies simply because they are there to use. A more cautious approach would likely be for those in the developing world to clarify what they wish to accomplish and to make some judgment as to how the new technologies are able or are not able to assist them in achieving these goals. In this respect, the developed world could not serve well as a role model, because schools in developed countries have rarely posed such a central question as they have incorporated the new technologies into their own programs.

SECTION FOUR

CONCLUSIONS AND RECOMMENDATIONS

CHAPTER THIRTEEN

IMPROVING THE QUALITY OF TEACHING

Val D. Rust
Per Dalin

A major intention of this book has been to assess the state of teaching in the developing world and to understand how we might improve the quality of teaching. To do this we have drawn together a wide range of thinking and research about teachers and teaching in the developing world.

To focus on quality issues associated with any facet of education raises an awareness of the desperate situation facing the entire educational enterprise in the developing world. According to Shaeffer (Chapter 4), the two most common contemporary characteristics of educational systems in the developing world are: (1) a leap in the quantity of education available, and (2) a steady deterioration in the quality of education available. How do we account for this quantity/quality shift.

Socially, schooling is just now becoming a part of the broader value system of many environments, with the consequence that enrollments are skyrocketing. Between 1970 and 1985 enrollments in the developing world more than doubled, and almost tripled in Africa (UNESCO, 1987). Even so, the participation and performance rates of young people beginning school continue to be so minimal that up to 40% of first-grade children in certain countries fail the program and are expected to repeat the first-grade. By the fourth-grade, over half of the children in many developing countries have already left school. At the age of 14 years, only 10 percent of developing world children are literate in their native language (Fuller, 1986, p. 2).

The wastage in terms of returns on educational investments to developing countries is astronomical. Whereas in the developed world almost everyone who begins school finishes primary school, in rural Haiti the frequent repetition and drop-out rates of pupils require that 20 student-years of attendance are required to produce a single primary school graduate (Fuller, 1986, p. 3). Coutinho (Chapter 2, Case Study) reminds us that the situation is so drastic in rural Brazil that the very functions of the school are changing, so that teachers now struggle as much with physical care and health of the children as with intellectual nourishment.

Economically, the resources available for education in developing countries are negligible when compared with the developed world. Fuller reminds us, for example, that the difference between recurrent expenditures per pupils in low-income countries in 1980 ($59) was less than 2.6% of industrialized countries ($2,297), and expenditures on instructional materials per pupil in low-income countries ($1.69) was less than 1.9% of industrialized countries ($92.32). In addition, teachers in low income countries must instruct 2.5 times as many students at any given time (44) as teachers in industrialized countries (18) (Fuller, 1986, p. 5).

There is ample evidence that the situation has actually deteriorated in recent years. Whereas industrialized countries almost doubled per pupil expenditures between 1970 and 1980, per pupil expenditures in low-income countries declined (Fuller, 1986, p. 11).

Administratively, as the educational systems expand, the funds available for teachers' salaries and other traditional costs actually diminish because of the expansion of the educational bureaucracy which is attempting to establish a communications infrastructure, provide school facilities and materials, supervise teachers, and oversee the system. Ghani (Chapter 2) has painted a graphic picture of educational policy in many areas that intentionally holds down the number of certified teachers in the system in an attempt to reduce costs.

As the bureaucracies expand, their complexity causes them to fragment and crumble, preventing teachers from being placed, and when placed, paid on a regular basis (Verspoor & Leno, 1986, p. 1). Teachers are lost in the system and begin to feel isolated, separated from colleagues and the rest of the population. The growing bureaucracy attempts to maintain some semblance of contact and supervision by establishing systems of reports and record-keeping that create new demands on the teachers while filtering information in ever distorted forms through the various administrative levels.

This is all occurring at a time when more and more pupils are entering the classroom, which requires teachers to adjust their teaching styles to cope with the realities of the larger class-size conditions.

Pedagogically, the developing world is in the throws of reform. Ministries see the necessity of instituting more up-to-date textbooks, which probably contain topics and approaches unfamiliar to many teachers. In Indonesia and elsewhere, teachers are expected to shift from traditional teaching modes to "student active learning"; they are expected to stop lecturing to students and start asking open-ended questions (Chapter 3, Case Study). Science classes must now incorporate experimentation and manipulation of complex equipment.

Professionally, teachers are also experiencing difficult times. Cummings (Chapter 1) has suggested that as societies evolve, a dramatic shift takes place in terms of the characteristics of teachers toward lower social-class origins, more females, and lower academic achievement. Much more information is necessary before we can firmly validate or discredit this assertion, but it is clear that little understood shifts are taking place that make some difference in terms of the quality of teachers.

In terms of teachers in the community of nations, the evidence is overwhelming that socioeconomic conditions place enormous constraints on the ability of ministries of education to provide the resources and means to insure that qualified and talented teachers are teaching in the schools and the ability to make available the resources necessary to promote productive working conditions and stimulate a learning climate.

IMPROVING THE QUALITY OF TEACHING

While the above observations are becoming a part of our common wisdom, the crucial question is how the situation can be altered. Is it possible to redirect the deteriorating quality of education and actually improve the quality of teaching in the developing world? Three general possibilities may be computed in a quality equation:

1.   Reduce the educational services being provided.
2.   Increase the human and/or material resources going into education.
3.   Increase the efficiency of the present resources in the educational process.

It should be noted that these possibilities can each be manipulated in a variety of ways, and they may all be manipulated simultaneously. We shall rely mainly on the contributions to this volume in addressing the three above possibilities.

REDUCE THE EDUCATIONAL SERVICES BEING PROVIDED

In theory, quality might be improved by reducing some services so that energies and resources could be directed toward a more limited number of students or programs. None of the authors in this volume even consider the possibility of any reduction of educational services. In fact, any realistic appraisal of educational history would suggest that once an educational service has been made available, public officials and the general population will not allow it to be reduced. The developing world has not even begun to realize universal primary education and if the developed world provides any indication of things to come, enrollment figures will continue to expand in terms of the percentage of young people in school, the number of years the young are expected to attend, and the days per year young people will attend (Rust, 1977, p. 36).

Consequently, this part of our equation is crucial in a negative sense. That is, expansion rather than reduction of services will continue to be the norm contributing to a continued deterioration of the quality of education.

There may be one escape clause in this factor.   Public resources may be concentrated somewhat through the expansion of the private sector. If greater private resources are channeled into the development of private schooling, then the public sector could actually restrict the services it is expected to provide. Such an option may have some viability at the secondary level, but the public sector appears to be the only viable option at the primary level.

INCREASE HUMAN AND/OR MATERIAL RESOURCES GOING INTO EDUCATION

An obvious aspect of increased educational quality would clearly be to increase human and material resources, and indeed Fuller's review of school quality confirms that student performance is related to per pupil and total school expenditures. The basic issue is how to increase these resources, and a number of possibilities present themselves, related both to national and international inputs.

National Inputs

There is no question that national governments are theoretically able to provide greater resources to education and the financing of teacher related costs. However, Hurst and Rust (Chapter 6) point out that central governments in the developing world are making far greater relative efforts to support education than are occurring in most industrialized countries, and it is unlikely that future efforts will assume such great priority that governments will begin channeling a much greater portion of their limited resources into education.

Some additional public resources might be identified at the local level that could supplement central government contributions. Local communities could provide housing without cost or at a reduced rental rate. Land could be made available for small farming or gardening purposes, and other amenities might be made available to make teaching more attractive and entice better people into the profession. In some countries, where education is not yet free, the children of teachers might be provided with a free education. Those in isolated areas might also be given additional allowances in the form of services from other public agencies and systems. Teachers could have access to public utilities for reduced cost or use this available communications systems. Teachers in the Andaman Islands of India, for example, receive free passage on public transportation systems to visit relatives on the mainland at least once a year (ILO, 1978, p. 62), which provides some incentive to participate in such programs. Our point here is that while direct government contributions to education are not likely to be increased substantially, there remains the possibility that additional national resources could be channeled into the educational system.

International Inputs

One of the pervasive distinctions we would draw between most of the developed world and the developing world is that the sense of insularity of the developed world thinking concerning its sense of connectedness with the developing world, while the developing world operates consciously on the assumption of an integral connectedness with the metropolitan world.

This sense of connectedness derives, in part, from a growing dependence on the part of the developing world. There are those who have identified enormous problems with this sense of dependence. Coutinho (Chapter 2, Case Study), for example, challenges the assumptions of financial and technocratic inputs from the metropolitan countries, reminding us that Brazil has been incorporated into the structure of dependency on international capitalism that has actually exploited Brazil rather than contributed to it, helping to explain much of Brazilian underdevelopment.

While these problems are real and even explosive in nature, there remains a commitment on the part of developed countries to assist the developing world, and any attempt to expand resources for education in the developing world must include the possibility of further provision from donor agencies through development aid projects and technological transfer. Nielson (Chapter 12) gives us some hint of a confusing and complex array of agencies engaged in education and teaching at some level of commitment in South and Southeast Asia, all of which are making substantial inputs into national development programs. These inputs are already in place, and the fiscal crisis of the last decade in the developed world bodes ill against the likelihood that the developed world will expand its development resources appreciably. Of course, certain countries are in an expansion mode, but the overall contributions are unlikely to shift dramatically (OECD, 1979).

The major hope for any increase in international funding for teaching would probably have to come through cuts in other funding provisions. While such decisions would be mainly political in nature, there remains some commitment to fund projects that show evidence of greater payoffs. Verspoor and Leno recently assessed World Bank projects directed toward educational change between 1964 and 1983, and they concluded that "teachers are at the core of the educational change process." Any effective change that has occurred has included, among other things, a successful inservice component and a high teacher commitment and motivation for the change (Verspoor & Leno, 1986, p. 5). And yet, the average project allocation for in-service training is less than 4% of project costs. If quality change is to occur, it is clear that greater commitments must be made for those components of projects that show evidence of contributing to success. A greater portion of project funds must go for teachers and their training.

While the first two elements of our quality equation are extremely problematic in terms of their potential to reverse the slippage occurring in quality, the third factor shows the greatest potential to begin improving the quality of teachers and teaching.

INCREASE THE EFFICIENCY OF THE RESOURCES GOING INTO THE EDUCATIONAL PROCESS

If we are to increase the effective use of resources going into the educational process, a major focus must be on teaching effectiveness. Avalos (Chapter 8), has given us a brief review of the concept of teacher effectiveness from the vantage point of contemporary researchers, pointing out that the concept must ultimately be connected with student outcomes but is also related to presage, context, and teacher process variables. Current thinking places stress on the teacher as a thinking, problem-solving human being rather than someone possessing a set of competencies that are applied universally and mechanically to the teaching situation. Jones and Bhalwankar (Chapter 7) have given us a conceptual framework for identifying various models of teaching and indicate the way choices among them might be made. Simply put, a competent teacher possesses a repertoire of options and the wisdom to know when one option is more appropriate than another.

According to Lee Shulman (1987, pp. 19-20), in the developed world, current reform measures related to teacher policy generally call for the following:

> greater professionalization of the teacher, with higher
> standards for entry, greater emphasis on the scholarly
> bases for practice, more rigorous programs of
> theoretical and practical preparation, better strategies
> for certification and licensure, and changes in the
> workplace that permit greater autonomy and teacher
> leadership.

While all of these elements have face-value validity, not only for the developed but also the developing world, the question remains which spheres represent more efficient use of very scarce resources. Many of those measures, in fact, represent rather expensive means toward quality improvement. Those concerned with the developing world may not have the resources to adopt what may be thought of as the best quality practices; however, the authors of this volume have collectively explored a number of efficiency options that are closely connected to the reality base of the developing world. We have clustered some of these under four headings: Teacher Preparation, The Teaching Process, System Factors, and The Management of Change.

Teacher Preparation

The most extensive literature on teachers and teaching in the developing world centers on teacher preparation. Our volume reflects this focus as three chapters, each with an accompanying case study, are devoted to pre-service, on-service, and in-service education. Because so many practicing teachers in the developing world are uncertified, we have chosen to describe teacher certification activities for them as on-service education.

Ghani (Chapter 2) has described a wide range of teacher preparation practices throughout the world. He has chosen time as his single most important descriptive variable but has avoided making judgments about the variations he finds. At this stage in our understanding of teachers, this seems to have been a sensible way to portray the variations in teacher education, because most studies which try to relate teacher preparation with student outcomes have also used the length of training as the most critical measure.

One possibility of increasing teacher competence might be to extend the general primary and secondary schooling time future teachers receive. Such a notion would be particularly significant in those countries where teacher preparation is equivalent to secondary school education. Fuller concludes, however, that this would require extraordinary cost increases, and the studies he has reviewed are mixed, most of them showing negligible effects (1986, p. 34).

To the contrary, achievement effects are more consistent for the number of teacher training courses teachers take, particularly in connection with those less-advantaged children (Husen, Saha, & Noonan, 1978, p. 26). McGinn, Warwick, and Reimners (1989, p. 22) maintain that the best single predictor of student achievement in primary schools is the degree of formal teacher education. If this is the case, then policies of placing unqualified teachers in classrooms as a cost-saving measure may not be terribly sound. It also reinforces the importance of on-service programs in the case of large numbers of teachers who fail to satisfy even minimum credentialing requirements. Andrews, Housego, and Thomas (Chapter 3) have provided the reader with an extensive outline of options available but have also made specific judgments, based on expert opinion, as to their relative value. In other words, while authors of most studies dealing with the relationship between teacher courses and student achievement have been satisfied to consider only the time teachers have spent or the number of courses they have taken, Andrews, Housego, and Thomas claim that some courses of action may be more productive than others, not only for on-service but for in-service programs.

Shaeffer (Chapter 4) and Vera (Chapter 4, Case Study) argue that one more positive approach to in-service training is what they call participatory teacher training where the teacher behaves as a self-directed, active agent, as a decision maker, and as a problem solver in the context of the training rather than as a recipient of information and skills decided from on high.

We emphasize that some of the options available may require more initial expense but could ultimately be more cost efficient within the overall educational process. Teacher education must ultimately be judged within the framework of the actual teaching process.

The Teaching Process

Limited resources require people to make difficult choices involving pedagogically sound options and cost-saving options. Within this volume, different authors have come to different decisions about what choices might be most appropriate. One approach to improving the teaching process has been suggested by Guthrie (Chapter 9), who makes a case for improving what he calls "formalistic teaching," which characterizes most of traditional education throughout the world. According to Guthrie, most innovations intending to improve the teaching process place a double burden on teachers in that they not only expect the teachers to improve their instructional skills but they expect teachers to alter their teaching styles in some fundamental manner.

In areas of the world where most teachers possess marginal professional skills and academic backgrounds, it might be more efficient if we concentrate on formalistic teaching skills rather than expecting teachers to shift to a radically different teaching style. The reviews by Avalos and Haddad (1981) and Fuller (1987) signal tentative support for Guthrie's position, in that more than half the studies they reviewed, which included teacher experience as a variable, indicated that a positive relationship exists between teacher experience and student achievement. In other words, as teachers learn how to function as conventional, traditional teachers, their experience appears to have a positive influence on student learning.

One important in-service mode might simply be to help teachers be the best of what they are rather than challenge them to be something quite different. In this manner, teacher activities would also tend to be appreciated and reinforced rather than challenged by parents who adhere to more traditional cultural orientations (Spratt, 1984). In addition, cost-effective changes might be made in the system that are compatible with formalistic teaching, including modification of examination systems, improved textbooks, supplementary materials, and distance programs for in-service programs.

Such a line of argument would be challenged by writers such as Shaeffer (Chapter 4), Vera (Chapter 4, Case Study), and Coutinho (Chapter 2, Case Study) who argue that quantitative improvement of present teaching practice is not enough. A whole new style of teaching is necessary if inroads in quality are to be achieved. A number of examples of improved practice are outlined in this volume.

The Cianjur Project is one case in point. Gardner (Chapter 3, Case Study) provides a startling case study of a project in Indonesia that grew out of research showing that in certain classrooms all the children were doing well, while in other classrooms of children of similar backgrounds, few children were doing well, which indicated that certain teaching environments were, indeed, better than others. The classrooms in the project were changed to make the children active participants in the lessons. The children were placed in different grouping configurations, and active interaction between children and teachers was encouraged. In addition, adequate supervision and in-service activities were adopted for participants.

A final approach to teaching efficiency has evolved out of the realization that teaching to this point has always been heavily labor intensive. Third World countries devote up to 95% of their recurrent costs to personnel expenses, with most of these funds going for teacher expenses (Avalos & Haddad, 1978, p. 7). As long as it remains so labor intensive, little possibility exists for greater efficiency, and Rust and Semali (Chapter 12) review the various promises of communication technology to reduce costs while improving teaching.

At the one extreme are what technology proponents describe as "unreasonable" and even "outrageous" proposals for changing the entire teaching format because they recognize that any "reasonable" proposal remains programed to failure. The most outrageous proposal for change is that teachers be replaced by electronic devices. Of course, more conventional options are also available.

Rust and Semali express tempered optimism in the potential of electronic delivery systems to assist teachers in the teaching process, but they conclude that their ability to provide education more efficiently and effectively than conventional schooling has yet to be demonstrated. Technology is already able to supplement the teacher in becoming better prepared (e.g., UNESCO, 1984; UNESCO, 1981; Sobeih, 1984) and in learning how to instruct (Masota, 1982), but it will be some time before serious consideration can be given to replacing the live teacher, who will remain, at least for some time, the core of the educational process.

Even if teachers were to gain extraordinary competence and be filled with extraordinary idealism and devotion to teaching, unless other factors were altered, their influence would likely be neutralized. Teaching effectiveness is not totally dependent on the teacher, and it must be considered in a much wider perspective.

System Factors

The history of education in the developing world has, until very recently, been mainly concerned with building a national system of education. The major emphasis of this activity has been on finding mechanisms to build schools, hire teachers, and enroll a substantial number of children in the schools. While an educational infrastructure is now somewhat in place in most countries, there remain enormous problems associated with that infrastructure and its management.

One of the curious observations we make in reviewing the various essays of this book is the lack of attention authors have given to the structure of educational systems. Most authors, when dealing with teachers and teaching, either do not recognize the importance of system factors in relation to the teaching process or they have chosen to focus on other central issues. Thompson (Chapter 5) is one exception as he reminds readers of the practical weaknesses of centralized bureaucratic structures that pervade the scene in the developing world, and he optimistically notes that many governments have begun seeking ways to modify their centralized management structures.

Many system factors are directly related to identifying the most qualified teachers, placing them in appropriate environments, and keeping track of them once they are assigned. Cummings

(Chapter 1) notes that information of the most basic kind, dealing with teachers in the developing world, is simply not widely available, and more adequate record keeping could facilitate the management process.   Thompson (Chapter 5) points out that a rich resource in terms of qualified teachers already exists, but much of this resource is wasted because administrators have failed to consider how teachers might best be deployed within the educational system.

Hurst and Rust (Chapter 6) are unequivocal that the working conditions in which teachers are expected to function condition what they are able to accomplish as much as the teaching competence which they possess.   If teachers are to be more effective, their physical and social surroundings will require improvement.

The Management of Change

Closely related to general management issues is the fact that any improvements in education imply innovation and change. Those students of change are acutely aware that change does not happen automatically.   The best of ideas, programs, and practices are doomed to fail unless desired change is properly understood and managed.   Dalin (Chapter 10) devotes an entire chapter to issues of educational renewal and staff development processes.   He outlines a model of effective change and the stages innovative proposals go through when effective change actually takes place. He rejects assumptions that large external costs are involved in effective change.   It is most effective when schools are liberated to discover their own needs and use their own resources to meet these needs.   On a national level, such a change orientation costs very little.   However, central bureaucracies must give up some of their power if local change has any possibility of success.

Others in the book also look at specific issues related to change. Hurst and Rust (Chapter 6) develop an argument that helps explain why teachers are often reluctant to accept change proposals.   They concur with Dalin that the mainstream assumptions about change are faulty, one assumption being that teachers are simply not motivated or interested in change. It is their view that teachers act as rational decision makers in terms of the relative advantages these innovations have for them and their students.

CONCLUDING REMARKS

We have been concerned with the improvement of teachers and teaching in the developing world. We have noted that the situation for teachers is far from ideal, and any efforts toward improvement are fraught with enormous challenges. The resources are simply not available to do what our best understanding of teaching requires. Even with resources, our knowledge base is presently so thin that we must be very tentative about what to do. However, we do know enough that improvement is not impossible, though it will be difficult.

One thing we have confidence in is that teachers in general are willing to do what is necessary to improve, if the challenges put before them seem in the best interests of the young people with whom they work. The major responsibility, however, lies with managers and policy makers to create a climate and provide the resources necessary to assist teachers in their quest to improve the teaching process.

SECTION FIVE

COMPREHENSIVE BIBLIOGRAPHY

COMPREHENSIVE BIBLIOGRAPHY

Aarons, A. (1981). Teachers and children as researchers. *Education Gazette* (Papua New Guinea), 98-99.

Abiri, J. O. O. (1976). Preparation of the secondary school mother tongue teacher. *West African Journal of Education, 20*, 7-16.

ACEID. (1984). Clustering of primary schools: A growing trend in Asia and the Pacific. *ACEID Newsletter, 28*, 13-17.

Adaralegbe, A. (1975). Preparing the primary school social studies teacher. *West African Journal of Education, 19*, 24-47.

Adeyinka. (1973). The coming of western education to Africa. *West African Journal of Education, 15*, 21-33.

Ahmad, S. H. B. (1986). *Implementing a new curriculum for primary schools: A case study from Malaysia.* Unpublished doctorial dissertation, London University.

Akinyemi, K. (1986). A study of technophobia among primary school teachers in Nigeria. *Programmed Learning and Educational Technology, 23*, 263-69.

Al-Shammarv, E. A. S. (1984). *A study of motivation in the learning of English as a foreign language in intermediate and secondary schools in Saudi Arabia.* Unpublished doctoral dissertation, Indiana University, Bloomington, IN.

Ale, S. O. (1981). Difficulties facing mathematics teachers in developing countries: A case study of Nigeria. *Educational Studies in Mathematics, 12*, 479-89.

Altbach, P. G. (1983). Key issues of textbook provision in the third world. *Prospects: Quarterly Review of Education, 13*, 315-325.

Altbach, P. G. (1987). Teaching: International concerns. *Teachers College Record, 88*, 326-29.

Anicet, M. (1982). *An examination of the structure and organisation of teaching practice in primary teachers training colleges in the People's Republic of the Congo* (African Studies in Curriculum Development & Evaluation, No. 57). Nairobi, Kenya: Nairobi University, Institute of Education.

Ankrah-Dove, L. (1982). The deployment and training of teachers for remote rural schools in less-developed countries. *International Review of Education, 28*, 3-27.

APEID (Asian Programme of Educational Innovation for Development). (1975). *Science in basic functional education: Philosophy, approaches, methods, and materials.* Bangkok: UNESCO.

APEID. (1980a). *Biology education in Asia.* Bangkok: UNESCO.

APEID. (1980b). *Linking science education to real life.* Bangkok: UNESCO.

APEID. (1980c). *Linking science education to the rural environment: Some experiences.* Bangkok: UNESCO.

APEID. (1981a). *Educational innovations in Asia and the Pacific.* Bangkok: UNESCO.

APEID. (1981b). *Development of professional support services in innovations* (Occasional Paper, No. 6). Bangkok: UNESCO.

APEID. (1985). *Grassroots networking for primary education: Case studies.* Bangkok: UNESCO.

Arishi, A. Y. (1984). *A study of EFL teachers' behaviors in EFL classes in Saudi Arabia.* Unpublished doctoral dissertation, Indiana University, Bloomington, IN.

Ariyadasa, K. D. (1976a). *In-service training of teachers in Sri Lanka* (Experiments and Innovations in Education, No. 23). Bangkok: UNESCO, Asian Centre of Educational Innovation for Development.

Ariyadasa, K. D. (1976b). *Management of educational reforms in Sri Lanka* (Experiments and Innovations in Education, No. 25). Prepared for the Asian Centre of Educational Innovation for Development. Paris: UNESCO.

Atcon, R. (1973). *Uma proposta de reforma da UFES.* Vitoria, ES: UFES.

Ausubel, D. (1963). *The psychology of meaningful verbal learning.* New York: Grune and Stratton.

Avalos, B. (1980). Teacher effectiveness: Research in the third world: Highlights of a review. *Comparative Education, 16*, 45-54.

Avalos, B. (1985). Training for better teaching in the third world: Lessons from research. *Teaching and Teacher Education, 1*, 289-299.

Avalos, B. (Ed.) (1986). *Teaching children of the poor in Latin America: An Ethnographic approach.* Ottawa, Canada: International Development Research Center.

Avalos, B., & Haddad, W. (1981). *A review of teacher effectiveness research in Africa, India, Latin America, Middle East, Malaysia, Philippines and Thailand: Synthesis of results.* Ottawa, Canada: International Development Research Center.

Awuor, M. O. (1982). *An examination of teaching practice as a component of primary teacher training in Kenya* (African Studies in Curriculum Development & Evaluation, No. 66). Nairobi Kenya: Nairobi University, Institute of Education.

Ayot, H. (1983). Teacher advisory centres in Kenya. In J. Greenland (Ed.), *The in-service training of primary school teachers in English-speaking Africa.* London: Macmillan.

Babalola, B. A. (1974). Conceptual analysis of instruction as a model for teaching plan. *West African Journal of Education, 18*, 375-81.

Badri, H. K. (1979). Distance teaching in the Sudan. *Educational Broadcasting International, 12*, 164-66.

Bagunywa, A. M. K. (1975). The changing role of the teacher in African educational renewal. *Prospects: Quarterly Review of Education, 5*, 220-6.

Barker, J. (1977). A package approach to distance teaching for developing countries. *Teaching at a Distance, 9*, 36-42.

Barrington, J. M. (1980). The teacher and the stages of educational development. *British Journal of Teacher Education, 6*, 100-114.

Basu, C. K. (1985). *In-service teacher education for universal primary education: An experimental model from Bangladesh.* Unit for Cooperation with UNICEF and WFP, UNESCO, UPEL 13.

Basu, C. K. (1986). In-service teacher training as part of the universal primary education World Bank project in Bangladesh. *Performance and Instruction, 25,* 17-18.

Bazo, M. (1987). *Modeling teacher training through the teachers who promote student learning: A review of studies on Latin America.* Cambridge, MA: Unpublished paper.

Beeby, C. E. (1965). *The quality of education in developing countries.* Cambridge, MA: Harvard University Press.

Beeby, C. E. (1966). *The quality of education in developing areas.* Cambridge: The University Press.

Beeby, C. E. (1977/78). Teachers, teacher education, and research. In R. Gardner (Ed.), *Teacher education in developing countries: Prospects for the eighties.* London: University of London, Institute of Education.

Beeby, C. E. (1979). *Assessment of Indonesian education: A guide in planning.* Wellington, NZ: Council for Educational Research.

Beeby, C. E. (1980a). Reply to Gerard Guthrie. *International Review of Education, 26,* 439-44.

Beeby, C. E. (1980b). The thesis stages fourteen years later. *International Review of Education, 26,* 451-474.

Beltran, L. R. (1976). Some structure and rural development communication in Latin America: The radiophonic schools in Colombia. Paper presented at the Summer Conference on Communication and Group Transformation for Development, East-West Communication Institute, Hawaii. In Chu, G., Rahim, S., & Kincaid, D. L. (Eds.), *Communication for Group Transformation* (Communication Monograph No. 2). Honolulu: East-West Center.

Berger, M. (1976). *Educacao e dependencia.* Porto Alegre: Difusao Europeia do livro.

Berstecher, D. (Ed.) (1985). *Education and rural development: Issues for planning and research.* Paris: UNESCO, International Institute for Educational Planning.

Bhalwankar, A. G. (1984). *A study of effects of expository and guided discovery methods of teaching mathematics on the achievement of students of different levels of intelligence.* Unpublished doctoral dissertation, University of Poona, Pune, India.

Bhargava, R. (1986). *Communicative language teaching: A case of much ado about nothing.* Paper presented at the Annual Meeting of the International Association of Teachers of English as a Foreign Language (20th, Brighton, England, April 1986).

Biddle, B., & Ellena, W. (1967). *Contemporary research on teacher effectiveness.* New York: Holt, Rinehart and Winston.

Biniakunu, D. D. (1982). In-service teacher training improves eighth graders' reading ability in Zaire. *Journal of Reading, 25,* 662-65.

Birdsall, N., & Fox, M. J. (1985). Why males earn more: Location and training of Brazilian school teachers. *Economic Development and Cultural Change, 34,* 533-56.

Blakemore, K. & Cooksey, B. (1980). *A sociology of education for Africa.* London: George Allen & Unwin.

Block, C., Gilmore, C., & Anzalone, S. (1987). *Computers in classrooms in LDs: Strategies and an update on some work in progress.* Washington, DC: Office of Education and Technology, U.S. Agency for International Development.

Bolam, R. (1981). *In-service education and training of teachers and educational change.* Paris: OECD.

Bork, A. (1987). Potential for Interactive Technology. *B.Y.T.E.* (February).

Bourke, S. F. (1985). The study of classroom contexts and practices. *Teaching and Teacher Education, 6,* 33-49.

Boyer, E. L. (1983). *High school: A report on secondary education in America*. New York: Harper and Row.

BP3K (Office of Educational Development). (1975). *Educational innovation in Indonesia*. Paris: UNESCO.

Brekka, L. T., & Revani, B. (1976). *Use of television and teacher training* (Technical Report No. 20). Stanford, CA: Stanford University, Stanford Electronics Labs.

British Council. (1981). *Focus on the teacher: Communicative approaches to teacher training* (ELT Documents 110). London: British Council, English Language and Literature Division.

Brophy, J. E. (1979). Teacher behavior and its effects. *Journal of Educational Psychology, 71*, 733-750.

Brophy, M., & Dudley, B. (1982). Patterns of distance teaching in teacher education. *Journal of Education for Teaching, 8*, 156-62.

Brophy, M., & Dudley, B. (1989). Training teachers in the third world. *Teaching at a Distance, 23*, 40-45.

Brophy, J. E., & Good, T. (1985). Teacher behavior and student achievement. In M. Wittrock (Ed.), *Handbook of research on teaching*. New York: Macmillan.

Bruce, M. (1979). Notes on European education. *Phi Delta Kappan, 61*, 389-91.

Bruner, J., Goodnow, J., & Austin, G. (1977). *A study of thinking*. New York: John Wiley.

BSSC (Biological Sciences Curriculum Study). (1965). *Biology teacher's handbook*. New York: John Wiley.

Bude, U. (1982). Towards a realistic definition of the teacher's role in primary schooling: Experiences and research evidence from Cameroon. *Compare, 12*, 105-120.

Bude, U. (1983). The adaptation concept in British colonial education. *Comparative Education, 19*, 341-55.

Bude, U. (1985). *Information seminar for headmasters, headmistresses* (Pak-German Bas-Education Project Schools). Peshawar, Pakistan: Northwest Frontier Province Education Department.

Bude, U., & Greenland, J. (1983). *In-service education and training of primary school teachers in anglophone Africa*. Baden-Baden: Deutsche Stiftung fuer internationale Entwicklung.

Burns, R. B. (1984). The process and context of teaching. In D. W. Ryan and L. W. Anderson (Eds.), *Rethinking research on teaching: Lessons from an international study* (Evaluation in Education), *8*, 95-112.

Cardoso, F. H. (1980). *As ideias e seu lugar: Ensaios sobre as teorias de desenvolvimento* (Cadernos CEBRAP, N. 33). Editora Vozos, Ltda. CEHRAP, 1980.

Carnoy, M., & Levin, H. (1976). *The limits of educational reform*. New York: McKay.

Chale, E. (1983). *Teaching and training in Tanzania*. Unpublished doctoral thesis, University of London, Institute of Education.

Chapman, D. W., & Boothroyd, R. A. (1986). *Programmed instruction as a means of improving student achievement: A look at the Liberian IEL project*. Paper presented at the IMTEC Annual Seminar, October 26-31, Denpasar, Indonesia.

Chaudhry, F. I., & Fakhro, S. Q. (1986). Computer education in Bahrain's secondary schools (a Pilot Project). *Computers and Education, 10*, 439-43.

Cheong, L. P. (1976). *Report on the experimental schools*. Singapore: Institute of Education.

Christensen, P. R., & Mugiri, E. M. (1983). *The intensive use of radio for teaching English in Kenyan rural primary schools. Exploring a cost-effective application of educational technology* (AID/DSPE-C-0051). Washington, DC: Academy for Educational Development, Inc.

Churchill, S. (1976). *The Peruvian model of innovation: The reform of basic education* (Experiments and Innovations in Education, No. 22). Paris: UNESCO.

Clark, C. M., & Peterson, P. (1986). Teachers' thought processes. In M. C. Wittrock (Ed.), *Handbook of research on teaching* (3rd edition) (pp. 255-296). New York: Macmillan.

Clark, C. M., & Yinger, R. (1979). Teachers' thinking. In P. Peterson & H. Walberg (Eds.), *Research on teaching.* New York: McCutchan.

Coker, H., Medley, D. M., & Soar, R. S. (1980). How valid are expert opinions about effective teaching? *Phi Delta Kappan, 62*, 131-134.

Cole, M. J. A. (1975). Science teaching and science curriculum development in a supposedly non-scientific culture. *West African Journal of Education, 19*, 313-22.

Coleman, J. S., et al. (1966). *Equality of educational opportunity.* Washington, DC: Department of Health, Education, and Welfare.

Coleman, J. S. (1987). "Social capital" and schools. *Momentum, 18*, 6-8.

Comber, L. C., & Keeves, J. P. (1973). *Science education in nineteen countries.* New York: John Wiley.

Cooksey, B. (1986). Policy and practice in Tanzanian secondary education since 1967. *International Journal of Educational Development, 6*, 183-202.

Council of Europe. (1970). *School systems: A guide* (rev. ed.). Strasbourg: Council of Europe, Council for Cultural Cooperation.

Crossley, M. (1980). Relevance education, strategies for curriculum change and pilot projects: A cautionary note. *International Journal of Educational Development, 4*, 245-250.

Crossley, M. (1984). Strategies for curriculum change and the question of international transfer. *Journal of Curriculum Studies, 16*, 75-88.

Crossley, M., et al. (1985). INSET: Prospects and practice in developing countries. *Journal of Education for Teaching, 11,* 120-32.

Crossley, M., & Guthrie, G. (1987). Current research in developing countries: INSET and the impact of examinations on classroom practice. *Teaching and Teacher Education, 3,* 65-76.

Cruickshank, D. R. (1986, Winter). Profile of an effective teacher. *Educational Horizons, 1,* 81-86.

Cuadra, E. (1987). *Credible data: The uses of computer technologies in legitimate educational policies, the case of Honduras.* Paper presented at the 31st Annual Meeting of the Comparative and International Education Society, March.

Cummings, W. K. (1984). *The conceptualization and diffusion of an experiment in low-cost education: A six-nation study.* An unpublished document at the International Development Research Centre, Ottawa, Canada.

Cury, C. R. J. (1984). *Ideologia e educacao Brasileira catolicos e liberais.* Sao Paulo: Cortez.

Dalin, P. (1973). *Case studies in educational innovation: Strategies for innovation in education.* Paris: OECD.

Dalin, P. (1978). *Limits to educational change.* London: Macmillan.

Dalin, P. (1986). *Skoleutvikling.* Oslo: Universitetsforlaget.

Dalin, P., & Rust, V. D. (1983). *Can schools learn?* London: Windsor. Nelson-NFER.

Dave, P. N. (in press). Teaching and teacher behavior--A trend report. In M. B. Buch (Ed.), *Third survey of research in education.* New Delhi: National Council of Educational Research and Training.

Denham, C. (1985, Summer). The expanding knowledge base of the teacher education curriculum. *Teacher Education Quarterly,* 84-94.

Dickinson, R. J. (1984). A structured approach to the production of teacher education materials: The ZeSTT experience. *Journal of Educational Television, 10,* 79-83.

Dove, L. A. (1981, June). How the World Bank can contribute to basic education given formal schooling will not go away. *Comparative Education, 17*, 173-183.

Dove, L. A. (1982a). The deployment and training of teachers for remote rural schools in less-developed countries. *International Review of Education, 28*, 3-27.

Dove, L. A. (1982b). *Lifelong teacher education and the community school* (UIE Monographs, 10). Hamburg: UNESCO Institute for Education.

Dove, L. A. (1985). *The development and training of teachers for remote rural schools in less developed countries* (Notes, Comments, Child Family Community, NS 164). Paris: UNESCO.

Dove, L. A. (1986). *Teachers and teacher education in developing countries.* London: Croom Helm.

Doyle, W. (1977). Paradigms for research on teacher effectiveness. In L. S. Shulman (Ed.), *Review of research in education* (Vol. 5). Itasca, IL: Peacock.

Doyle, W. (1983a). Paradigms for research. In M. Dunkin (Ed.), *The international encyclopedia of teaching and teacher education.* Oxford, Pergamon.

Doyle, W. (1983b). Academic Work. *Review of Educational Research, 53*, 159-199.

Doyle, W. (1987). Paradigms for research. In M. Dunkin (Ed.), *The International encyclopedia of teaching and teacher education.* Oxford: Pergamon.

Doyle, W., & Ponder, G. (1977). The practicality ethic in teacher decision making. *Interchange, 8*, 1-12.

Duck, L. (1981). *Teaching with charisma.* Boston: Allyn and Bacon.

Duncan, W., & Loefstedt, J.-I. (1982). *School building, teacher training and village development in Bangladesh.* Stockholm: University of Stockholm, Institute of International Education.

Dunkin, M. J., & Biddle, B. (1974). *The Study of Teaching.* New York: Holt, Rinehart and Winston.

Eaker, R., & Huffman, J. (1980). *Helping teachers use research findings: The consumer-validation process.* East Lansing, MI: Michigan State University, Institute for Research on Teaching.

Eddy, C. L. (1981). *OECD in the Caribbean: A review and a look forward.* Unpublished material.

Edelfelt, R. (1985). *An analysis of policy needs for in-service education in Indonesia.* Oslo, Norway: IMTEC.

Edman, M. (1968). *A self-image of primary school teachers.* Detroit: Wayne State University Press.

Ekanayake, S. B. (1980). Training teachers for changing roles in Sri Lanka. *Prospects: Quarterly Review of Education, 10,* 504-11.

Elley, W. B., & Mangubhai, F. (1981a). *The impact of a book flood in Fiji primary schools.* Wellington, NZ: New Zealand Council for Education Research and University of the South Pacific, Institute of Education.

Elley, W. B., & Mangubhai, F. (1981b). The long-term effects of a book flood on children's language growth. *Directions* [Suva, Fiji: University of South Pacific, Institute of Education], *7,* 15-24.

Elliott, J. (1976-77). Developing hypotheses about classrooms from teachers' practical constructs. *Interchange, 7*(2), 2-26.

Elton, L., & Manwaring, G. (1981). Training and education of teachers in higher education in developing countries. *Higher Education, 10,* 131-40.

Encyclopedia Britannica, (1985). *Yearbook.* Chicago: Encyclopedia Britannica, Inc.

Erdos, R. F. (1975). *Establishing an institution teaching by correspondence* (International Bureau of Education Series, No. 17: Experiments and Innovations in Education). Paris: UNESCO.

Eshiwani, G. S. (1979). The goals of mathematics teaching in Africa: A need for re-examination. *Prospects: Quarterly Review of Education*, *9*, 346-52.

ETS (Educational Testing Service). (1976). *Teachers make a difference*. Princeton, NJ: ETS.

Evans, D. (1976). Technology in nonformal education: A critical appraisal. *Comparative Education Review*, *20*, 305-326.

Evans, D. (1979). *Dependent development: The alliance of multinational, state, and local capital in Brazil*. Princeton: Princeton University Press.

Farnes, N. (1973). Distance teaching for developing countries. *Teaching at a Distance*, *5*, 34-39.

Faure, E. (1972). *Learning to be*. Paris: Unesco.

Fensham, P. J. (1986). *Science for all*. Paper presented at the annual meeting of the American Educational Research Association, San Francisco.

Ferede, Y. (1981). *The role of elementary school teachers in curriculum development and implementation in selected government elementary schools of Addis Ababa* (African Studies in Curriculum Development & Evaluation No. 11). Nairobi, Kenya: Nairobi University Institute of Education.

Fernau, C. (1984). Methods and techniques. Student involvement in the production of teaching aids. *Labour Education*, *54*, 35-39.

Field, S. (1981). *Generalist teaching policy and practice* (Research Report No. 36). Port Moresby: University of Papua New Guinea, Educational Research Unit.

Flanders, N. (1970). *Analyzing teacher behavior*. New York: Addison Wesley.

Florio, S., & Walsh, M. (1978). *The teacher as colleague in classroom research*. East Lansing, MI: Michigan State University, Institute for Research on Teaching.

Florio-Ruane, S., & Burak-Dohanich, J. (1984). *Communicating research findings: Teacher-research deliberations.* East Lansing, MI: Michigan State University, Institute for Research on Teaching.

Freire, P. (1979). *Educacao e mudanca.* Rio de Janeiro: Paz e Terra.

Fretwell, D. H. (1978). Teacher training in developing nations. *School-Shop, 38,* 62-63.

Fretwell, D. H. (1981). *Technology transfer and vocational teacher training in developing countries.* Paper presented at the Annual Convention of the American Vocational Association (Atlanta, GA, December 1981).

Fullan, M. (1982). *The meaning of educational change.* Toronto: OISE Press.

Fuller, B. (1987). *Raising school quality in developing countries: What investments boost learning?* (Discussion Papers, No. 2). Washington, DC: World Bank.

Gage, N. (1978). *The scientific basis of the art of teaching.* New York: Columbia University, Teachers College Press.

Gage, N. (1984). What do we know about teaching effectiveness? *Phi Delta Kappan, 66,* 87-93.

Gagne, R. M. (1985). *The conditions of learning* (4th ed.). New York: Holt Rinehart and Winston.

Gallegos, A. M. (1982, Jan.). The growing education crisis in developing countries: Conditions affecting improvement and some new perspectives. *Educational Technology, 22,* 1.

Galton, M., Simon, B., & Croll, P. (1980a). *Inside the primary school.* London: Routledge & Kegan Paul.

Galton, M., Simon, B., & Croll, P. (1980b). *Progress and performance in primary classroom.* London: Routledge & Kegan Paul.

Gama, E. M. P., et al. (1985). *Diagnostico estadual da educacao no Espirito Santo.* Vitoria, Espirito Santo: PPGE-UFES.

Gardner, R. (Ed.) (1979). *Teacher education in developing countries: Prospects for the eighties.* London: University of London Institute of Education.

Gianordoli, R. L. (1987). Valiacao do curso de pedagogia da UFES atraves da percepcao de professores. *Alunos e Egressos do Curso, 1,* Vitoria: UFES.

Garrison, J. W., & Macmillan, C. J. B. (1983). A philosophical critique of the process-product research on teaching. *Educational Theory, 34,* 255-274.

Gimeno, J. B., & Ibanez, R. M. (1977). *The education of primary and secondary school teachers.* Paris: UNESCO.

Gitau, B. K. (1987). Achievement motivation in distance education: An experimental study to measure students' achievement motive as elicited by achievement arousal conditions given in reference to, and with emphasis on written assignments. *International Council for Distance Education Bulletin, 14,* 37-47.

Goad, L. H. (1984). *Preparing teachers for lifelong education.* Hamburg: UNESCO, Institute for Education.

Goble, N. M., & Porter, J. F. (1977). *The changing role of the teacher: International perspectives.* Paris: UNESCO.

Good, T. (1983, April). *Classroom research: A decade of progress.* Paper presented at the meeting of the American Educational Research Association, Montreal, Canada.

Good, T., & Brophy, J. (1984). *Looking in classrooms.* New York: Harper and Row.

Goode, T. (1963). *Classroom research: A decade of progress.* Paper presented at the meeting of the American Educational Research Association, Montreal, Canada.

Goodings, G. R., Byram, M., & McPartland, M. (Eds.) (1982). *Changing priorities in teacher education.* London: Croom Helm.

Graham, J. W., & Paige, D. D. (1980). Research and evaluation in radio education in Nepal. Report filed on 20 February.

Gray, R. A. (1988, May). Educational technology use in distance education: historical review and future trends. *Educational Technology, 28*, 38-42.

Greenland, J. (Ed.) (1983). *The in-service training of primary teachers in English-speaking Africa.* London: Macmillan.

Grenholm, L. H. (1975). *Radio study group campaigns in the United Republic of Tanzania* (International Bureau of Education Series, No. 15: Experiments and Innovations in Education). Paris: UNESCO.

Grimmelt, P. (Ed.) (1984). *Research in teacher education: Current problems and future prospects in Canada.* Vancouver: University of British Columbia.

Guthrie, G. (1980a). Stages of educational development? Beeby revisited. *International Review of Education, 26*, 411-438.

Guthrie, G. (1980b). Response [to C. E. Beeby] from Gerard Guthrie. *International Review of Education, 26*, 445-449.

Guthrie, G. (1984). Secondary teacher training effectiveness in Papua New Guinea. *Studies in Educational Evaluation, 10*, 205-08.

Guthrie, G. (1985). Current research in developing countries: Teacher credentialling and distance education. *Teaching and Teacher Education, 1*, 81-90.

Guthrie, G. (1986). Current research in developing countries: The impact of curriculum reform on teaching. *Teaching and Teacher Education, 2*, 81-89.

Haddad, W. D. (1985). *Teacher training: A review of World Bank experience* (Discussion Paper, No. EDT 21). Washington, DC: World Bank.

Hadiatamadja, S. (1976). *Higher education and development in Indonesia: The viability of the multi-purpose function of the community college at the undergraduate level of the university system.* Unpublished doctoral dissertation, University of Southern California, Los Angeles, CA.

Hall, B. (1973). *Wakati wa furaha: An evaluation of a radio study group campaign*. Uppsala: The Scandinavian Institute for African Studies.

Hall, G. E. (1979). *A national agenda for research and development in teacher education: 1979-1984*. Austin, TX: University of Texas, Research and Development Center for Teacher Education.

Halliwell, J. (1987, Jan.). Is distance education by radio outdated? A consideration of the outcome of an experiment in continuing medical education with rural health care workers in Jamaica. *British Journal of Educational Technology, 18*(1).

Harley, G. S. E. (1982). *Instructional design models and teaching models in tertiary education with reference to distance education*. Unpublished doctoral dissertation, University of South Africa, Pretoria, South Africa.

Harris, H. T. B. (n.d.). *The administrative structures of education: Case studies of sixteen countries* (Reports, Studies C 105). Paris: UNESCO.

Hawes, H. W. R. (1976). *Locally based educational research and curriculum development in developing countries--the teacher's role* (IIEP Occasional Papers, No. 40). Paris: UNESCO, International Institute for Educational Planning.

Hawes, H. W. R. (1979). The curriculum of teacher education. In R. Gardner (Ed.), *Teacher education in developing countries: Prospects for the eighties*. London: University of London Institute of Education.

Hawes, H. W. R. (1982, Dec.). *Professional support for teachers in schools: An Indonsian case study* (EDC Occasional Papers, No. 3). London: University of London, Institute of Education.

Hawkridge, D. (1988). Distance education and the World Bank. *British Journal of Educational Technology, 19*, 84-95.

Hebenstreit, J. (1984). *Computers in education in developing countries*. Paris: UNESCO, Div. of Structures, Content, Methods, and Techniques of Education.

Henderson, K. B. (1973). Research on teaching secondary school mathematics. In N. L. Gage (Ed.), *Handbook of research on teaching*. Chicago: Rand McNally.

Heyneman, S. (1984). Research on education in the developing countries. *International Journal of Educational Development, 4*, 293-304.

Heyneman, S., Farrell, J. P., & Sepulveda-Stuardo, M. A. (1978). *Textbooks and achievement: What we know* (Staff Working Paper, No. 298). Washington, DC: World Bank.

Heyneman, S., & Loxley, W. A. (1983). Influences on academic achievement across 29 high and low income countries. *American Journal of Sociology, 88*, 1162-1194.

Holderness, W. L. (1986). *Upgrading primary education in the senteen circuits, 1980-85* (Occasional Publication, No. 2). Mafeking: University of Bophuthatswana, Institute of Education.

Holmberg, B. (1985). Applications of distance education in Kenya. *Distance Education, 6*, 242-47.

Hough, J., & Duncan, J. (1970). *Teaching description and analysis*. New York: Addison Wesley.

Hoyle, E. (1973). Strategies of curriculum change. In R. Watkins (Ed.), *In-service training: Structure and content*. London: Ward Lock.

Hoyle, E., & Megarry, J. (Eds.) (1980). *Professional development of teachers. World Yearbook of Education 1980: Professional Development of Teachers*. London: Kogan Page.

Huberman, A. M. (1973). *Understanding change in education: An introduction*. Paris: UNESCO, IBE.

Huberman, A. M., & Miles, M. (1984). *How school improvement works*. New York: Plenum.

Hunt, D. E. (n.d.). *In-service training as persons-in-relation*. Ontario: Ontario Institute for Studies in Education.

Hunter, M. (1981). *Teach more--Faster*. El Segundo, CA: TIP Publications.

Huq, M. (1965). *Education and development strategy in South and Southeast Asia.* Honolulu: East-West Center Press.

Huq, M. (1975). *Education, manpower and development in South and Southeast Asia.* New York: Praeger.

Hurst, P. (1983). *Implementing educational change: A critical review of the literature* (EDC Occasional Paper, No. 5). London: University of London, Institute of Education.

Husen, T., Saha, L. J., Noonan, R. (1978, Dec.). *Teacher training and student achievement in less developed countries* (Staff Working Paper, No. 310). Washington, DC: World Bank.

IBE (International Bureau of Education). (1979). *Teachers and educational research.* Geneva: IBE.

IBE. (1985). In-service teacher education. *IBE Bulletin,* 234/5, 1-2nd quarter. Paris: UNESCO.

Ibe-Bassey, G. S. (1988). How Nigerian teachers select instructional materials. *British Journal of Educational Technology, 19,* 17-27.

IBGE. (1980). *Censo Demografico.*

ILO. (1978). *Teachers' pay.* Geneva: International Labour Office.

ILO. (1981a). *Employment and conditions of work of teachers.* Geneva: International Labour Office.

ILO. (1981b). *Report of the joint meeting on conditions of work of teachers.* Report of a meeting held at Geneva from 27 Oct. to 4 Nov., 1981.

ILO/UNESCO. (1976). *Report of the joint ILO / UNESCO Committee of experts on the application of the recommendation concerning the status of teachers* (Doc. 19C/23; CEART/III/1976/10) (Third session, Geneva, 8-19 March, 1976).

ILO/UNESCO. (1983). *Joint ILO / UNESCO committee of experts on the application of the recommendation concerning the status of teachers.* Geneva: International Labour Office.

ILO/UNESCO. (1984). *The status of teachers: An instrument for its improvement: The international recommendation of 1966: Joint commentaries by the ILO and Unesco.* Geneva: International Labour Office.

Inkeles, A., & Sirowy, L. (1979). *Cross-national comparison of student-to-teacher ratios: An example in convergence theory.* Stanford, CA: Stanford University, Institute for Research on Educational Finance and Governance.

International Federation of Teachers. (1963). Difficulties facing primary school teachers in seven new nations. *Panorama, 5,* 2-4.

Islam, A, K. M. A. (1975). Physics teaching in developing countries. *Physics Education, 12,* 334-335.

Jackson, P. (1968). *Life in classrooms.* New York: Holt, Rinehart and Winston.

Jain, S. C. (1977). Biology teachers in Indian schools and their training. *Journal of Biological Education, 11,* 91-4.

Jamison, D., & McAnany, E. (1978). *Radio for Education and Development.* Beverly Hills: Sage.

Jamison, D. T., & Orivel, F. (1978). The cost-effectiveness of distance teaching projects. *Educational Broadcasting International, 11,* 169-75.

Jangira, N., & Sharma, S. (1974). Teaching and teacher behavior. In *Survey of research in education.* Baroda: M. S. University, Center of Advance Study in Education.

Jenkins, C. (1978). *Formal and informal education for national development in Indonesia.* Unpublished doctoral dissertation, University of Massachusetts, Amherst, MA.

Jenkins, J., et al. (1986). *Distance teaching: A catalyst for curriculum change for introducing vocational subjects.* Paper presented at the Vocationalising Education Conference (London, England, May 7-9, 1986).

Jennings-Wray, Z. D. (1980). A comparative study of influences and constraints on decision-making in the primary school curriculum: Some implications for the teacher as an agent of change in third world countries. *Journal of Curriculum Studies, 12,* 231-44.

Jennings-Wray, Z. D. (1982). Agricultural education and work experience programmes in schools in a third world country: What prospects for human resources development. *Comparative Education, 18,* 281-292.

Jennings-Wray, Z. D., & Wellington, P. I. (1985). Educational technology utilization in Jamaica's secondary school system: Present problems and future prospects. *British Journal of Educational Technology, 16,* 169-83.

Johnston, S. A. (1985). An Approach to the teaching of academic writing. *ELT Journal, 39,* 248-52.

Johnstone, J., & Jiyono. (1983). Out-of-school factors and educational achievement in Indonesia. *Comparative Education Review, 27,* 278-295.

Joyce, B., Hersh, R. H., & McKibbin, M. (1983). *The structure of school improvement.* New York: Longman.

Joyce, B., & Showers, B. (1980, Feb.). Improving in-service training: The messages of research. *Educational Leadership, 37,* 379-84.

Joyce, B., & Showers, B. (1983). *Power in staff development through research on teaching.* Washington, D. C.: ASCD.

Joyce, B., & Weil, M. (1986). *Models of teaching.* Englewood, Cliffs, NJ: Prentice-Hall.

Junge, B., & Shrestha, S. M. (1984). Another barrier broken: Teaching village girls to read in Nepal. *Reading Teacher, 37,* 846-52.

Kaewdang, R. (1983). *A study of the school cluster system.* Bangkok: Office of the National Primary Education Commission.

Kaneko, M. (1987). *Enrollment expansion in postwar Japan.* Hiroshima: Hiroshima University Research Institute for Higher Education.

Karasawa, T. (1955). *Kyoshi no rekishi*. Tokyo: Sobunsha.

Karnick, K. (1981). *Developmental Television in India*. Educational Broadcasting International.

Keleher, J. (1975). Primary and teacher education in the Kano State of Nigeria. *West African Journal of Education, 19*, 247-54.

Kenya, Republic of. (1971). *Report of the Commission of Enquiry*. Nairobi.

Kindervatter, S., et al. (1985). Training of trainers and adult educators: Case studies. *Convergence: An International Journal of Adult Education, 18*, 116-42.

King, K. (1982). Formal, nonformal, and informal learning: Some North-South contrasts. *International Review of Education, 28*, 177-187.

King, F. S. (1985). Teaching aids at low cost. *Media in Education and Development, 18*, 68-72.

Kinyanjui, P. (1977). In-service training of teachers through radio and correspondence in Kenya. In P. Spain, D. Jamison, & E. McAnany, (Eds.), *Radio for Education and Development: Case Studies* (Working Paper No. 226) (Vol. 1). Washington, DC: World Bank.

Kiray, M. B. (1979). Teaching in developing countries: The case of Turkey. *International Social Science Journal, 31*, 40-48.

Kitchen, R. D. (1969, May). Helping teachers to further their education through university external courses. *Teacher Education in New Countries, 10*, 35-42.

Knamiller, G.W. (1981). Environmental education and the north-south dialogue. *Comparative Education, 17*, 87-94.

Kohlberg, L. (1976). The cognitive developmental approach to moral education. In D. Purpel & K. Ryan (Eds.), *Moral education . . . It comes with the territory*. Berkeley: McCutchen.

Komenan, A., & Grootaert, C. (1988). *Teacher-nonteacher pay differences in Cote D'Ivoire* (Policy, Planning, and Research Working Paper, No. 12). Washington, DC: World Bank.

Kouraogo, P. (1987). Curriculum Renewal and INSET in Difficult Circumstances. *ELT Journal, 41*, 171-78.

Kouyate, M. (1978). The teacher shortage and peer teaching in Africa. *Prospects: Quarterly Review of Education, 8*, 33-46.

Kraig, A. B. (1980). State of the art instructional technology. *International Journal of Instructional Media, 8*(1).

Kulshrestha, S. P. (1979). *Emerging value-pattern of teachers and new trends of education in India.* New Delhi: Light and Life Publishers.

LaBelle, T. J. (1973). *The new professional in Venezuelan secondary education.* Los Angeles: University of California, Los Angeles, Latin American Studies Center.

Lacson, J. D. (1987). *Cost-effective national schemes.* Paper presented at the Regional Workshop on Technical/Vocational Teacher Training (Chiba City, Japan, May 11-22, 1987).

Lalor, G. C., & Marrett, C. (1986). *University of the West Indies Distance Teaching Experiment.* Report of the University of the West Indies, Mona (Jamaica).

Lalor, G. C. (1983). *The University of the West Indies Distance Teaching Project* (Report to the advisory council, ACEP 7). Mona, Jamaica: University of the West Indies.

Lanier, J. (1984). *The future of teacher education: Two papers* (Occasional Paper, No. 79). East Lansing, MI: Michigan State University, Institute for Research on Teaching.

Lanier, J. (1986). Research in teacher education. In M. C. Wittrock (Ed.), *Handbook of research on teaching* (3rd ed.). New York: Macmillan.

Lewin, K. (1984). Selection and curriculum reform. In J. Oxenham (Ed.), *Education versus qualifications?* (pp. 115-46). London: Allen and Unwin.

Lewis, G., & Ransley, R. (1977). Piagetian testing in the South Pacific: Implications for teacher education. *South Pacific Journal of Teacher Education, 5*, 191-198.

Lillis, K. M. (1983). Processes of curriculum innovation in Kenya. *Comparative Education, 19*, 89-107.

Lindvall, M. (1984). Individual differences and school learning environments. In E. W. Gordon (Ed.), *Review of research in education*. Washington, DC: American Educational Research Association.

Lo, B. L. C. (1984). Teacher education in the eighties. In R. Hoyboe (Ed.), *Contemporary Chinese education*. New York: M. E. Sharpe.

Lopez, G., Assael, J., & Neumann, E. (1986). School failure: Who is responsible? In B. Avalos (Ed.), *Teaching children of the poor: An ethnographic study in Latin America*. Ottawa: IDRC.

Lortie, D. C. (1975). *School-teacher: A sociological study*. Chicago: University of Chicago Press.

Loucks, S., & Hall, G. B. (1979). *Implementing innovations in schools: A concern-based approach*. Washington, DC: AERA.

Lowe, J., Grant, N., & Williams, T. D. (1971). *Education and nation building in the third world*. Edinburgh: Scottish Academic Press.

Lucas, J., & Lorayne, H. (1974). *The memory book*. New York: Ballentine.

McAnany, E. (1973). *Radio's role in development: Five strategies of use*. Washington, DC: Academy for Eductional Development, Information Center on Instructional Technology.

McConnelogue. (1975). In P. Taylor (Ed.), *Aims, influences, and change in the primary school curriculum*. London/Slough: NFER.

McCormick, B. (1984). Prospects and problems for China's TVUs. *Media in Education and Development, 17*, 136-39.

McGinn, N., Warwick, D. P., & Reimers, Fernando. (1989). *Policy choices to improve school effectiveness in Pakistan*. Paper presented at the VIIth World Congress of Comparative Education, Montreal, Canada, June, 1989.

Malkawi, F. H. (1984). *A case study of chemistry teaching and learning in a tenth grade classroom in Jordan.* Unpublished doctoral dissertation, Michigan State University, East Lansing, MI.

Mampouya, G. (1982). *A study of the effectiveness of the teaching of the English language in the Congo* (African Studies in Curriculum Development & Evaluation, No. 53). Nairobi, Kenya: Nairobi University, Institute of Education.

Mandeville, G. K. (1987). Reanalysing teaching research data: Problems and promises. *Evaluation in Education, 8*(2).

Mani, A. (1980). *Determinants of educational aspirations among Indonesian youth.* Unpublished doctoral dissertation, University of Wisconsin, Madison, WI.

Marquez, A. D. (1975). The educator in the Latin American context. *Prospects: Quarterly Review of Education, 5,* 227-29.

Marshall, D. G. (1984). Computer technology in third world education. *Computers and Education, 8,* 377-81.

Martaamidjaja, A. S. (1981). *A study of verbal interaction patterns of agricultural vocational high school teachers in West Java, Indonesia.* Unpublished doctoral dissertation, East Texas State University, Commerce, TX.

Marx, K. (1867). *Das Kapital: Zur kritik der politischen oekonomie.* Hamburg: Otto Meissner.

Masota, L. A. (1982). *Investigation of the Effectiveness of Teacher-Education Curriculum in Primary School Mathematics in Tanzania Mainland* (African Studies in Curriculum Development and Evaluation, No. 64). Nairobi, Kenya: Nairobi University, Institute of Education.

Medley, D. (1982a). *Teacher competence and teacher effectiveness: A review of process-product research.* Washington, DC: AACTE.

Medley, D. (1982b). Teacher effectiveness. In H. E. Mitzel (Ed.), *Encyclopedia of educational research.* New York: Free Press.

Menezes-de-Figueiredo, N., & Menou, M. J. (1988). Assessing needs for teaching information science in Brazil. *Journal of Education for Library and Information Science, 28*, 188-200.

Meyer, J. W., & Hannah, M. (1980). *National development.* Chicago: University of Chicago Press.

Miles, M. B. (1964). *Innovation in education.* New York: Teachers College, Columbia University.

Miles, M. B. (1980). *Common properties of schools in context: The backdrop for knowledge utilization and school improvement.* Washington, DC: National Institute of Education.

Miller, E. L. (1981). "Teachers of Survival"--The task of teacher education. *Caribbean Journal of Education, 8*, 194-215.

Miller, L. E., & Dlamini, B. M. (1987). *The Swaziland agriculture teacher education program as perceived by professionals in agricultural education.* Paper presented at the Annual Meeting of the Association for International Agricultural Education (3rd, Chevy Chase, MD, April 24-26, 1987).

Mitzel, H. E. (1960). Teacher effectiveness. In C. H. Harris (Ed.), *Encyclopedia of educational research* (3rd. ed.). New York: Macmillan.

Mitzel, H. E. (1970). The Impending instructional revolution. *Phi Delta Kappa, 52*, 434-39.

Mody, B. (1978). *Lessons from the Indian satellite experiment.* Educational Broadcasting International.

Molomo, R. (1983). The Botswana in-service team: A mobile support service for primary schools. In J. Greenland (Ed.), *The in-service training of primary teachers in English-speaking Africa* (pp. 138-152). London: Macmillan.

Morgan, V., & Dunn, S. (1981, Spring). Teacher recruitment: Regional patterns. *Oideas, 23*, 5-21.

Morris, P. (1985). Teachers' perceptions of the barriers to the implementation of a pedagogic innovation: A South East Asian case study. *International Review of Education, 31*, 3-18.

Mukhalu, F. (1982). *Techniques and strategies of improving the supervision, assessment and evaluation of the competence of student teachers in the Kenya primary teachers' training colleges* (African Studies in Curriculum Development & Evaluation, No. 44). Nairoby, Kenya: Nairobi University, Institute of Education.

Mulay, V. (1978). The teacher in the sky. *Prospects: Quarterly Review of Education, 8,* 531-34.

Murphy, P. *The Lesotho Distance Teaching Centre: Five years' learning* (IEC Broadsheets on Distance Learning No. 16). Cambridge, England: International Extension College.

Musto, S., et al. (1971, June). *Los medios de communicacion social al servicio del desarrollo: Analisis de eficiencia de "accion cultural popular" radio sutatenza.* Bogota, Colombia: Accion Cultural Popular.

Mutiso, M. A. (1982). *Towards determining and developing an appropriate video programme for in-service training of primary school teachers in Kenya* (African Studies in Curriculum Development & Evaluation. No. 52). Nairobi, Kenya: Nairobi University, Institute of Education.

Muyeed, A. (1982). Some reflections on education for rural development. *International Review of Education, 28,* 228-238.

National Research Council. (1987). *Microcomputer applications in education and training for developing countries.* Boulder, CO: Westview Press.

Namuddu, C. (1986). *Teaching and learning biology: Teacher participation in research for professional growth* (Draft report No. 3). Nairobi: Kenyatta University.

Nguchu, R. R. (1981). *The extent to which radio is used in teaching of home science in urban primary schools in Kenya* (African Studies in Curriculum Development and Evaluation, No. 30). Nairobi, Kenya: Nairobi University, Institute of Education.

Nichols, J. C. (1982, May). Aspects de la radiodiffusion directe par satellite. *Revue de L'UER, 18*(3).

Nitsaisook, M. (1985). *Classroom environment study, phase I: The correlational study: Thailand.* Bangkok: Ministry of Education, Department of Teacher Education.

Novak, J., & Gowin, D. B. (1984). *Learning how to learn.* Cambridge: Cambridge University Press.

Nunn, A. (1987). *The Peruvian educational reform of 1972 and its implementation in Ayacucho.* Unpublished doctoral dissertation, University of Sussex, Sussex, England.

Nwagwu, N. A. (1976). African students' attitudes towards school teaching as a career. *Educational Review, 29,* 47-57.

Nwagwu, N. (1981). The Impact of changing conditions of service on the recruitment of teachers in Nigeria. *Comparative Education, 17,* 81-94.

Obidi, S. S. (1975). Towards the professionalization of teaching in Africa. *West African Journal of Education, 19,* 239-46.

OECD (Organization for Economic Cooperation and Development). (1971). *Training, recruitment, and utilization of teachers in primary and secondary education.* Paris: OECD.

OECD. (1975). *Classification of educational systems: Summary volume.* Paris: OECD.

OECD. (1979). Development assistance. *OECD Observer, 17.*

Ogunsola, A. F. (1975). Teacher education programme in Nigeria. *West African Journal of Education, 19,* 229-38.

Okwudishu, C. O., & Klasek, C. B. (1986). An analysis of the cost-effectiveness of educational radio in Nepal. *British Journal of Educational Technology, 17,* 173-85.

Oliveros, A. (1975a). Change and the Latin American teacher: Potential and Limitations. *Prospects: Quarterly Review of Education, 5,* 230-238.

Oliveros, A. (1975b). *La formacion de los profesores en America Latina* (Barcelona: Promocion Cultural, S.A.). Paris: UNESCO.

Onganga, O. O. (1982). *An Evaluation of the Effectiveness of Radio Programmes in Teaching English Language to Class Six Pupils in Primary Schools in South Nyanza, Kenya* (African Studies in Curriculum Development & Evaluation, No. 46). Nairobi, Kenya: Nairobi University, Institute of Education.

Orungbemi, O. O. (1987). *An investigation of some problems of teaching social studies at primary school level in Ondo State, Nigeria.* Unpublished doctoral thesis, University of Wales, Cardiff, Wales.

Oxenham, J. (1975). *Non-formal education approaches to teaching literacy: Program of study in non-formal education* (Supplementary Series, Paper No. 2). East Lansing, MI: Michigan State University, Institute for International Studies in Education.

Padma, M. S. (1979). Teaching and teacher behavior. In M. B. Buch (Ed.), *Second survey of research in education.* Baroda: Society for Educational Research and Development.

Pedro, E. (1984, Sept.). Rebuilding teacher attitudes in a climate of transition. *Bernard van Leer Foundation Newsletter*, 8-10.

Peiris, K. (1983). *Tiny sapling, sturdy tree: The inside story of primary education reforms of the 1970s in Sri Lanka.* Oslo: Universitetsforlaget.

Perraton, H. (1983). *Secondary education at a distance* (IEC Broadsheets on Distance Learning, No. 12). Cambridge, England: International Extension College.

Perrott, E., & Padma, M. S. (1981). The transfer of a self-instructional teacher-training course from Britain to India. *Programmed Learning and Educational Technology*, *18*, 136-43.

Phillips, D. C. (1980, Dec.). What do the researcher and the practitioner have to offer each other? *Educational Researcher*, *9*, 17-20, 24.

Piaget, J. (1952). *The origins of intelligence in children.* New York: International University Press

Pillai, J. K. (1976). Teacher education programmes and personal growth of teachers. *New Frontiers in Education, 6*, 32-38.

Poonwassie, D. H. (1987, July). *International co-operation to provide teacher education in the small islands of the Caribbean.* Paper presented to the VIth World Congress of Comparative Education, Rio de Janeiro, Brazil.

Popper, K. R. (1966). *The open society and its enemies: Hegel and Marx* (Vol. 2). Princeton: Princeton University Press.

Postlethwaite, T. N., & Thomas, R. M. (1980). *Schooling in the ASEAN region.* Oxford: Pergamon.

Powell, K., & Berd, J. M. (1984). *Teacher effectiveness: An annotated bibliography and guide to research.* New York: Garland.

Powell, J. L. (1985). *The teacher's craft: A study of teaching in primary school.* Edinburgh: The Scottish Council for Research in Education.

Pritchard, R. M. O. (1983, Oct.). The status of teachers in Germany and Ireland. *Comparative Education Review, 27*, 341-350.

Pynn, M. E. (1978). *Special education in developing nations: A proposal for teacher training in Ecuador.* Paper presented at the World Congress on Future Special Education (First, Stirling, Scotland, June 25 - July 1, 1978).

Quansah, K. B. (1985). Current testing in Africa: Selection or measure of real performance? *Prospects: Quarterly Review of Education, 31*, 281-288.

Rappaport, R., et al. (1986). Learning resources. *Media in Education and Development, 19*, 61-79.

Rasheed, M. A. (1986). *Teachers education development in the Arab Gulf States.* Paper presented at the World Assembly of the International Council on Education for Teaching, Kingston, Jamaica, July 20-24, 1986.

Reed, R. J. (1975). *Characteristics of teachers; A survey tool for policy making: A descriptive study in Liberia.* Berkeley: University of California, Program in International Education Finance.

REPELITA IV. (1984). *Policies and prospects for sustained development under challenging conditions.* Jakarta: Republic of Indonesia.

Reuksuppasompon, K. (1983). *A study of the teaching of literature written in English in selected universities in Thailand.* Unpublished doctoral dissertation, University of Southern Illinois, Carbondale, IL.

Robson, M. (1982). Developing teacher education resource materials in Zimbabwe. *Median Education and Development, 15,* 85-91.

Ringer, F. K. (1979). *Education and society in modern Europe.* Bloomington: Indiana University Press.

Rosenshine, B. (1983). Teaching functions in instructional programs. *Elementary School Journal, 83,* 335-330.

Rosenshine, B. V., & Berliner, D. C. (1978). Academic engaged time. *British Journal of Teacher Education, 4,* 3-16.

Rotimi, B. O. (1975). Adeyemi College of Education: 1964-1974 (A decade of experiment in the supply of middle level manpower in teacher education). *West African Journal of Education, 19,* 503-16

Ruiz, T., & Ruiz, E. (1976). Some applications of educational technology for teacher education in Peru. *Educational Broadcasting International, 9,* 75-6.

Russell, T. (1984). The importance and the challenge of refection in action by teachers. In P. Grimmelt (Ed.), *Research in teacher education: Current problems and future prospects in Canada.* Vancouver: University of British Columbia.

Russell, T. (1985). *Re-framing the theory-practice relationship in in-service teacher education.* Paper presented at the conference on "Rethinking Teacher Education," Toronto, April 28-30.

Rust, V. D. (1977). *Alternatives in Education: Theoretical and historical perspectives*. London: Sage.

Rust, V. D. (1984). What can we learn from others? *Wilson Quarterly, 8*, 78-90.

Rust, V. D. (1985). Academic ability among teachers: The unusual case of Norway. *Teaching and Teacher Education, 1*, 263-271.

Ryan, D. W., & Anderson, L. W. (1987). Rethinking research on teaching: Lessons learned from an international study. *Evaluation in Education, 8*(2).

Salamone, V. A., & Salamone, F. A. (1982). Student teachers and change. *Anthropology and Education Quarterly, 13*, 61-72.

Saunders, M., & Vulliamy, G. (1983). The implementation of curricular reform: Tanzania and Papua New Guinea. *Comparative Education Review, 27*, 351-373.

Schiefelbein, E., and Simmons, J. (1981). *The determinants of school achievement: A review of the research for developing countries*. Ottawa: International Development Research Centre.

Schmuck, R., Runkel, P., & Arends, J. (1977). *The second handbook of organizational development in schools*. Palo Alto, CA: Mayfield.

Schon, D. (1983). *The reflective practitioner*. New York: Basic Books.

Schuck, R. (1981). The impact of set induction on student achievement and retention. *Journal of Educational Research, 74*, 227-232.

SEAMEO (Southeast Asian Ministries of Education Organization) INNOTECH. (1980a). *Project impact: A terminal report*. Manila, Innotech.

SEAMEO INNOTECH. (1980b). *Project impact: The curriculum and the delivery system*. Manila: Innotech.

Searle, B., et al. (1975). *Application of radio to teaching elementary mathematics in a developing country* (Second Annual Report). Stanford, CA: Stanford University, Institute for Mathematical Studies in Social Science.

Searle, B., et al. (1976). *Application of radio to teaching elementary mathematics in a developing country* (Third Annual Report). Stanford, CA: Stanford University, Institute for Mathematical Studies in Social Science.

Searle, B, Friend, J, & Suppes, P. (1976). *The Radio Mathematics Project, 1974-75.* Stanford: Stanford University, Institute for Mathematical Studies in the Social Sciences.

Searle, B., et al. (1977). *Application of radio to teaching elementary mathematics in a developing country* (Fourth Annual Report). Stanford, CA: Stanford University, Institute for Mathematical Studies in Social Science.

Shalaway, L., & Lanier, J. (1978). *Teachers attaining new roles in research: A challenge to the education community.* East Lansing, MI: Michigan State University, Institute for Research on Teaching.

Sharpes, D. K. (1983, Oct.). *Methodological issues in researching teacher education in developing countries.* Paper presented to the Northern Rocky Mountain Educational Research Association, Jackson, WY.

Shavelson, R., & Dempsey-Atwood, N. (1976). Generalizability of measures of teaching behavior. *Review of Educational Research, 46,* 553-611.

Shavelson, R., & Stern, P. (1981). Research on teachers' pedagogical thoughts, judgments, decisions and behavior. *Review of Educational Research, 51,* 455-498.

Shimizu, Y. (1975). *Chiiki shakai to kokuritsu daigaku.* Tokyo: Tokyo Daigaku Shuppankai.

Shulman, L. S. (1987). Knowledge and teaching: Foundations of the new reform. *Harvard Educational Review, 57,* 1-22.

Sibanda, D. (1981). The Zimbabwe integrated teacher education course (ZINTEC). In J. Greenland (Ed.), *The in-service training of primary school teachers in English-speaking Africa*. London: Macmillan.

Singh, N. (1983). *A study of five schools which have shown significant academic improvements* (Working paper). Singapore: Ministry of Education.

Smart, N. (1979). Teachers, teacher education and the community. In R. Gardner (Ed.), *Teacher education in developing countries: Prospects for the eighties*. London: University of London, Institute of Education.

Smith, B. O., & Maux, M. O. (1970). *A study of the logic of teaching*. Urbana: University of Illinois Press.

Sobeih, N. A. A. (1984). *Education for national development in Asia: Priorities in teacher education: A comparative analysis*. Paper presented at the International Symposium on Asian Studies in July, 1984.

Soepaat. (1982). *An investigation to determine the open and closed-mindedness of agricultural technical secondary teachers in East Java, Indonesia*. Unpublished doctoral dissertation, East Texas State University, Commerce, TX.

Sohoni, B. K., Bhalwankar, A. G., Ketkar, S. R., & Purandare, P. S. (1979). *A study of the development of teacher effectiveness through teaching practice*. Bombay: SNDT Women's University.

Spaulding, S. (1975). Are teachers facing a crisis of identity? *Prospects: Quarterly Review of Education, 5*, 209-19.

Spaulding, S. (1987). *Technology, education, information and development*. Paper presented at the New York University Conference sponsored by the Society for International Development on New Information Technologies in Education and Publishing, Nov., 1986.

Spodek, B. (1987). *Reform in Chinese kindergartens: The preparation of kindergarten teachers.* Paper presented at the Annual Meeting of the American Educational Research Association (Washington, DC, April 20-24, 1987).

Spratt, J. E., & Wagner, D. (1984). *The making of a Fqih: The transformation of traditional Islamic teachers in modern times.* Cambridge, MA. Harvard University, Graduate School of Education.

Stebbins, R. A. (1975). *The teachers and meaning.* Leiden: E. J. Brill.

Stewart, I. (1978). Problems of teacher education in developing countries, with special reference to Papua New Guinea: Some current strategies. *British Journal of Teacher Education, 4,* 186-201.

Stone, E. (1986). Towards a systemic approach to research on teaching: The place of investigative pedagogy. *British Educational Research Journal, 12,* 167-181.

Streat, W. L. (1981). *Development of professional support services.* In APEID, Development of professional support services in innovations (Occasional Paper, No. 6, pp. 1-6). Bangkok: UNESCO.

Stuart, J., et al. (1986). *Case studies in development studies teaching in Lesotho classrooms.* Maseru: National University of Lesotho, Centre for African Studies.

Suchman, J. R. (1962). *The elementary school training program in scientific inquiry.* Urbana: University of Illinois Press.

Sudame, G. R., Roy, S., & Arunkumar, P. (1985). School broadcasts in India. *Perspectives in Education, 1,* 123-127.

Sultan Idria Training College. (1985). *Keeping diaries during teaching practice.* Tanjung Malim, Malaysia: Sultan Idria Training College.

Sykes, G. (1985). Teacher education in the United States. In B. R. Clark (Ed.), *The school and the universities.* Berkeley: University of California Press.

Taba, H. (1966a). *Teacher's handbook for elementary social studies.* Reading, MA: Addison-Wesley.

Taba, H. (1966b). *Teaching strategies and cognitive functioning in elementary school children* (Cooperative Research Project No. 2404). San Francisco: San Francisco State College.

Tanbanjong, A. (1983). *A comparison of the effectiveness of using and not using manipulative materials in teaching addition and subtraction to first grade students in Bangkok, Thailand.* Unpublished doctoral dissertation, University of Houston, Houston, TX.

Tarigan, T. E. (1975). Teaching English in Indonesia. *English Language Teaching Journal, 30,* 61-66.

Tavares, N. (1980). Educacao e Imperialismo no Brasil. *Educacao & Sociedade CEDES, Cortez Editoria,* 2(7), 5-53.

Tedesco, J. C. (1983). Pedagogical model and school failure. *Cepal Review, 2,* 133-146.

Thompson, A. R. (1984). *Teacher education: The staff development context.* A paper presented at the ICET 31st World Assembly, Bangkok.

Thompson, A. R., & Greenland, J. J. (1983). The implications of UPE for teacher education. *International Review of Education, 29,* 199-213.

Tilson, T., et al. (1978). *Application of radio to teaching elementary mathematics in a developing country* (Fifth Annual Report). Stanford, CA: Stanford University, Institute for Mathematical Studies in Social Science.

Triosi, N. (1983). *Effective teaching and student achievement.* Reston, VA: National Association of Secondary School Principals (NASSP).

Trow, M. (1967). The transition to mass secondary education. In S. M. Lipset & R. Bendix (Eds.), *Class, status, and power.* New York: Free Press.

Tsuneo, H. (Ed.) (1856). *Kyoshi no shakai-teki chii.* Tokyo: Yukikaku.

Tucker, J. L. (1981). Teacher education policy in contemporary China: The socio-political context. *Theory and Research in Social Education, 8,* 1-13.

Tugade, M., & Winarno Surakhamad. (1986). *Post-project evaluation of NRT.* Manila: INNOTECH.

Turner, J. (1978). Teacher education in predominantly rural countries. *British Journal of Teacher Education, 4,* 176-86.

Turney, C. (1977). *Sydney micro skills.* Sydney: Sydney University Press.

Tyack, D. B. (Ed.) (1967). *Turning points in American educational history.* New York: John Wiley.

U. S. Department of Education. (1987). *Japanese education today.* Washington, DC: U. S. Government Printing Office.

Udoh, C. O. (1976). Preparation of physical and health education teachers for primary schools in the African environment. *West African Journal of Education, 20,* 28-45.

UNESCO (United Nations Educational, Scientific, & Cultural Organization). (1975a). *Abridged version of the international standard classification of education.* Paris: UNESCO.

UNESCO. (1975b). *A systems approach to teaching and learning procedures: A guide for educators in developing countries.* Paris: UNESCO.

UNESCO. (1975c). *Alternative structures and methods in teacher education* (Report of a Technical Working Group, Kathmandu, Nepal, October 21-30, 1975). Bangkok: UNESCO, Regional Office for Education in Asia.

UNESCO. (1975d). *Teacher education and curriculum for development* (Report of a Regional Planning Workshop, Quezon City, Philippines, May 19-31, 1975). Bangkok: UNESCO, Regional Office for Education in Asia.

UNESCO. (1976a). *Continuing education for teacher educators; Advanced-level workshops* (Report of a Task Force Meeting (Tokyo, March 13-25, 1976). Bangkok: UNESCO, Regional Office for Education in Asia.

UNESCO. (1976b). *Exploring new directions in teacher education: Experiments in the preparation and training of teachers in Asia.* Bangkok: UNESCO, Regional Office for Education in Asia.

UNESCO. (1976c). *Educational reforms and innovations in Africa* (Experiments and Innovations in Education, No. 34). Paris: UNESCO.

UNESCO. (1979). *In-service teacher education: Developing innovatory strategies and instructional materials* (Report of a Study Group. Bangkok, Thailand, September 20-29, 1979). Bangkok: UNESCO, Regional Office for Education in Asia and Oceania.

UNESCO. (1980, 1983, 1986a, 1987). *Statistical yearbook.* Paris: UNESCO.

UNESCO. (1981, 1982). *Distance learning for teacher education* (Report of a Technical working group meeting at Islamabad, Pakistan) (3 volumes). Bangkok: UNESCO, Regional Office for Education in Asia and the Pacific.

UNESCO. (1984). *Training of science teachers and teacher educators* (Report of a Technical Working Group, Quezon City, Philippines, July 17-27, 1984). Bangkok: UNESCO Regional Office for Education in Asia and the Pacific.

UNESCO. (1985). *Teachers and Their Use of Educational Technology* (Report of a Regional Training Workshop, Seoul, South Korea, September 16-27, 1985). Bangkok: UNESCO, Regional Office for Education in Asia and the Pacific.

UNESCO. (1986b). *Preparing multi-media teaching materials. A source book.* Bangkok: UNESCO: Regional Office for Education in Asia and the Pacific.

UNESCO. (1986c). *Operational teacher training objectives and raising achievement levels.* Bangkok: UNESCO Regional Office for Education in Asia and the Pacific.

UNESCO. (1986d). *Asia and the Pacific programme of educational innovation for development, teacher development for better pupil achievement.* Bangkok: UNESCO.

Unoh, S. O. (1975). Training primary school teachers of reading and the language arts. *West African Journal of Education, 19*, 49-60.

Valadian, M., & Randall, A. (1980). Aboriginal and islander teacher aide in-service programme. *The Aboriginal Child at School, 8*(2), 22-35.

Valle, V. M. (1982). *Technical guidelines for in-service teacher training* (For Latin American and Caribbean Countries). Washington, DC: Dept. of Educational Affairs.

Valtin, H. (1987). Teaching physiology in Africa. *Physiologist, 30*, 1-7.

Vera, R. (1982). *Teacher training workshops: An approach for the analysis and transformation of teacher practices.* A paper prepared at the Teacher training workshop, Santiago, Chile.

Verspoor, A., & Leno, J. L. (1986, Oct.). *Improving teaching: A key to successful educational change: Lessons from World Bank Experience.* Paper presented at the Annual IMTEC Seminar, Bali, Indonesia.

Vivian, S. (1968, May). In-service education for primary teachers in Uganda. *Teacher Education in New Countries, 9*, 40-49.

Vocational and technical teacher preparation in Asia and the Pacific (Report of Two Regional Workshops in Bangkok, Thailand, March 6-28, 1981 and January 28-February 19, 1982). Tokyo: National Institute for Educational Research.

Wagner, R. V. (1978). Teaching in South America: Some generalities. *Teaching of Psychology, 6*, 31-35.

Walberg, H. (1985). Synthesis of research on teaching. In M. C. Wittrock (Ed.), *Handbook of research on teaching.* New York: Macmillan.

Wanasinghe, J. (1983). The concept of cluster schools and its relevance to educational development in Sri Lanka. *International Journal of Educational Development, 3*, 247-252.

Wang, M. C., & Lindvall, C. M. (1984). Individual differences and school learning environments. In E. W. Gordon (Ed.), *Review of research in education, 11*, Washington, DC: AERA.

Waskito Tjiptosasmito, & Cummings, W. K. (1981). *The status and deployment of teachers in Indonesia.* Jakarta: Ministry of Education.

Watson, K. (1983). Rural primary school teachers as change agents in the Third World: Three case studies. *International Journal of Educational Development, 3*, 47-59.

WCOTP (World Confederation of Organizations of the Teaching Profession). (1962). *Survey of the status of the teaching profession in Africa.* Washington, DC: World Confederation of Organizations of the Teaching Professions.

WCOTP. (1964). *Survey of the status of the teaching profession in the Americas.* Washington, DC: World Confederation of Organizations of the Teaching Professions.

WCOTP & Japan Teacher's Union (JTU). (1972). *Struggle for the status of the teaching profession in Asia.* Tokyo: JTU.

Weiler, H. N. (1979). *Education and development: From the age of innocence to the age of skepticism* (Program Report 79-80). Stanford, CA: Stanford University, Institute for Research on Educational Finance and Governance, School of Education.

Weiler, H. N. (1983). *Aid for education: The political economy of international cooperation in educational development.* Stanford, CA: Stanford University.

Wells, G., & Chang, G. L. (1986). *Effecting educational change through collaborative research.* Toronto: Ontario Institute for Studies in Education.

White, P. (1984). *AUSSAT and education: Has education missed the boat?* Paper presented at the Film and Television School Seminar, After AUSSAT...?" in Sydney, Australia, March.

White, R. (1977). Mass Communication and the Popular Promotion Strategy of Rural Development in Honduras. In P. Spain, D. Jamison, & E. McAnany (Eds.), *Radio for Education and Development Case Studies* (Working Paper 226) (Vol. 2), Washington, DC: World Bank.

White, R. A. (1983). The Latin American Association for Radiophonic Education. *Media in Education and Development, 16*, 122-28.

Williams, P. (1974, Sept.). *Ghana's teaching service.* West Africa, 1074-5.

Williams, P. (1979). *Planning teacher demand and supply: Fundamentals of educational planning.* Paris: UNESCO, International Institute for Educational Planning.

Woods, P. (1983). *Sociology and the school: An interactionist viewpoint.* London: Routledge & Kegan Paul.

Wright, C. (1985). *Reflections on collaborative action research in education.* Freetown, Sierra Leone: Milton Margai Teachers College, CREST.

Yinger, R. (1980). A study of teacher planning. *The Elementary School Journal, 80*, 107-127.

Young, B. (1985). *The primary education project, in education and development.* Kathmandu, Nepal: Tribhuvan University, Research Centre for Educational Innovation and Development.

Zahlan, A. B. (1988). Issues of quality and relevance in distance-teaching materials. *Prospects: Quarterly Review of Education, 18*, 75-83.

Zughoul, M. R. (1987). Restructuring the English department in third world universities: Alternative approaches for the teaching of English literature. *IRAL, 25*, 221-37.

Zymelman, A, & DeStefano, J. (1988). *Teacher salaries in Sub-Saharan Africa* (Report of the Population and Human Resources Division). Washington, DC: World Bank.

INDEX